MULTIPLE-CHOICE & FREE-RESPONSE QUESTIONS WITH DBQ IN PREPARATION FOR THE AP WORLD HISTORY EXAMINATION

Ethel Wood
Princeton High School
Princeton, NJ

Copyright © 2004 by D & S Marketing Systems, Inc.

All rights reserved.

No part of this book may be reproduced or transmitted in any form or by any means, electronic or mechanical, including photocopying and recording, or by any information storage or retrieval systems, without written permission from the publisher.

Printed in the U.S.A.

Preface

The study of world history is a daunting task. So much has happened in the past that it seems almost impossible to know where or how to begin. However, after a long discussion among scholars and teachers, the College Board has defined the curriculum that students are responsible for on the examination in May.

MULTIPLE-CHOICE AND FREE-RESPONSE QUESTIONS WITH DBQ IN PREPARATION FOR THE AP WORLD HISTORY EXAMINATION assists students in assessing their level of understanding of both concepts and factual information that the AP World History course covers. The questions simulate as closely as possible the AP World History Examination. Part I of the book gives a brief overview of the course and explains both the necessary content themes and skills. Part II includes an overview of each of the eras covered on the exam, as well as multiple-choice questions and a free-response question for each unit. Part III includes three complete practice exams of 70 multiple-choice questions and three free-response questions each. The exams include concepts and facts in the following proportions as recommended by the College Board:

Foundations (8000 B.C.E. to 600 C.E.)	19-20%
600 - 1450 C.E.	22%
1450 - 1750 C.E.	19-20%
1750 - 1914 C.E.	19-20%
1914 - Present	19-20%

The book prepares the students for both the multiple-choice and free-response portions of the AP Examination. The narrative review will help students understand the concepts that both multiple-choice questions and free-response questions cover.

All communications concerning this book should be addressed to:

D&S Marketing Systems, Inc.
1205 38th Street
Brooklyn, NY 11218

TABLE OF CONTENTS

PART I

The World History Course and Examination..i

PART II

UNIT I: Foundations (to 600)

    Review...1
    Multiple Choice Questions...28
    DBQ Essay Question..38

UNIT II: 600-1450 C.E.

    Review...43
    Multiple Choice Questions...72
    Comparative Essay...81

UNIT III: 1450-1750 C.E.

    Review...83
    Multiple Choice Questions...112
    Change Over Time Essay...122

UNIT IV: 1750-1914 C.E.

    Review...123
    Multiple Choice Questions...153
    Comparative Essay...162

UNIT V: 1914-Present

    Review...163
    Multiple Choice Questions...191
    Change Over Time Essay...201

PART III

SAMPLE EXAMINATION I..209

SAMPLE EXAMINATION II...237

SAMPLE EXAMINATION II...265

PART I

THE WORLD HISTORY COURSE AND EXAMINATION

The World History Course and Examination

The study of world history is a daunting task. So much has happened in the past that it seems almost impossible to know where or how to begin. Indeed, world history courses vary widely from one high school to the next, making the situation even more challenging. After a long discussion among history scholars on both the university and secondary levels, the Advanced Placement Program has managed to put in place a curriculum that is comprehensive both in its world coverage and time sequence. An early word of caution to students taking the exam is to pay close attention to the guidelines provided by the College Board that are followed in this study book. Many textbooks and secondary courses on "world history" still emphasize the history of the west and do not focus on the themes outlined in the AP curriculum. While the education they provide may be sound, they will not necessarily prepare you for the exam.

The pages that follow include a description of the course, the broad themes that it follows, the "habits of mind" that it requires, and something about the examination itself. Read through this part very carefully because it will provide you with an overview of the course that will help keep you from getting lost in the complexities and challenges that the study of world history always presents.

A DESCRIPTION OF THE COURSE

Does history seem like just one fact after another to you? If so, you need to reconsider the way that you view it. The AP World History course does not expect you to know a lot of details. However, the curriculum does require you to make connections between broad, sweeping patterns in history and the particular events that occur in specific cultures. For example, you may know that Christopher Columbus sailed across the Atlantic Ocean in 1492, and that his ships were the Santa Maria, the Nina, and the Pinto. What if you forget the name of one of the ships? The AP World History curriculum doesn't mind, but what you do need to understand is that Columbus' voyage was an early example of a massive movement of Europeans to the "New World" that resulted in a major turning point in world history. You need to know something about the forces that converged to make his voyage possible and the consequences it had on *world* history, not just the United States. And then, you might want to compare the consequences of his voyage to those of the Chinese explorer, Zheng He. So if you don't already think of history in these terms, begin to change your perspective right now.

GOALS

In a nutshell, the goals of the course include:

1. **To develop an understanding of the *story* of history** – History has evolved over eons of time. Any event must be placed in the sequence of the story and cannot be understood without knowing what happened earlier. How did the Romans develop Latin, a language that came to be the root for many modern languages today? Their accomplishment rested on the knowledge and skills of earlier civilizations, and their language was also a part of the broader Roman culture. Once the language spread to other areas, its influence broadened and outlived the empire that created it. The development and influence of Latin is part of the broader story of human development of written language in all of its many forms.

2. **To focus on interactions among human societies** – Studying one country, kingdom, empire, or area in particular is fine, but the focus of AP World History is on interactions among societies. For example, the religion of Islam started in the Arabian Peninsula in the 7th century C.E. It greatly impacted the lives of the Bedouins and the other Arabian groups that first encountered it. However, the spread of Islam to other areas is a much more significant event in terms of impact on world history. In some places, such as India, the introduction of Islam sparked conflict that resonates through time and has led to violence in the modern world. In other areas, such as northern Africa, Islam spread slowly, encompassing local traditions, so that the religion itself was transformed. In both cases, you should notice that the focus is on *interaction* among societies, not on one society in isolation.

3. **To interpret history in terms of historical evidence** – We know what happened in the past because someone somehow passed knowledge down from one generation to the next. Usually knowledge is transmitted through writing, but oral traditions also may be important methods of transfer. We also may learn about history by looking at cultural objects that have survived through the years. Many pieces of history obviously are lost, and we are left with only those that filter their way through time. As a result, we must reconstruct the past based on imperfect relics and accounts. Historians must be sleuths as they investigate such questions as these: Who said it? When? Why? What point of view did the person have, and can I find another piece of evidence that either agrees or disagrees with it?

4. **To understand the nature of change over time** – We know that the world changed a great deal between 1900 and 2000 C.E. But how and why? Did it happen through violent, sudden actions, like invasions or strikes, or did change slowly evolve? The nature of change is important to investigate because it is part of the broad story of history. Changes that start in one area – like technology – may cause change in other areas, such as government, the economy, and/or family life. Tracing and analyzing the thread of change through time is an important focus of the AP World History course.

5. **To make comparisons among major societies** – The human story can best be understood by comparing similar events, trends, customs, or influences in different parts of the world. The Incas managed to raise food for an empire in an inauspicious mountain environment, whereas the Aztecs were able to do the same thing in the middle of a swamp. Their different environments led to similar outcomes, but they did it through different farming techniques and they produced both different and similar crops. Those comparisons help us to understand the broader accomplishments and challenges of both civilizations.

THEMES

These goals may be translated into several themes that the course follows. You should be able to see them in every era in every part of the world and make connections over all eras of time and from civilization to civilization.

1. **patterns and impacts of interactions among societies** – These interactions may take the form of trade, war, or diplomacy, and they may also include the involvement of international organizations.

2. **relationships between change and continuity over time** – Change is sometimes easier to see than continuity, but they are always interrelated. What stays the same, and why, especially when other things change? For example, customs may stay the same even though environments and/or technology changes.

3. **the impact of technology and demography** – Technology includes inventions from the wheel to computer science, and demography is the study of people and their relationship to the environment. Demography includes migration, population increase or decrease, disease, and agriculture.

4. **systems of social structure and gender structure** – These include a study of social statuses and class, as well as differing statuses of and division of labor between men and women. The course traces changes in these areas over time, and invites students to make comparisons among societies.

5. **cultural and intellectual developments and interactions** – This theme includes belief systems, such as philosophies and religions, as well as arts and literature. It emphasizes the impact of these developments across civilizations and through time.

6. **changes in functions and structures of governments and attitudes toward them** – Governments have always existed in human society, but they have taken many different shapes and have performed various functions. People have always expected something of government, but those expectations have changed over time as well.

HABITS OF MIND

History scholars must develop a set of skills that are necessary to develop in order to understand the major themes. The AP curriculum refers to these skills as "Habits of Mind" that may be divided into two categories:

1. **Habits of Mind for the study of any history:**

   - building and evaluating arguments based on evidence

   - using documents and other primary data to understand history; analyzing bias, point of view, and context

   - assessing change and continuity over time

   - handling diverse interpretations of similar phenomena through interpreting bias, point of view, and context

2. **Habits of Mind for studying World History:**

   - seeing and understanding global patterns, yet connecting them to local specific events in particular places

   - comparing within and among societies, including comparisons of different or similar reactions to global processes

   - developing historical understanding by assessing claims of universal standards, while noting commonalities and differences; putting cultural diversities within historical context

The AP World History Examination assesses both content and habits of mind in all types of questions, both multiple choice and essay.

THE TIME PERIODS

The course encompasses five eras in time beginning in 8000 B.C.E. and extending to the present. B.C.E. (before the common era) is the same thing as B.C. (before Christ), and C.E. (the common era) corresponds to A.D. (anno Domini). The time periods and their percentages on the examination are as follows:

Foundations (8000 B.C.E. to 600 C.E.)	19-20%
600 -1450 C.E.	22%
1450 -1750 C.E.	19-20%
1750 -1914 C.E.	19-20%
1914 -Present	19-20%

THE IMPORTANCE OF PERIODIZATION

Periodization is the process of dividing history into manageable "chunks" so as to avoid the pitfall of thinking about history as just one fact after another. It may apply to any period of time, long, in-between, or relatively short. For example, you may periodize your life so far by creating categories that describe your life during a particular period, like "when I lived in Denver," or "when I was in elementary school." On reflection, you can see change and continuity, and most of us can see distinct eras. United States history may be periodized as well into chunks like "the Revolutionary Era," or "the Industrial Revolution." In all cases, particular events, trends, and/or people characterize the era and make it distinct from other eras. Sometimes eras end and new ones begin with **"Marker Events"** that produce many important changes, such as the Civil War in U.S. history. Other times the change is more gradual, but is apparent, especially in hindsight.

Of course, world history is much more difficult to periodize than an individual's life or one country's history. Breaking down thousands of years into chunks is a very challenging task, especially when you must consider *all* civilizations in every corner of the globe. However, world historians have attempted to do just that. As you can imagine, they don't always agree with one another, but the AP World History curriculum is based on periodization into the five eras: Foundations, 600-1450, 1450-1750, 1750-1914, and 1914 to the present. Even though they are all part of the long story of history, each era is different from the others. In a way, periodization is something of a mind trick that allows us to find order in the myriad of events, people, and societies that have existed in all of human history.

"Marker events" in world history are also much more difficult to assess in world history than for single-country histories. Is the American Civil War a marker event in world history? Maybe so, but it is much less obvious than it is for U.S. history. Since marker events often characterize eras, it is important to set up some criteria for judging them, such as:

- The event or series of events must cross national or cultural borders, affecting many civilizations.

- Later changes or developments in history must be at least partially traced to this event or series of events.

- The event or series of events must have impact in other areas. For example, if it is a change in belief systems, it must impact some other major area, like government, social classes, the economy, and/or technology.

In this book, each era begins with a Periodization Overview that notes broad characteristics and changes that make the era different from others. The overview will help you put the facts into perspective and make judgments about what is important to remember in order to understand interactions, connections, and change over time.

THE STRUCTURE OF THE EXAMINATION

The College Board AP World History Examination offered every year in May is intended to measure a student's mastery of both content reflected in the six Overarching Themes and skills outlined in the seven Habits of Mind. The test is three hours and five minutes long, and includes the following types of questions:

- **multiple-choice questions** – The test has 70 multiple-choice questions and allows 55 minutes for students to complete them.

- **document-based question (DBQ)** – This question requires students to read several documents (maps, charts, cartoons, and/or quotes), and respond to a question that asks them to analyze and interpret the documents. Students are allowed a ten-minute mandatory reading period, and 40 minutes to write the essay (a total of 50 minutes).

- **change-over-time essay** – This question requires a student to follow a particular topic or issue over time, generally through at least one of the specified eras. Students are expected to complete the essay in 40 minutes.

- **comparative essay** – This question asks students to compare a broad issue in world history in at least two societies or areas of the world. Students are allowed 40 minutes to complete this essay.

Section I of the test consists of the 70 multiple-choice questions. They cover the five eras in approximately the percentages designated (19-20% for Foundations, 22% for 600-1450, 19-20% for 1450-1750, 19-20% for 1750-1914, and 19-20% for 1914). Some of the questions ask about cross-era comparisons or change-over-time. The questions cover all areas of the globe. Section I counts as 50% of the student's final score on the examination.

Section II, the free-response section, includes the three essay questions, which together count for the remaining 50% of the final exam score. The essays are all equally weighted, and no choices are allowed. All three questions are mandatory. Part A begins with the ten-minute reading period for the DBQ, and follows with a forty-minute period for answering the question. In Part B, students are allowed forty minutes to answer the change-over-time essay. Finally, Part C is the forty-minute comparative essay.

Important note: The AP World History examination tests your knowledge of civilizations around the globe. No more than 30% of the examination covers topics in European history, and the history of the United States is important only as it affects global patterns and trends. For example, the American Revolution is seen as one of a number of revolutions that occur in many countries during the late 18th and early 19th centuries. Of course, the United States played a vital role in world history during the 20th century, and world history students are expected to know something about it.

MULTIPLE-CHOICE QUESTIONS

Throughout this book you will find comparably difficult multiple-choice questions about topics that you will encounter when you take the AP World History Examination. Students sometimes wonder whether or not it might help their exam score if they guess the answers to questions that they don't know. Random guessing usually doesn't help because one-fourth of the number of questions answered incorrectly will be subtracted from the number of questions answered correctly. However, if you have some knowledge of a question and are able to eliminate one or more choices, it is usually a good idea to guess from among the remaining choices.

THE ESSAYS

For essay questions, follow this mantra carefully: Answer the whole question, and nothing but the question! Spend a minute of your allotted time to literally tear the question apart and take note of *everything* that it asks you to do. If you don't get around to answering part of the question, you will be punished in the score, sometimes severely. Part of the challenge of the essay questions is to remember all the things that you are supposed to do in a limited amount of time. On their AP Central Website (www.apcentral.collegeboard.com), the College Board urges you to pay particular attention to the verbs:

- **Analyze** means to first identify component parts of the question and then examine their nature and relationship.

- **Assess/evaluate** asks you to make a judgment, consider negative and/or positive points (or advantages and disadvantages), or give an opinion.

- **Compare** requires you to note both similarities and differences.

- **Describe** simply asks you to tell about something. It generally isn't as difficult as analyzing, assessing, evaluating, or comparing.

- **Discuss** means to talk through and consider a topic from different points of view, or possibly debate.

- **Explain** means to clarify. It involves making clear the causes or reasons for the issue or topic, as well as some historical evidence to illustrate your main points.

Part A: the Document-Based Question (DBQ)

Historians interpret events and issues from the past by sifting through, reading, and gaining understanding of documents. In other words, they must have "Habits of Mind" that allow them to objectively and accurately reconstruct history. A DBQ requires students to demonstrate some of these skills. In addition, it requires students to develop an overall sense of what the documents all together say about the topic. In the essay, then, students must *synthesize*, or put together pieces of the documents that help them to answer the question. The DBQ's intent is much more to test your ability to analyze, determine points of view, and detect bias than to measure your content knowledge of the subject. The process differs from the actual challenge to the historian in that the documents are pre-selected and presented to you. Historians actually have to find and put them together themselves.

Important notes:

- Do *not* just list the documents and explain what each one says. That will not earn you even a mediocre grade on the essay.

- You do *not* have to use every part of every document, and there is never any one correct way to answer the question. However, you do have to use all or all but one of the documents in your essay. That means that there are no "trick" or irrelevant documents.

- You may cite documents in different ways – by number ("Document 4"), by author, or by some other part of the document that makes it easily recognizable (for example, "the excerpt from the New Testament").

- You will be asked to "wish for" additional documents. In other words, you will need to explain what other type of document would help to answer the question more completely and why. Consider what points of view may be missing or incomplete. As a historian, this skill would help to direct any further research on the topic.

Although the DBQ theoretically does not require prior knowledge about the topic, you will be better able to determine the document's significance and possible purpose if you understand the historical contexts in which each is written.

Part B: the Change-Over-Time Essay (COT)

Most students think that the Change-Over-Time Essay is the hardest one of them all. It not only requires you to have knowledge about particular societies and trends that exist during any one era of world history, it asks you to trace how a particular topic or issue has changed across eras or from the beginning to the end of an era. Students in most classes study the eras chronologically, so while you are studying one time period, it is easy to forget what happened in a previous era. This essay will be much easier if you keep up with changes as you go through the course. For example, if you are studying trade during the Song Dynasty of China, ask yourself what trade was like during the Han (an earlier) Dynasty, and note the change and continuity. To make the question even tougher, the COT Essay may ask you to identify change in more than one society or area of the world. Mercifully, you probably will have some choice of what areas of the world that you write about.

The essay focuses on your content knowledge of one or more of the six themes, but skills are important, too, because you must make judgments about what to choose and you have to be able to think across time periods.

Part C: the Comparative Essay

Think carefully about the six themes in preparing to answer the Comparative Essay. By its, very name, the question will ask you to focus on developments in at least two societies interaction with each other or with global themes or events. But what do you compare?

Think of different areas identified in the themes, such as:

- government
- the economy
- belief systems (philosophies, religion)
- agriculture
- migrations
- trade and cultural exchange
- culture (customs, language, values, arts, literature)

- technology
- impact/concerns
- gender structure/roles
- social classes/statuses

Important note: For all of you that like to make differences between comparing and contrasting, please understand that in order to get a top score, the Comparative Essay expects you to address *both* similarities and differences.

THE "GENERIC" RUBRICS

Rubrics are guidelines that College Board readers for all subjects use as standards to score students' essays. They are intended to insure that all essays are scored in the same way, so that a student's score would not vary significantly depending on which reader happens to make a judgment on his/her paper. For AP World History, the College Board publishes "generic" rubrics that apply to all essay questions of each of the three types: DBQ, Change-over-time, and Comparative. Each question has its own specific notes and requirements, but knowledge of the generic rubric allows you to understand how your essays will be scored.

All essays are graded on a 9 point scale, with 9 being the highest possible score, and 0 the lowest. The three rubrics are divided into two parts:

the basic core – These are points that show that students are "competent" in their skills and knowledge of world history. For the DBQ, 7 of the 9 points form the basic core, and for the COT and Comparative Essays, 6 of 9 points make up the core.

the expanded core – These remaining points are awarded to students that show "excellence" in their skills and knowledge of world history. Students may *not* gain any expanded core points without first getting all the points available from the basic core.

This scoring configuration makes it even more important that students address all parts of the essay because losing a point from the basic core precludes any hope of gaining points from the expanded score.

Other common characteristics of all three generic rubrics include:

BASIC CORE	EXPANDED CORE
an acceptable thesis	a clear, comprehensive, and analytic thesis
supports thesis with historical evidence (documents for DBQ)	supports thesis with ample historical evidence

An acceptable thesis is one that adequately answers all parts of the essay. That does not mean that you can just regurgitate the question in statement form. A thesis should give a brief overview of what the rest of the essay says.

The DBQ "Generic" Rubric

These characteristics are particular to the DBQ question:

BASIC CORE (7 points)	EXPANDED CORE (2 points)
uses all or all but one of the documents	"careful and insightful" analysis of documents."
basically understands the meaning of the documents, although misinterpretation of one document is allowed	"persuasive use" of documents
	analyzes bias or point of view in most documents
analyzes bias or point of view in three of the documents	more sophisticated, more groupings of documents
groups the documents in two or three ways for proper analysis	uses outside knowledge effectively
identifies one appropriate type of additional document	identifies more than one additional document

The Change-Over-Time "Generic" Rubric

These characteristics are particular to the COT question:

BASIC CORE (6 Points)	EXPANDED CORE (3 Points)
addresses all parts of the question (allows some unevenness) provides appropriate historical evidence effectively shows change-over-time and/or continuities.	addresses all parts of the question thoroughly and from different perspectives as appropriate (global issues, chronology, causation, change, continuity, content) provides ample historical evidence provides links to relevant ideas, events, trends

The Comparative "Generic" Rubric

These characteristics are particular to the Comparative Essay, although notice that some are similar to those for the COT Essay:

BASIC CORE (6 Points)	EXPANDED CORE (3 Points)
addresses all parts of the question (allows some unevenness) provides appropriate historical evidence makes one or two relevant, direct comparisons	addresses all parts of the question thoroughly and from different perspectives as appropriate (comparisons, chronology, causation, connections, themes, interactions, content.) provides ample historical evidence relates comparisons to larger global context shows similarities and differences makes consistent comparisons

OVERVIEW OF THE REVIEW BOOK

Part II of this book takes each of the five eras of the AP World History curriculum and address major themes and patterns as they interact during the time frame. Each review narrative is followed by 35 multiple-choice questions and one essay intended to help students assess their comprehension of the era. This part may be studied throughout the year, and the later units assume that students have knowledge from the previous units.

Part III consists of three sample exams that students may take as they prepare for the exam in May. Each sample exam is modeled after the AP test, with 70 multiple-choice questions, one DBQ, one COT essay, and one Comparative Essay.

The purpose of the book is to help students make their way through the myriad of information – events, trends, people, places – that constitute world history in order to see the overall patterns and themes. Additionally, students will have the opportunity to test and improve the skills, or Habits of Mind, that will help them to understand the content. The book is as concise as possible. Most world history textbooks are huge, so you don't need another text. Instead, this book provides help in rethinking history, identifying important world themes and changes, and applying historians' tools to help broaden and deepen an understanding of the past.

PART II

Unit Reviews and Questions

UNIT ONE

Foundations (8000 B.C.E.-600 C.E.)

Of all the time periods covered in the AP World History curriculum, Foundations (8000 BCE - 600 CE) spans the largest number of years. It begins with an important Marker Event – the **Neolithic Revolution** – and ends after the fall of three major classical civilizations – Rome in the Mediterranean region, Han China, and the Gupta Empire of India.

Broad topics addressed in the Foundations time period are:

- **Environmental and periodization issues**

- **Early development in agriculture and technology**

- **Basic cultural, political, and social features of early civilizations: Mesopotamia, Egypt, Indus Valley, Shang China, and Meso/South America**

- **The rise and fall of classical civilizations: Zhou and Han China, India (Gupta Empire), and Mediterranean civilizations (Greece and Rome)**

- **Major belief systems, including polytheism, Hinduism, Judaism, Confucianism, Daoism, Buddhism, and Christianity**

A NOTE ABOUT PREHISTORY (BEFORE 3500 CE)

A basic type of periodization is to divide all of time into "prehistory" and "history." Usually the distinction is based on whether or not the people left written records, but the presence of written records is very closely tied to the beginnings of agriculture. Scholars are not entirely sure about when human beings first appeared on earth, but new discoveries continue to push the date further back in time. So "prehistory" lasted for millions of years.

The first humans probably emerged in eastern Africa, due to a happy confluence of availability of food and domesticable animals and favorable climate. For thousands of years humans sustained themselves as hunters and gatherers, and as a result were quite dependent on the abundance of food. Hunters gained skills in capturing and killing animals, and gatherers learned which plants and fruits were edible and nutritious. Technological inventions generally supported the fulfillment of these basic activities. Stones (and eventually metals) were shaped as tools and weapons, and techniques were developed for efficient gathering and storage of food.

By 8000 BCE, humans had migrated to many other areas, probably following the herds and other available food sources. Major migrations include:

- **Early Africans to Australia, the Middle East, Europe, and Asia**

- **Asians across the land bridge to the Americas**

Our knowledge of prehistoric people is limited, partly because they lived so long ago, and partly because they left no written records. However, archaeologists have found evidence of these generally shared characteristics of prehistoric people:

1) **Social structure** – Most people traveled in small bands, and authority was based on family relationships. Men took leadership roles, but women were highly valued for their gathering skills. Labor was generally divided based on gender, with men as hunters and women as gatherers. However, status differences between men and women were generally not wide, with relative gender equality apparently characterizing their group life.

2) **Beliefs** – Archaeological evidence suggests that prehistoric people were guided by their beliefs in spirits and sacred places. Their cave drawings and traces of their cultural objects indicate that they believed in an afterlife, although they probably did not practice **polytheism**, or a belief in many gods. Instead, **polydaemonism**, or the belief in many spirits (not specific gods), probably describes their religion more accurately. Bushes, rocks, trees, plants, or streams could be inhabited by these spirits, who often appeared to communicate with humans.

The prehistoric era includes the early stages of agriculture from about 10,000 to 4,000 BCE, but once settlement began, the stage was set for the development of reading and writing and the period known as "history."

ENVIRONMENTAL AND PERIODIZATION ISSUES

When, how, and why did people give up their wandering and settle to live in one place? First of all, it happened in different parts of the world at different times, but settled communities had developed in many places by 8000 BCE. The ability to settle was based almost entirely on successful cultivation of crops and domestication of animals. These drastic changes in human life are known collectively as the **Neolithic Revolution** that almost certainly happened independently in different places over a large span of time. For example, the people settling along the major rivers in China did not learn to farm because they were in contact with the people in the Indus River area. Instead, people in both areas probably figured out the advantages of settled life on their own. Although the Neolithic Revolution was one of the most significant Marker Events in world history, it occurred gradually and probably by trial and error.

Foundations (8000 B.C.E.-600 C.E.) — Unit One

The changes that resulted include:

- **Increase in reliable food supplies** – Agricultural skills allowed people to control food production, and domestication of animals both helped to make agricultural production more efficient and increased the availability of food.

- **Rapid increase in total human population** – Reliable food supplies meant that people were less likely to starve to death. With increasing life spans came increasing reproduction, and more children meant that there were more people to tend the land and animals.

- **Job specialization** – Other occupations than farming developed, since fewer people were needed to produce food. Some early specialized jobs include priests, traders, and builders.

- **Widening of gender differences** – Status distinctions between men and women increased, as men took over most agricultural cultivation and domestication of animals. Women were responsible for raising children, cooking food, and keeping the house, but in virtually all of the early civilizations men became more and more dominant. A **patriarchal system** commonly developed, with men holding power in the family, the economy, and the government.

- **Development of distinction between settled people and "nomads"** – All people did not settle into communities but remained as hunters and gatherers. As more settled communities developed, the distinction between agriculturalists and hunters and gatherers grew.

THE IMPORTANCE OF GEOGRAPHY

American students are often criticized for their lack of knowledge of geography, but it is essential in the study of world history. Although you will not have to specifically identify places on the AP Exam, you cannot follow change over time nor make accurate comparisons unless you know something about both physical and political geography.

Our concepts of geography have been shaped by western historians of the past, and in recent years some scholars have questioned very basic assumptions about the ways that the globe is divided. For example, take the concept of a continent. Why is Europe considered a continent? What actually separates Europe from Asia? Certainly, physical geographical separation of the two continents is far from clear. Historians Martin Lewis and Karen Wigen refer to *cartographic ethnocentrism* in their controversial book, *The Myth of Continents*. This ethnic point of view is centered around Europe, and a little later, around the United States. For example, where did the name "Middle East" come from? From the European perspective, this area is east of Europe, but it is not as far away as China is. If we look at the Middle East from a cultural point of view, we certainly can see commonalities that extend throughout northern Africa, the Arabian Peninsula, Europe, and Asia. So why do we divide the area up into several continents?

Biased divisions that Lewis and Wigen identify include:

- **East vs. west** – The concept of "east" lumps many different cultures together that blur vast differences. Some of this occurs in considering the west, but cultural distinctions are generally more readily acknowledged.

- **South vs. north** – The history of the southern part of the globe has often been ignored in the telling of world history, and the northern half has been highlighted.

Even maps that we use reflect these biases. Most map projections center around the Atlantic Ocean, clearly showing Europe and North America in the middle. Inventors of the relatively new Peders' projection claim that older, more familiar projections (like Mercator and Robertson's) actually short change "less important" countries in terms of land space. Of course, we cannot talk about world history without labels, biased though they may be. However, it is essential to use objective criteria in determining what events, places, and people have shaped the course of history. Do not automatically assume that one part of the world is inherently more important than another at any particular time without thinking it through carefully and objectively.

THE NATURE OF CIVILIZATION

These changes in turn allowed the development of "civilization," a basic organizing principle in world history. Civilization may be defined in many ways, but it is generally characterized by:

- **Large cities that dominate the countryside around them** – Growing populations required more food production, so the cities controlled their hinterlands in order to guarantee a reliable and continuous supply of food for their inhabitants.

- **Monumental architecture and public building projects that take many forms** – They may include temples, palaces, irrigation projects, city walls, public arenas, government buildings, and aqueducts.

- **A complex political organization** – In order to coordinate activities and provide protection for the cities and hinterlands, governments developed. The larger the area and population, the more demanding political positions became, and control of the government began to move away from kinship ties. Although many early rulers passed their authority down to their sons, other factors became important, such as military prowess and ability.

- **A written language** – This important development in human history allowed societies to organize and maintain the growing political, social, and economic structure that followed settlement into agricultural areas. Those societies that developed a written language were able to communicate multiple ideas and large amounts of information that in turn encouraged greater complexity and growth.

- **Specialization of labor** – With basic food needs taken care of by fewer people, others may specialize in jobs that help to improve the quality of life. For example, engineers may construct bigger and better irrigation systems, and bureaucrats may increase their level of government services.

- **Advanced art and literature** – In prehistoric times and in simple communities, most artwork and literature was (is) produced by people who were preoccupied with activities that sustained their lives, such as hunting and gathering or farming. Art consisted of simple drawings, and literature usually took the form of oral stories passed down from one generation to the next. With the advent of civilization, some people had the time to concentrate on art and literature, making them their primary occupation.

- **Long distance trade** – As technologies improved and specialization increased, trade with other civilization centers began. This trade led to **cultural diffusion**, or the spreading and sharing of cultural characteristics. Not only was **material culture** – objects such as pottery, tools, and textiles – shared, but **nonmaterial culture** – such as beliefs, customs, and values – also spread, contributing to the cosmopolitan nature of cities.

THE CIVILIZATION CONTROVERSY

The term "civilization" is derived from Latin, the language of the ancient Roman Empire. The Latin word *civilis* means "of the citizens," and the Romans used it to distinguish between themselves from the "inferior" people who lived on the fringes of their empire. However, the distinctions that the word implies began long before the time of the Romans. The process of civilization, or the development of the characteristics listed above, indisputably occurred in several parts of the world before 1500 BCE, and the feelings of superiority that urban folks displayed probably began just as early.

Civilization as an organizing principle in world history is actually quite controversial. Traditionally historians have seen the development of civilization in a positive light, or as improvements in the quality of human life. So they refer to some societies as more "advanced" than others that remain more "backward." However, other scholars have cautioned against ignoring the "dark side" of the distinctions that the word "civilization" implies.

The Civilization Controversy: a Building Block for Human Society?	
Advantages of Civilization	**Disadvantages of Civilizations**
Development of specialized skills, inventions, arts, and literature	Increase in class and gender distinctions, creating oppression for some
Building of economically and politically coordinated cities	Overproduction of land, depletion of soil, eventual destruction caused by increase in population
Increased ability to protect people from dangers both inside and outside the city	Increased attacks from outsiders attracted to wealth; internal crime promoted by crowded conditions
Growth of prosperity, improving quality of life	Creation of life-threatening congestion, pollution, disease, and decrease in sanitation

Today most historians try to steer away from the question of whether the advent of civilization led to a higher level of human life or started us on the road to ultimate destruction. The important thing to remember is that it dramatically changed the course of world history, whether for good or for bad. No matter what the location or time period, the division between urban and rural lifestyles is a recurring theme throughout time, and biases toward one lifestyle or the other remain as a great continuity throughout eras and among many societies around the world.

PERIODIZATION

The Foundations time period (8000 BCE to 600 CE) is so vast that there are many ways to divide it into periods or eras. However, some major breaks within the time period are these:

1) **Early agricultural and technological development** (about 8000 BCE to 3500 BCE) – Small groups of settlers grew into kinship-based villages that practiced both crop cultivation and domestication of animals. Tools and inventions helped villages to stabilize and eventually grow.

2) **Development of the earliest civilizations** (about 3500 to 1500 BCE) – Villages grew into cities that came to dominate the land around them. Collectively known as the "river valley" civilizations, they include:

   - **Mesopotamia** (developed by 3500 BCE or so) – between the Tigris and Euphrates Rivers in the Middle East

   - **Egypt** (developed by 3000 BCE or so) – along the Nile River in northeastern Africa

   - **Indus Valley people** (developed by 2500 BCE or so) – along the Indus River in south central Asia

Foundations (8000 B.C.E.-600 C.E.) — Unit One

- **Shang China** (developed by 1700 BCE or so) – along several rivers in the north China plains

3) **Classical civilizations** (approximately 1000 BCE to 600 CE) – These civilizations were generally much larger than the earlier ones, and their political economic, cultural, and military organizations usually were more complex. All traded extensively with others, and conquered many new territories. Classical civilizations include Zhou and Han China, the Roman Empire, and the Gupta Empire in India.

EARLY AGRICULTURAL AND TECHNOLOGICAL DEVELOPMENTS

Sedentary agricultural communities were usually the forerunners to the development of the earliest river valley civilizations. However, the shift away from hunting and gathering societies took many other forms.

ALTERNATIVES TO SEDENTARY AGRICULTURE

1) **shifting cultivation** – Often referred to as "slash and burn" agriculture, this farming method developed primarily in rain forest zones of Central and South America, West Africa, eastern and central Asia, and much of southern China and Southeast Asia. The obvious destruction to the environment was worsened by the frequency of the farmers' movement. At first, the soil in the burnt areas was very fertile, but when soil nutrients were depleted, farmers moved on to slash and burn another piece of jungle.

2) **pastoral nomadism** – This alternative to sedentary agriculture is characterized by following the herds, just as the earlier hunters and gatherers did. However, the herds were domesticated, and consisted of sheep, goats, cows, reindeer, camels, and/or horses. **Nomadism**, or the practice of moving frequently from one place to the other, was dictated by the need for pasture for the animals. This life style developed across the grassy plains of central Eurasia and nearby desert areas of the Arabian peninsula and the Sudan. Pastoral nomads may be categorized by the animals that they tended:

- **Horse nomads** – The first nomads did not ride them, but devised chariots for horses to pull. Some of these nomads formed empires (Hyksos, Hittites).

- **Reindeer herders** – These nomads populated Scandinavia and were generally far away from civilization centers.

- **Camel herders** – The main animal herded in the Sudan and the Arabian peninsula was the camel.

- **Cattle nomads** – Cattle were herded in the upper reaches of the Nile River and the southern Sudan, grass areas far away from civilization centers.

The life style of nomads by necessity means that they do not settle into villages, and therefore do not form the basis for the later development of cities. Settled agriculturalists generally saw them as "barbarians," an inferior lot that needed to be kept out of their villages. However, despite this designation, nomadic groups, especially when they have embarked on major migrations, have had a significant impact on the course of world history. Do not make the mistake of discounting them, because nomads have often sparked major changes that have greatly affected and sometimes dominated settled communities.

EARLY AGRICULTURE

By about 5000 BCE agriculture had become well established in several areas. In Southwest Asia, wheat and barley were raised, and sheep and goats were domesticated. In Southeast Asia, yams, peas, and early forms of rice were grown, and pigs, oxen, and chickens were kept. In the Americas, corn (maize), squash, and beans were staples of the diet, and in South America, potatoes were also grown. Domesticated animals were far less important in the Americas than they were elsewhere, but South Americans did domesticate llamas and alpacas.

As agriculture began to take hold in various parts of the world, the population grew rapidly. For example, world population in 3000 BCE was probably about 14 million humans, but by 500 BCE, the total had risen to about 100 million.

TECHNOLOGICAL ADVANCEMENTS

The time period that followed the advent of agriculture and preceded the earliest civilizations is known as the **Neolithic era** (in contrast to the earlier Paleolithic – or "Stone Age" – era). The name means "new stone age", and it is characterized by the refinement of tools, primarily for agricultural purposes. The time period spans roughly from 10,000 to 4000 BCE.

Early labor specialization is based on three craft industries:

- **Pottery** – Once agriculture began, pots were needed for cooking and storage, so pottery making was probably the first craft industry to develop. Early on, people discovered that designs could be etched into the clay before it hardened, so pottery became a medium for artistic expression.

- **Metallurgy** – The first metal used was copper that could be hammered into shapes for tools and jewelry. No heat was required, but someone discovered that heating separated the metal from its ores and improved the malleability and overall quality of the product. Early tools such as knives, axes, hoes, and weapons were made of copper.

- **Textile production** – Textiles decay much more readily than pottery, metal tools, and jewelry do, but the earliest textiles can be documented to about 6000 BCE. Through experimentation with plant and animal fibers, they developed methods of spinning thread and weaving fabrics, jobs done primarily by women at home while tending to children and other domestic duties.

THE DEVELOPMENT OF THE EARLIEST CIVILIZATIONS (3500 BCE-1200 BCE OR SO)

Somewhere around 4000 BCE, a series of technological inventions forged the way for a new phase of development within some of the agricultural societies. Three important changes were:

- **The introduction of the plow** – Plows meant that more land could be cultivated more efficiently. Greater productivity led to the growth of towns into cities.

- **The invention and use of bronze** – Bronze is an alloy of copper and tin that led to vast improvements in equipment and tools.

- **The advent of writing** – Apparently, the first people to use writing were the Sumerians in the Tigris-Euphrates valley. Not coincidentally, this area was the site of perhaps the oldest civilizations in history, beginning about 3500 BCE.

The Sumerians were the first of a series of people to inhabit Mesopotamia, and they developed all of the major characteristics of "civilization": cities, public buildings, job specialization, complex political organization, writing, arts and literature, long-distance trade. Other early civilizations were Egypt, the Indus Valley people, and Shang China.

COMMON CHARACTERISTICS OF THE RIVER-VALLEY CIVILIZATIONS

Each early civilization developed its own unique ways of life, but they all shared some common characteristics:

- **Location in river valleys** – Rivers provided water for crops, as well as the easiest form of transportation. All four river valleys of the earliest civilizations had very fertile soil called *loess*, or alluvial soil carried and deposited as river water traveled downstream.

- **Complex irrigation systems** – Controlling the flow of the rivers was a major issue for all of the civilizations, and all of them channeled the water for agricultural use through irrigation systems.

- **Development of legal codes** – The most famous set of laws was ***Hammurabi's Code***, but all wrote and implemented laws as political organization and long-distance trade grew more complex.

- **Use of money** – Long distance trade made the **barter system** (trading one type of good for another) impractical, so all the civilizations developed some form of money for economic exchanges.

- **Elaborate art forms and/or written literature** – These took different forms, but all civilizations showed advancements in these areas. For example, Egyptians built pyramids and concentrated on decorate arts, and Mesopotamians wrote complex stories like the *Epic of Gilgamesh*.

- **More formal scientific knowledge, numbering systems, and calendars** – Developments in these areas varied from civilization to civilization, but all formalized knowledge in at least some of these areas.

- **Intensification of social inequality** – In all river valley civilizations, gender inequality grew, and all practiced some form of slavery. Slaves were often captives in war or hereditary, and they were used for household work, public building projects, and agricultural production.

In addition to the river valley civilizations, early civilizations appeared in Mesoamerica and South America, and though they shared many characteristics above, they did not develop along river valleys. The **Olmecs** appeared by about 1200 BCE in what is now Mexico. Their trade and culture influenced other parts of Central America and shaped the development of later civilizations in the area. Between 1800 and 1200 BCE, an elaborate culture developed in the Andes area of South America. The **Chavin** people in particular spread widely throughout the area from their center in present-day Peru.

All of the civilizations varied greatly, as the chart on the next page reflects. For the exam, you only need to be able to accurately compare two of the civilizations.

Foundations (8000 B.C.E.–600 C.E.) — Unit One

COMPARISONS OF EARLY RIVER VALLEY CIVILIZATIONS			
	CULTURE	**POLITICAL ORGANIZATION**	**SOCIAL STRUCTURE**
MESOPOTAMIA (developed by 3500 BCE)	Cuneiform writing with wedge shaped characters; 2000 symbols reduced to 300 Extensive trade with Egypt and the Indus Valley *Epic of Gilgamesh* Early use of bronze tools, chariots Advanced astronomy; math based on 60 Pessimistic view of world, perhaps due to irregular, unpredictable flooding of the rivers Polytheism – gods powerful and often cruel Kings powerful, but not divine	City-states and warrior kings in almost constant conflict with one another Large empires in later times *Hammurabi's Code* and *lex talionis* (law of retaliation) Competition among city states as well as frequent invasions led to less political stability than in Egypt	Job specialization – farmers, metallurgist, merchants, craftsmen, political administrators, priests Social classes: 1) free land-owning class 2) dependent farmers and artisans 3) slaves for domestic service (could purchase freedom) Merchant class important Marriage contracts, veils for women; women of upper classes less equal than lower class counterparts
EGYPT (developed by 3000 BCE)	No epic literature Concerned with decorative arts, shipbuilding, some medical knowledge Less advanced in math and astronomy than Mesopotamians Less extensive trade, especially in earlier eras Polytheism, with pharaoh as a god Optimistic view of life (regular, controllable flooding of the river) Strong belief in the afterlife; *Book of the Dead* Hieroglyphics – complex, pictorial language	Divine kingship – the pharaoh; highly centralized, authoritarian government Generally stable government throughout the 3 kingdoms Extensive bureaucracy; pharaoh's power channeled through regional governors	Smaller nobility than Mesopotamia; fewer merchants Some social mobility through the bureaucracy Priests have high status (only ones who understand the complex hieroglyphic written language) Women – probably higher status than in Mesopotamia; love poetry indicates some importance placed on male/female relationships One female pharaoh – Hatshepsut Influential wife of pharaoh – Nefertiti
INDUS VALLEY (developed by 2500 BCE)	Writing system only recently decipherable Soapstone seals that indicate trade with both Mesopotamians and China Pottery making with bulls and long-horned cattle a frequent motif Small figurines of women Cruder weapons than Mesopotamians – stone arrowheads, no swords Polytheism – naked man with horns the primary god; fertility goddesses Two cities: Harappa and Mohenjo-Dara	Assumed to be complex and thought to be centralized Limited information, but large granaries near the cities indicate centralized control	Priests have highest status, based on position as intermediaries between gods and people Differences in house sizes indicate strong class distinctions Statues reflect reverence for female reproductive function

	CULTURE	POLITICAL ORGANIZATION	SOCIAL STRUCTURE
SHANG CHINA (developed by 1700 BCE)	Oracle bones used to communicate with ancestors Pattern on bones formed basis for writing system; writing highly valued, complex pictorial language with 3000 characters by end of dynasty Uniform written language became bond among people who spoke many different languages Bronze weapons and tools, horse-drawn chariots Geographical separation from other civilizations, though probably traded with the Indus Valley	Centralized government, power in the hands of the emperor Government preoccupied with flood control of the rivers	Job specialization – bureaucrats, farmers, slaves Social classes – warrior aristocrats, bureaucrats, farmers, slaves Patriarchal society; women as wives and concubines; women were sometimes shamans
MESO AND SOUTH AMERICA (developed by 1200 BCE)	Olmecs in Mesoamerica: Highly developed astronomy; used to predict agricultural cycles and please the gods Polytheism; religious rituals important, shamans as healers Ritual ballgames Irrigation and drainage canals Giant carved stone heads; probably with religious significance Jaguar symbol important Chavin in Andean region: Polytheism; statues of jaguar men Square stone architecture, no mortar Well-developed agriculture based on maize Unique geography: lived on coast, in mountains, and in jungle	Olmecs: apparently not united politically; unusual for ancient civilizations Chavin: probably political unification; public works operated by reciprocal labor obligations; had a capital city	Olmec: craft specializations; priests have highest status; most people were farmers Chavin: Priests have highest status; capital city dominated the hinterlands; most people were farmers

CHANGE OVER TIME – EGYPT AND WESTERN ASIA

The river valleys where civilizations first developed have been home to many people continuously over time right up to present day. In ancient times all of the areas changed significantly from their early beginnings through golden days to their eventual demise. The chart on the next page reflects change over time in two of the areas – Egypt and Western Asia, concentrating on the era from 1500 to 500 BCE.

CHANGE OVER TIME – EGYPT AND WESTERN ASIA CHANGES BY 1500-500 BCE		
	EGYPT	**WESTERN ASIA**
Political systems	Outside invaders took over; political fragmentation challenged power of the pharaoh; foreign rule for the first time – Hyksos; reunified into New Kingdom, when Hyksos expelled; in contrast to Old Kingdom, aggressive and expansionist; building of army/fortifications; female pharaoh – Hatshepsut; Ramesses II – expansionist, dominated age for 66 year reign	Outside invaders took over, control city states; two distinct political zones: Babylonia in south, Assyria in north; Assyria was expansionist; Hittites; larger states interacted – a geopolitical sphere
Trade, contact	Increased amount of trade, contact; control of Syria/Palestine and Nubia – brought new resources – timber, gold, copper; myrrh and resin from punt	Increased amount of trade, contact; Assyrians brought in tin and textiles in exchange for silver; Hittites took over copper, silver, and iron deposits
Culture, including languages and writing	Hyksos intermarried with Egyptians, assimilation of Egyptian ways; Amarna letters – reflect contacts among cultures; "superiority" of Egyptian culture	More diverse languages – Hittites, Kassites (non-Semitic); diffusion of Mespotamian political and cultural concepts, including Akkadian as language of international diplomacy; cuneiform writing spread; mythology, arts and architecture spread
Religion	Akhenaton – perhaps monotheism, devotion to sun god Aten	Spread of Sumerian mythology to entire area
Architecture	No more pyramids, but colossal statues and temples, and underground tombs	
Military	Clashes between Egypt and the Hittites	Clashes between Egypt and the Hittites
Transportaton	Horses by 1500 BCE; horse drawn chariots; enabled larger kingdoms	Horses by 2000 BCE; horse drawn chariots; enabled larger kingdoms; camels arrived

THE DECLINE OF THE EARLIEST CIVILIZATIONS

Throughout history, no matter what the era, virtually all civilizations that have come to power eventually decline and die. Historians have always been intrigued with the question of why decline appears to be inevitable. The experience of the earliest civilizations provides some answers to the question of why empires fall.

If you study the chart on page 13 carefully, you will notice that by the era from 1500 to 500 BCE, both Egypt and Western Asia were showing signs of conflict and weakness. Ironically, the problems began at a time when both areas were prosperous from trade. Their cities were cosmopolitan, arts and literature flourished, and the civilizations were in frequent contact with one another. So what happened?

An important change occurs around 1200 BCE for all of the civilizations except for China. Without exception the others experienced a major decline or destruction during this Marker Era in world history. Examples include:

- **Egypt** – Egypt experienced strong attacks from the north, and the government lost control of Nubia, a region to the south. Egypt survived, but was considerably weaker than before.

- **The Hittites** – This powerful group that occupied and controlled what is now Turkey fell apart when attacked from the northeast, never to appear as a unified empire again.

- **The Indus Valley people** – This civilization disappeared as Aryans from the north spilled into the area and took control.

- **Mycenaens** – These people who were the precursors to the later Greek civilization collapsed shortly after their famous conflict with Troy in the Trojan Wars.

In all cases, the very infrastructure of civilization collapsed, remarkably all about the same time. Why? Or a better question may be why China was spared the debacle. A common denominator is invasion, and one answer is that **Indo-Europeans** from an area north of Mesopotamia migrated south into Western Asia and the Indus Valley. This massive migration began in the mid-2nd millennium BCE, and for more than a thousand years thereafter, they threatened all of the early civilizations except for China. However, a more intriguing idea is that the very thing that brought strength also destroyed them – trade and contact with others. Interactions among the societies led to shared prosperity – the more trade, the more money people made. Trade also brought about cultural diffusion, which contributed to the diversity and sophistication of the cities. However, weaknesses may be shared as easily as strengths. When one weakened, the others felt the impact. Only China survived because it was not as involved in the trade loop as the others were.

The fall of empires around 1200 BCE is an excellent example of the role that interactions among societies play in determining the course of world history. As we will see as we go through time, interactions, both positive and negative, have been a major force that shape broad, important changes over time.

NOMADS AND MIGRATIONS (3500-500 BCE)

During the era of the earliest river valley civilizations, numerous nomadic groups migrated to new areas, with many resulting repercussions. Many of the kingdoms and empires themselves were founded by nomadic groups that took control and settled into the area of

Foundations (8000 B.C.E.-600 C.E.) — Unit One

the people that they conquered. Mesopotamia in particular, largely because of its geography, was always subject to frequent invasions from outsiders. As we saw earlier, nomads also played a large role in the fall of empires around 1200 BCE. Other groups migrated westward to Europe, setting the stage for later developments there.

Three major migrations of the era from 3500-1100 BCE are:

- **Phoenicians** – By about 2000 BCE this small group of seafaring people from a coastal area of the eastern Mediterranean Sea had set up colonies in North Africa and southern Europe. Pressured by both lack of space in their homeland and desire for prosperity from trade, the Phoenicians traveled widely over the entire Mediterranean area. To facilitate their trading, they simplified the cuneiform system, producing an alphabet with 22 characters that was far easier to learn and use. Not only did the Phoenicians spread their maritime skills, but their alphabet became the basis for alphabets in Greece, Rome, and eventually for many modern languages.

- **Israelites** – According to Judaism, the Israelites actually originated about 2000 BCE in the Mesopotamian city of Ur with the founder of the religion, Abraham. Abraham and his family migrated to the eastern Mediterranean, where they settled in a land they called Canaan. The Jews were distinctly different from other people of the area because they were **monotheistic**, believing in only one god. They later migrated to Egypt to escape a spreading drought. There they became slaves, and under their leader Moses, they returned to Canaan where they eventually formed the kingdom of Israel. The Jewish religion greatly influenced the people that they contacted, although it did not actively encourage conversion of non-Jews. Jewish beliefs and traditional stories were written down and later became basic to Christianity and Islam. The religion stressed the importance of prayer, worship, and good behavior – tenets that have become characteristic of many other monotheistic religions.

- **Aryans** – These herding peoples originated in the Caucasus area, but they began migrating in many directions about the mid 2nd millennium BCE. Waves of Aryan migrants invaded the Indian subcontinent, decimating the cities of the Indus Valley. The Aryans remained a nomadic people for many years, but eventually pushed eastward, settling in the fertile Ganges River area as agriculturalists. The Aryans imposed their **caste system** on the natives, a complex social structure with strict social status differences and virtually no social mobility. Their stories also became the basis for Hinduism.

THE CLASSICAL CIVILIZATIONS (1000 BCE-600 CE)

The period after the decline of river valley civilizations (about 1000 BCE-600 CE) is often called the **classical age**. During this era world history was shaped by the rise of several large civilizations that grew from areas where the earlier civilizations thrived. The classical civilizations differ from any previous ones in these ways:

1. They kept better and more recent records, so historical information about them is much more abundant. We know more about not just their wars and their leaders, but also about how ordinary people lived.

2. The classical societies provide many direct links to today's world, so that we may refer to them as **root civilizations**, or ones that modern societies have grown from.

3. Classical civilizations were expansionist, deliberately conquering lands around them to create large empires. As a result, they were much larger in land space and population than the river civilizations were.

Three areas where civilizations proved to be very durable were:

- **The Mediterranean** – Two great classical civilizations grew up around this area: the **Greeks** and the **Romans**.

- **China** – The classical era began with the **Zhou** Empire and continued through the **Han Dynasty**.

- **India** – Although political unity was difficult for India, the **Mauryan** and **Gupta Empires** emerged during the classical era.

COMMON FEATURES OF CLASSICAL CIVILIZATIONS

The three areas of classical civilizations developed their own beliefs, lifestyles, political institutions, and social structures. However, there were important similarities among them:

- **Patriarchal family structures** – Like the river valley civilizations that preceded them, the classical civilization valued male authority within families, as well as in most other areas of life.

- **Agricultural-based economies** – Despite more sophisticated and complex job specialization, the most common occupation in all areas was farming.

- **Complex governments** – Because they were so large, these three civilizations had to invent new ways to keep their lands together politically. Their governments were large and complex, although they each had unique ways of governing.

- **Expanding trade base** – Their economic systems were complex. Although they generally operated independently, trade routes connected them by both land and sea.

Foundations (8000 B.C.E.-600 C.E.) — Unit One

CLASSICAL CIVILIZATIONS

	Culture	Political Organization	Social Structure
Greece (about 800-300 BCE)	Most enduring influences come from Athens: Valued education, placed emphasis on importance of human effort, human ability to shape future events Interest in political theory: which form of government is best? Celebration of human individual achievement and the ideal human form Philosophy and science emphasized the use of logic Highly developed form of sculpture, literature, math, written language, and record keeping Polytheism, with gods having very human characteristics Cities relatively small Great seafaring skills, centered around Aegean, but traveling around entire Mediterranean area	No centralized government; concept of **polis**, or a fortified site that formed the centers of many city states Governing styles varied (Sparta a military state, Athens eventually a democracy for adult males) Athens government first dominated by **tyrants**, or strong rulers who gained power from military prowess; later came to be ruled by an assembly of free men who made political decisions. Both Athens and Sparta developed strong military organizations and established colonies around the Mediterranean.	Sparta theoretically equal; wealth accumulation not allowed Slavery widely practiced Men separated from women in military barracks until age 30; women had relative freedom; women in Sparta encouraged to be physically fit so as to have healthy babies; generally better treated and more equal to men than women in Athens Athens encouraged equality for free males, but women and slaves had little freedom. Neither group allowed to participate in polis affairs. Social status dependent on land holdings and cultural sophistication
Rome (about 500 BCE to 476 CE, although eastern half continued for another thousand years)	Perfection of military techniques: conquer but don't oppress; division of army into legions, emphasizing organization and rewarding military talent Art, literature, philosophy, science derivative from Greece Superb engineering and architecture techniques; extensive road, sanitation systems; monumental architecture – buildings, aqueducts, bridges Polytheism, derivative from Greeks, but religion not particularly important to the average Roman; Christianity developed during Empire period, but not dominant until very late Great city of Rome – buildings, arenas, design copied in smaller cities	Two eras: Republic – rule by aristocrats, with some power shared with assemblies; Senate most powerful, with two consuls chosen to rule, generally selected from the military Empire – non-hereditary emperor; technically chosen by Senate, but generally chosen by predecessor Extensive colonization and military conquest during both eras Development of an overarching set of laws, restrictions that all had to obey; Roman law sets in place principle of rule of law, not rule by whim of the political leader	Basic division between patricians (aristocrats) and plebeians (free farmers), although a middle class of merchants grew during the empire; wealth based on land ownership; gap between rich and poor grew with time *Paterfamilias* – male dominated family structure Patron-client system with rich supervising elaborate webs of people that owe favors to them Inequality increased during the empire, with great dependence on slavery during the late empire; slaves used in households, mines, large estates, all kinds of manual labor

	Culture	Political Organization	Social Structure
China (about 500 BCE to 600 CE)	Confucianism developed during late Zhou; by Han times, it dominated the political and social structure. Legalism and Daoism developed during same era. Buddhism appeared, but not influential yet Threats from nomads from the south and west sparked the first construction of the Great Wall; clay soldiers, lavish tomb for first emperor Shi Huangdi Chinese identity cemented during Han era: the "Han" Chinese Han – a "golden age" with prosperity from trade along the Silk Road; inventions include water mills, paper, compasses, and pottery and silk-making; calendar with 365.5 days Capital of Xi'an possibly the most sophisticated, diverse city in the world at the time; many other large cities	Zhou – emperor rules by **mandate of heaven**, or belief that dynasties rise and fall according to the will of heaven, or the ancestors. Emperor was the "son of heaven." Emperor housed in the forbidden city, separate from all others Political authority controlled by Confucian values, with emperor in full control but bound by duty Political power centralized under Shi Huangdi – often seen as the first real emperor Han – strong centralized government, supported by the educated shi (scholar bureaucrats who obtained positions through civil service exams)	Family basic unit of society, with loyalty and obedience stressed Wealth generally based on land ownership; emergence of scholar gentry Growth of a large merchant class, but merchants generally lower status than scholar-bureaucrats Big social divide between rural and urban, with most wealth concentrated in cities Some slavery, but not as much as in Rome Patriarchal society reinforced by Confucian values that emphasized obedience of wife to husband
India	Aryan religious stories written down into *Vedas*, and Hinduism became the dominant religion, although Buddhism began in India during this era; Mauryans Buddhist, Guptas Hindu Great epic literature such as the *Ramayana* and *Mahabarata* Extensive trade routes within subcontinent and with others; connections to Silk Road, and heart of Indian Ocean trade; coined money for trade So-called Arabic numerals developed in India, employing a 10-based system	Lack of political unity – geographic barriers and diversity of people; tended to fragment into small kingdoms; political authority less important than caste membership and group allegiances Mauryan and Gupta Empires formed based on military conquest; Mauryan Emperor Ashoka seen as greatest; converted to Buddhism, kept the religion alive "theater state" techniques used during Gupta – grand palace and court to impress all visitors, conceal political weakness	Complex social hierarchy based on caste membership (birth groups called *jati*); occupations strictly dictated by caste Earlier part of time period – women had property rights Decline in the status of women during Gupta, corresponding to increased emphasis on acquisition and inheritance of property; ritual of *sati* for wealthy women (widow cremated herself in her husband's funeral pyre)

GLOBAL TRADE AND CONTACT

During the classical era the major civilizations were not entirely isolated from one another. Migrations continued, and trade increased, diffusing technologies, ideas, and goods from civilization centers to more parts of the world. However, the process was slow. Chinese inventions such as paper had not yet reached societies outside East Asia by the end of the classical era. The Western Hemisphere was not yet in contact with the Eastern Hemisphere. Nevertheless, a great deal of cultural diffusion did take place, and larger areas of the world were in contact with one another than in previous eras.

One very important example of cultural diffusion was **Hellenization**, or the deliberate spread of Greek culture. The most important agent for this change was **Alexander the Great**, who conquered Egypt, the Middle East, and the large empire of Persia that spread eastward all the way to the Indus River Valley. Alexander was Macedonian, but he controlled Greece and was a big fan of Greek culture. His conquests meant that Greek architecture, philosophy, science, sculpture, and values diffused to large areas of the world and greatly increased the importance of Classical Greece as a root culture.

Trade routes that linked the classical civilizations include:

- **The Silk Road** – This overland route extended from western China, across Central Asia, and finally to the Mediterranean area. Chinese silk was the most desired commodity, but the Chinese were willing to trade it for other goods, particularly for horses from Central Asia. There was no single route, but it consisted of a series of passages with common stops along the way. Major trade towns appeared along the way where goods were exchanged. No single merchant traveled the entire length of the road, but some products (particularly silk) did make it from one end to the other.

- **The Indian Ocean Trade** – This important set of water routes became even more important in later eras, but the Indian Ocean Trade was actively in place during the classical era. The trade had three legs: one connected eastern Africa and the Middle East with India; another connected India to Southeast Asia; and the final one linked Southeast Asia to the Chinese port of Canton.

- **Saharan Trade** – This route connected people that lived south of the Sahara to the Mediterranean and the Middle East. The **Berbers**, nomads who traversed the desert, were the most important agents of trade. They carried goods in camel caravans, with Cairo at the mouth of the Nile River as the most important destination. There they connected to other trade routes, so that Cairo became a major trade center that linked many civilizations together.

- **Sub-Saharan Trade** – This trade was probably inspired by the Bantu migration, and by the end of the classical era people south of the Sahara were connected to people in the eastern and southern parts of Africa. This trade connected to the Indian Ocean trade along the eastern coast of Africa, which in turn connected the people of sub-Saharan Africa to trade centers in Cairo and India.

TRADE DURING THE CLASSICAL ERA (1000 BCE to 600 CE)					
Route	Description	What traded?	Who participated?	Cultural diffusion
Silk Road	Overland from western China to the Mediterranean Trade made possible by development of a camel hybrid capable of long dry trips	From west to east – horses, alfalfa, grapes, melons, walnuts From east to west – silk, peaches, apricots, spices, pottery, paper	Chinese, Indians, Parthians, central Asians, Romans Primary agents of trade – central Asian nomads	Chariot warfare, the stirrup, music, diversity of populations, Buddhism and Christianity, wealth and prosperity (particularly important for central Asian nomads)
Indian Ocean Trade	By water from Canton in China to Southeast Asia to India to eastern Africa and the Middle East; monsoon-controlled	Pigments, pearls, spices, bananas and other tropical fruits	Chinese, Indians, Malays, Persians, Arabs, people on Africa's cast coast	Lateen sail (flattened triangular shape) permitted sailing far from coast Created a trading class with mixture of cultures, ties to homeland broken
Saharan Trade	Points in western Africa south of the Sahara to the Mediterranean; Cairo most important destination Camel caravans	Salt from Sahara to points south and west Gold from western Africa Wheat and olives from Italy Roman manufactured goods to western Africa	Western Africans, people of the Mediterranean Berbers most important agents of trade	Technology of the camel saddle – important because it allowed domestication and use of the camel for trade
Sub-Saharan Trade	Connected Africans south and east of the Sahara to one another; connected in the east to other trade routes	Agricultural products, iron weapons	Diverse peoples in sub-Saharan Africa	Bantu language, "Africanity"

THE LATE CLASSICAL ERA: THE FALL OF EMPIRES (200 TO 600 CE)

Recall that all of the river-valley civilization areas experienced significant decline and/or conquest in the time period around 1200 BCE. A similar thing happened to the classical civilizations between about 200 and 600 CE, and because the empires were larger and more connected, their fall had an even more significant impact on the course of world history. Han China was the first to fall (around 220 CE), then the Western Roman Empire (476 CE), and finally the Gupta in 550 CE.

SIMILARITIES

Several common factors caused all three empires to fall:

- **Attacks from the Huns** – The Huns were a nomadic people of Asia that began to migrate south and west during this time period. Their migration was probably caused by drought and lack of pasture, and the invention and use of the stirrup facilitated their attacks on all three established civilizations.

- **Deterioration of political institutions** – All three empires were riddled by political corruption during their latter days, and all three suffered under weak-willed rulers. Moral decay also characterized the years prior to their respective falls.

- **Protection/maintenance of borders** – All empires found that their borders had grown so large that their military had trouble guarding them. A primary example is the failure of the Great Wall to keep the Huns out of China. The Huns generally just went around it.

- **Diseases that followed the trade routes** – Plagues and epidemics may have killed as many as half of the population of each empire.

DIFFERENCES

- The Gupta's dependence on alliances with regional princes broke down, exhibiting the tendency toward political fragmentation on the Indian subcontinent.

- Rome's empire lasted much longer than did either of the other two. The Roman Empire also split in two, and the eastern half endured for another 1000 years after the west fell.

- The fall of empire affected the three areas in different ways. The fall of the Gupta probably had the least impact, partly because political unity wasn't the rule anyway, and partly because the traditions of Hinduism and the caste system (the glue that held the area together) continued on after the empire fell. The fall of the Han Dynasty was problematic for China because strong centralized government was in place, and social disorder resulted from the loss of authority. However, dynastic cycles that followed the dictates of the Mandate of Heaven were well defined in China, and the Confucian traditions continued to give coherence to Chinese society. The most devastating fall of all occurred in Rome. Roman civilization depended almost exclusively on the ability of the government and the military to control territory. Even though Christianity emerged as a major religion, it appeared so late in the life of the empire that it provided little to unify people as Romans after the empire fell. Instead, the areas of the empire fragmented into small parts and developed unique characteristics, and the Western Roman Empire never united again.

COMMON CONSEQUENCES

The fall of the three empires had some important consequences that represent major turning points in world history:

- Trade was disrupted but survived, keeping intact the trend toward increased long-distance contact. Trade on the Indian Ocean even increased as conflict and decline of political authority affected overland trade.

- The importance of religion increased as political authority decreased. In the west religion, particularly Christianity, was left to slowly develop authority in many areas of people's lives. Buddhism also spread quickly into China, presenting itself as competition to Confucian traditions.

- Political disunity in the Middle East forged the way for the appearance of a new religion in the 7th century. By 600 CE Islam was in the wings waiting to make its entrance onto the world stage.

BELIEF SYSTEMS

Belief systems include both religions and philosophies that help to explain basic questions of human existence, such as "Where did we come from?" Or "What happens after death?" or "What is the nature of human relationships or interactions?" Many major beliefs systems that influence the modern world began during the Foundations Era (8000 BCE to 600 CE).

POLYTHEISM

The earliest form of religion was probably polydaemonism (the belief in many spirits), but somewhere in the Neolithic era people began to put these spirits together to form gods. In polytheism, each god typically has responsibility for one area of life, like war, the sea, or death. In early agricultural societies, quite logically most of the gods had responsibility for the raising of crops and domesticated animals. The most prominent god in many early societies was the Sun God, who took many forms and went by many names. Other gods supervised rain, wind, the moon, or stars. Many societies worshipped gods of fertility, as reflected in statues of pregnant goddesses, or women with exaggerated female features. Young male gods often had features of bulls, goats, or jaguars that represented power, energy, and/or virility. Perceptions of the gods varied from one civilization to the next, with some seeing them as fierce and full of retribution, and others seeing them as more tolerant of human foibles.

Religion was extremely important to the river-valley civilizations, and most areas of life revolved around pleasing the gods. Monotheism was first introduced about 2000 BCE by Israelites, but monotheism did not grow substantially till much later. Each of the classical civilizations had very different belief systems that partially account for the very different directions that the three areas took in succeeding eras. Rome and Greece were polytheistic, but Christianity had a firm footing by the time the Western Roman Empire fell. Hinduism dominated Indian society from very early times, although Buddhism also took root in India. From China's early days, ancestors were revered, a belief reinforced by the philosophy of Confucianism. Other belief systems, such as Daoism, Legalism, and Buddhism, also flourished in China by 600 CE.

HINDUISM

The beginnings of Hinduism are difficult to trace, but the religion originated with the polytheism that the Aryans brought as they began invading the Indian subcontinent sometime after 2000 BCE. Aryan priests recited hymns that told stories and taught values and were eventually written down in ***The Vedas***, the sacred texts of Hinduism. One famous story is ***The Ramayana*** that tells about the life and love of Prince Rama and his wife Sita. Another epic story is ***The Mahabharata***, which focuses on a war between cousins. Its most famous part is called ***The Baghavad Gita***, which tells how one cousin, Arjuna, overcomes his hesitations to fight his own kin. The stories embody important Hindu values that still guide modern day India.

Hinduism assumes the eternal existence of a universal spirit that guides all life on earth. A piece of the spirit called the **atman** is trapped inside humans and other living creatures. The most important desire of the atman is to be reunited with the universal spirit, and every aspect of an individual's life is governed by it. When someone dies, his or her atman may be reunited, but most usually is reborn in a new body. A person's caste membership is a clear indication of how close he or she is to the desired reunion. Some basic tenets of Hinduism are

- **Reincarnation** – An atman spirit is reborn in a different person after one body dies. This rebirth has no beginning and no end, and is part of the larger universal spirit that pervades all of life.

- **Karma** – This widely used word actually refers to the pattern of cause and effect that transcends individual human lives. Whether or not an individual fulfills his/her duties in one life determines what happens in the next.

- **Dharma** – Duties called dharma are attached to each caste position. For example, a warrior's dharma is to fight honorably, and a wife's duty is to serve her husband faithfully. Even the lowliest caste has dharma attached to it. If one fulfills this dharma, the reward is for the atman to be reborn into a higher caste. Only the atman of a member of the highest caste (originally the priests) has the opportunity to be reunited with the universal spirit.

- **Moksha** – Moksha is the highest, most sought-after goal for the atman. It describes the reunion with the universal spirit.

The universal spirit is represented by **Brahman**, a god that takes many different shapes. Two of Brahman's forms are **Vishnu** the Creator, and **Shiva** the Destroyer. Hinduism is very difficult to categorize as either polytheistic or monotheistic because of the central belief in the universal spirit. Do each of Brahman's forms represent a different god, or are they all the same? Brahman's forms almost certainly represent different Aryan gods from the religion's early days, but Hinduism eventually unites them all in the belief in Brahman.

BUDDHISM

Buddhism began in India in the Ganges River area during the 6th century BCE. Its founder was **Siddhartha Guatama**, who later became known as the Buddha, or the "Enlightened One." Siddhartha was the son of a wealthy Hindu prince who grew up with many advantages in life. However, as a young man he did not find answers to the meaning of life in Hinduism, so he left home to become an **ascetic**, or wandering holy man. His Enlightenment came while sitting under a tree in a deerfield, and the revelations of that day form the basic tenets of Buddhism:

- **The Four Noble Truths** – 1) All of life is suffering; 2) Suffering is caused by false desires for things that do not bring satisfaction; 3) Suffering may be relieved by removing the desire; 4) Desire may be removed by following the **Eightfold Path**.

- **The Eightfold Path to Enlightenment** – The ultimate goal is to follow the path to **nirvana**, or a state of contentment that occurs when the individual's soul unites with the universal spirit. The eight steps must be achieved one by one, starting with a change in thoughts and intentions, followed by changes in life style and actions, that prelude a higher thought process through meditation. Eventually, a "breakthrough" occurs when nirvana is achieved that gives the person a whole new understanding of life.

Note that Hinduism supported the continuation of the caste system in India, since castes were an outer reflection of inner purity. For example, placement in a lower caste happened because a person did not fulfill his/her dharma in a previous life. Higher status was a "reward" for good behavior in the past. Although Buddhism, like Hinduism, emphasizes the soul's yearning for understandings on a higher plane, it generally supported the notion that anyone of any social position could follow the Eightfold Path successfully. Buddhists believed that changes in thought processes and life styles brought enlightenment, not the powers of one's caste. Although the Buddha actively spread the new beliefs during his long lifetime, the new religion faced oppression after his death from Hindus who saw it as a threat to the basic social and religious structure that held India together. Buddhism probably survived only because the Mauryan emperor Ashoka converted to it and promoted its practice. However, in the long run, Buddhism did much better in areas where it spread through cultural diffusion, such as Southeast Asia, China, Korea, and Japan.

CONFUCIANISM

Three important belief systems (Confucianism, Daoism, and Legalism) emerged in China during the Warring States Period (403-221 BCE) between the Zhou and Han Dynasties. Although the period was politically chaotic, it hosted a cultural flowering that left a permanent mark on Chinese history.

Confucius contemplated why China had fallen into chaos, and concluded that the Mandate of Heaven had been lost because of poor behavior of not only the Chinese emperor, but all his subjects as well. His plan for reestablishing Chinese society profoundly affected the course of Chinese history and eventually spread to many other areas of Asia as well. He emphasized the importance of harmony, order, and obedience and believed that if five basic relationships were sound, all of society would be, too:

- **Emperor/subject** – The emperor has the responsibility to take care of his subjects, and subjects must obey the emperor.
- **Father/son** – The father takes care of the son, and the son obeys the father.
- **Older brother/younger brother** – The older brother takes care of the younger brother, who in turn obeys him.
- **Husband/wife** – The husband takes care of the wife, who in turn obeys him.
- **Friend/friend** – The only relationship that does not assume inequality should be characterized by mutual care and obedience.

Confucius also defined the "superior man" – one who exhibits **ren** (kindness), **li** (sense of propriety), and **xiao** (filial piety, or loyalty to the family).

Confucianism accepted and endorsed inequality as an important part of an ordered society. It confirmed the power of the emperor, but held him responsible for his people, and it reinforced the patriarchal family structure that was already in place in China. Because Confucianism focused on social order and political organization, it is generally seen as a philosophy rather than a religion. Religions are more likely to emphasize spiritual topics, not society and politics.

DAOISM

The founder of Daoism is believed to have been **Laozi**, a spiritualist who probably lived in the 4th century BCE. The religion centers on the *Dao* (sometimes referred to as the "Way" or "Path"), the original force of the cosmos that is an eternal and unchanging principle that governs all the workings of the world. The *Dao* is passive – not active, good nor bad – but it just is. It cannot be changed, so humans must learn to live with it. According to Daoism, human strivings have brought the world to chaos because they resist the *Dao*. A chief characteristic is *wuwei*, or a disengagement from the affairs of the world, including government. The less government, the better. Live simply, in harmony with nature. Daoism encourages introspection, development of inner contentment, and no ambition to change the *Dao*.

Both Confucianism and Daoism encourage self knowledge and acceptance of the ways things are. However, Confucianism is activist and extroverted, and Daoism is reflective and introspective. The same individual may believe in the importance of both belief systems, unlike many people in western societies who think that a person may only adhere to one belief system or another.

LEGALISM

The third belief system that arose from the Warring States Period is **legalism**, and it stands in stark contrast to the other beliefs. It had no concern with ethics, morality, or propriety, and cared nothing about human nature, or governing principles of the world. Instead it emphasized the importance of **rule of law**, or the imperative for laws to govern, not men. According to legalism, laws should be administered objectively, and punishments for offenders should be harsh and swift. Legalism was the philosophy of **Shi Huangdi**, the first emperor, whose Qin Dynasty rescued China from chaos. However, when he died, the Han emperors that followed deserted legalism and established Confucianism as the dominant philosophy.

JUDAISM

As noted earlier, Judaism was the first clearly monotheistic religion. At the heart of the religion was a belief in a Covenant, or agreement, between God and the Jewish people, that God would provide for them as long as they obeyed him. The **Ten Commandments** set down rules for relationships among human beings, as well as human relationships to God. Because they were specially chosen by God, Jews came to see themselves as separate from others and did not seek to convert others to the religion. As a result, Judaism has remained a relatively small religion. However, its influence on other major religions, including Zoroastrianism, Christianity, and Islam is vast, and so it remains as a very significant "root religion."

Zoroastrianism is an early monotheistic religion that almost certainly influenced and was influenced by Judaism, and it is very difficult to know which one may have emerged first. Both religions thrived in the Middle East, and adherents of both apparently had contact with one another. Zoroastrianism was the major religion of Persia, a great land-based empire that was long at war with Ancient Greece and eventually conquered by Alexander the Great. The religion's founder was **Zoroaster** or Zarathushtra, who saw the world immersed in a great struggle between good and evil, a concept that certainly influenced other monotheistic religions.

CHRISTIANITY

Christianity grew directly out of Judaism, with its founder **Jesus** of Nazareth born and raised as a Jew in the area just east of the Mediterranean Sea. During his lifetime, the area was controlled by Rome as a province in the empire. Christianity originated partly from a long-standing Jewish belief in the coming of a Messiah, or a leader who would restore the Jewish kingdom to its former glory days. Jesus' followers saw him as the Messiah who would cleanse the Jewish religion of its elitism and assure life after death to all that followed Christian precepts. In this way, its appeal to ordinary people may be compared to that of Buddhism, as it struggled to emerge from the Hindu caste system. Christianity's broad appeal to the masses, as well as deliberate conversion efforts by its early apostles, meant that the religion grew steadily and eventually became the religion with the most followers in the modern world.

Jesus was a prophet and teacher whose followers came to believe that he was the son of God. He advocated a moral code based on love, charity, and humility. His disciples predicted a final judgment day when God would reward the righteous with immortality and condemn sinners to eternal hell. Jesus was arrested and executed by Roman officials because he aroused suspicions among Jewish leaders, and he was seen by many as a dangerous rebel rouser. After his death, his apostles spread the faith. Especially important was **Paul**, a converted Jew who was familiar with Greco-Roman culture. He explained Christian principles in ways that Greeks and Romans understood, and he established churches all over the eastern end of the Mediterranean, and even as far away as Rome.

Christianity grew steadily in the Roman Empire, but not without clashes with Roman authorities. Eventually in the 4th century CE, the Emperor Constantine was converted to Christianity and established a new capital in the eastern city of Byzantium, which he renamed Constantinople. As a result, the religion grew west and north from Rome, and also east from Constantinople, greatly extending its reach.

By the end of the classical era, these major belief systems had expanded to many areas of the world, and with the fall of empires in the late classical era, came to be major forces in shaping world history. One major religion – Islam – remained to be established in the 7th century as part of the next great period that extended from 600 to 1450 CE.

UNIT ONE QUESTIONS

1. All of the following were changes to human societies brought about by the Neolithic Revolution EXCEPT:

   (A) Reliable food supplies increased.
   (B) The total human population rapidly increased.
   (C) Job specialization occurred.
   (D) Women and men grew to have more equal status.
   (E) The distinction between nomads and settled people became important.

2. Women were important contributors to the agricultural revolution because they were likely the gender who

   (A) owned property
   (B) wanted more leisure time
   (C) gathered edible plants and knew where grains grew
   (D) found carrying children on their backs too burdensome
   (E) liked farming

3. Which of the following is the best explanation for why the concept of civilization is controversial as an organizing principle of world history?

   (A) The concept is too broad to have any meaning.
   (B) The use of the concept assumes that settled people are superior to nomads.
   (C) The concept implies that eastern civilizations are superior to those in the west.
   (D) The concept assumes that nomadic people are civilized.
   (E) The concept ignores the importance of periodization in analyzing world history.

4. All of the following ancient civilizations were centered around a river valley EXCEPT:

   (A) Chavin
   (B) Egypt
   (C) Mesopotamia
   (D) China
   (E) Indus Valley

5. Which of the following most accurately compares the government structures of early Mesopotamia and Egypt?

(A) The governments of both civilizations were highly decentralized.
(B) Overall, Mesopotamian government was characterized by strong city-states, and Egypt was ruled by divine kingship.
(C) Mesopotamia had a highly developed bureaucracy; Egypt did not.
(D) In both civilizations power was concentrated in the hands of a king that was believed to be a god.
(E) Although priests were powerful in both societies, their authority was generally separated from the political power of the kings.

6. Which of the following best describes the basis of the ruler's authority in Zhou China?

(A) The ruler was chosen and favored by heaven, and held power as long as he was a wise and principled guardian of his people.
(B) The ruler was believed to be a god himself, and so his authority could not be questioned.
(C) The ruler depended heavily on his staff, so the real authority lay in the hands of the bureaucrats.
(D) The ruler was selected by a handful of elite aristocrats who also had the authority to remove him from office.
(E) The ruler was a military leader who held power as long as he was victorious on the battlefield.

7. Which of the following were common phenomena in early Mesopotamia, Ancient Egypt, and the Indus River Valley?

    I. a complex writing system
    II. extensive irrigation
    III. long distance trade
    IV. centralization of civilization around navigable rivers

(A) I and II only
(B) I and III only
(C) II, III, and IV only
(D) I, II, and III only
(E) I, II, III, and IV

(Questions 8 and 9 refer to the following diagram):

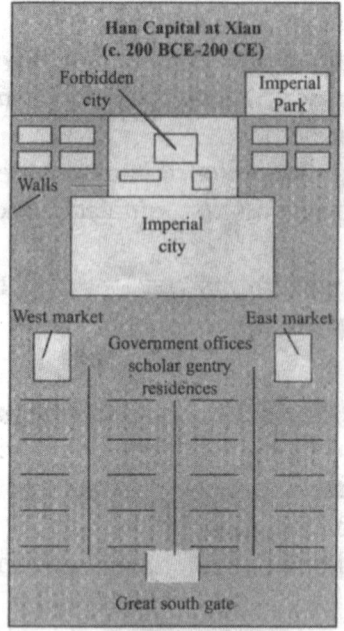

WORLD CIVILIZATIONS, 3rd ed. by Peter N. Stearns, Michael Adas, Stuart B. Schwartz and Marc Jason Gilbert. Copyright © 2001 by Addison-Wesley Educational Publishers Inc. Reprinted by Permission of Pearson Education, Inc.

8. The diagram shows the capital city of in ancient

    (A) Greece
    (B) Rome
    (C) Indus Valley
    (D) Babylonia
    (E) China

9. The "forbidden city" illustrated in the diagram reflects the political leader's status as

    (A) the son of heaven
    (B) a god (the divine ruler)
    (C) a superior man, but with no connections to spirituality
    (D) a tyrant
    (E) the head of the *paterfamilias*

10. All of the following commonly characterize the development of civilization EXCEPT:

    (A) large cities that dominate the countryside around them
    (B) public building projects
    (C) increasing equality among all citizens
    (D) a written language
    (E) long distance trade

Foundations (8000 B.C.E.-600 C.E.) Unit One

11. Confucianism encourages its followers to

    (A) learn from foreigners better ways to excel
    (B) experiment with new food crops
    (C) believe that their rulers were not in any way divine
    (D) seek principles of science
    (E) follow ethical rules that promote harmony and order

12. All of the following events happened at about the same time (1200 B.C.E.) EXCEPT:

    (A) The Hittite empire collapsed.
    (B) Major trade centers in Western Asia were destroyed.
    (C) Egypt was significantly weakened by a series of outside attacks.
    (D) The Zhou dynasty fell, and the Warring States period began.
    (E) The Mycenaean civilization was destroyed.

13. Which of the following factors best explains why the four events referred to in #12 happened about the same time?

    (A) destruction by a common attacker, the Huns
    (B) major environmental changes in all affected areas
    (C) similar life cycles of the four civilizations
    (D) a common tendency to rely too much on the authority of one ruler
    (E) interdependence

14. The continuing importance of written language in Chinese culture may be traced to its earliest use for

    (A) issuing mandates from the emperor to subject warlords
    (B) divination; communication with the ancestors
    (C) trade with nomads to the west of the river valley settlements
    (D) astronomical calculations that determine the planting and harvest seasons
    (E) organizing the political bureaucracy

15. The spread of Greek culture all over the eastern Mediterranean and the former Persian Empire is known as

    (A) hellenization
    (B) classicazation
    (C) Zoroastrianism
    (D) Olympization
    (E) Delianism

16. Which of the following civilizations had to acclimate to existing in a mountainous area with a narrow, dry coastline on one side of the mountain range and a rain forest on the other side?

   (A) Olmec
   (B) Indus
   (C) Nubian
   (D) Persia
   (E) Chavin

17. Shifting cultivation was generally practiced

   (A) around fertile river valleys
   (B) in rain forests and their peripheries
   (C) in mountainous areas
   (D) along dry coastal areas
   (E) in grassy plains

18. The polis is most closely associated with which of the following societies/civilizations?

   (A) The Mauryan Empire
   (B) Athens
   (C) Han China
   (D) Babylonia
   (E) Persian Empire

19. All of the following are accurate comparisons of Athens and Sparta EXCEPT:

   (A) Sparta demanded more subordination of its male citizens to the demands of the state.
   (B) The Athenians emphasized the importance of poetry, art, and philosophy; the Spartans did not.
   (C) Spartan women did not have as many freedoms as did Athenian women.
   (D) The Spartans placed the military at the center of their society; Athens generally did not.
   (E) Both Sparta and Athens dominated the countryside around them and were two of the largest city states.

Foundations (8000 B.C.E.-600 C.E.)   Unit One   33

20. All of the following are important principles of Greek culture that had wide influence on later civilizations EXCEPT:

    (A) new religious concepts that redefined the nature of god(s)
    (B) an interest in political theory that sought the best forms of government
    (C) an emphasis on the importance of human effort and ability to shape future events
    (D) celebration of human achievement, including the ideal human form
    (E) a philosophical and scientific tradition that emphasized the use of logic

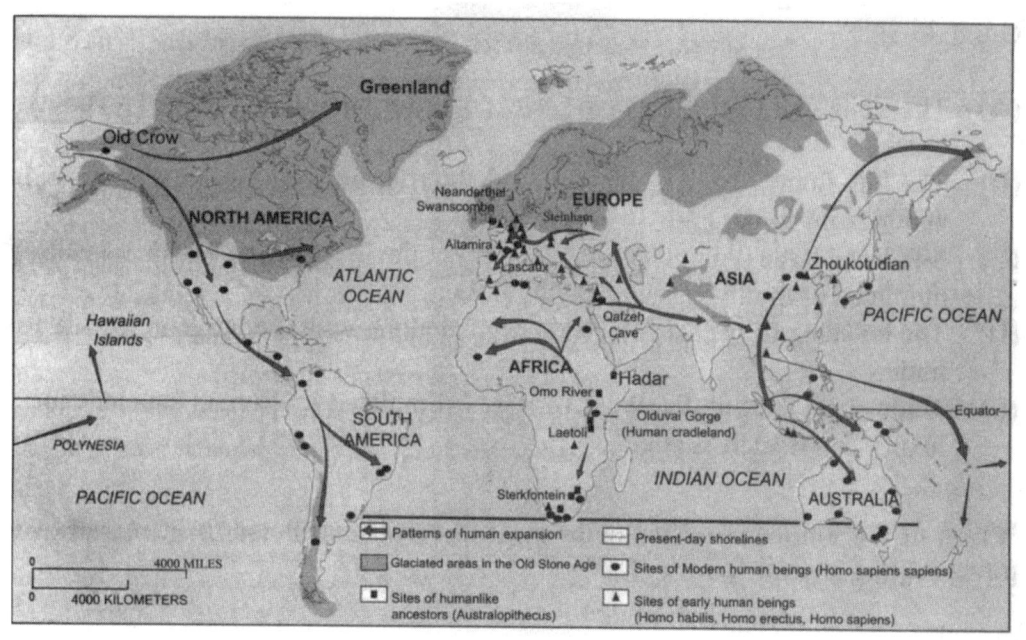

From World Civilizations, 3rd ed. by Peter N. Stearns, Michael Adas, Stuart B. Schwartz and Marc Jason Gilbert. Copyright © 2001 by Addison-Wesley Educational Publishers Inc. Reprinted by Permission of Pearson Education, Inc.

(Questions 21 and 22 are based on the above map):

21. The approximate date of the map is

    (A) 20,000 BCE
    (B) 10,000 BCE
    (C) 5,000 BCE
    (D) 3,500 BCE
    (E) 300 BCE

22. Which of the following is the most probable reasons for the migrations shown on the map?

   (A) Nutrients from the soil were being rapidly depleted.
   (B) Explorers were seeking gold and other riches.
   (C) Hunters were following their herds to better pasture.
   (D) Humans were escaping from powerful new breeds of carnivores.
   (E) Humans were seeking warmer climates.

23. All of the following are accurate descriptions of trade along the Silk Road before 600 C.E. EXCEPT:

   (A) The Chinese traded silk, pottery, and paper for horses, alfalfa, and a variety of crops.
   (B) The Silk Route linked China to the Mediterranean world via Central Asia, Iran, and Mesopotamia, Iran.
   (C) Silk Road trade did not significantly affect the lifestyles of Turkic nomads, the dominant pastoralist group in Central Asia.
   (D) The breeding of hybrid camels developed along with the burgeoning Silk Road trade.
   (E) Trade along the Silk Road network was stimulated by Roman demands for luxury goods such as silk.

24. Which of the following technologies most directly contributed to increased overland travel starting around 300 B.C.E.?

   (A) stirrups
   (B) camel saddles
   (C) wheeled chariots
   (D) horse collars
   (E) iron plows

25. Which of the following most helps to explain why the collapse of political institutions was more devastating to the Roman civilization than to Han China or Gupta India?

   (A) Political institutions in Rome were weaker to begin with.
   (B) The barbarian attacks destroyed more physical property and vital public works in Rome.
   (C) Roman emperors had more power than did Han or Gupta emperors, so their downfall eviscerated the Roman Empire.
   (D) Han China and Gupta India had strong religious/philosophical traditions to provide continuity.
   (E) The Romans were economically more self-sufficient than the Han or Gupta, so they had no long-distance trade to cushion their fall.

Foundations (8000 B.C.E.-600 C.E.)   Unit One   35

26. Which sailing technology allowed the sailors on the Indian Ocean to travel long distances by taking advantage of monsoon winds?

    (A) the square sail
    (B) the wooden rudder
    (C) the lateen sail
    (D) the caravel
    (E) lightweight masts

27. Which of the following was one of the most valuable commodities added to established trading systems by the trans-Saharan trade?

    (A) manufactured goods
    (B) copper
    (C) pottery
    (D) salt
    (E) spices

28. Why did the majority of the Chinese population during the Han dynasty live in eastern China?

    (A) They wanted access to sea trade and its accompanying wealth.
    (B) The best farmland was concentrated along rivers in eastern China.
    (C) They were more isolated from invasion from nomad peoples there.
    (D) The best Buddhist centers were in eastern China.
    (E) The Tibetans held control in the west, and they did not welcome Chinese settlement in their area.

29. The people who transported goods across the Sahara and dominated trade across the desert for centuries were the

    (A) Berbers
    (B) Bedouins
    (C) Malays
    (D) Ghanans
    (E) Bantu

30. Which of the following characteristics contributed most directly to a tendency toward political disunity in ancient India?

    (A) weak religious traditions
    (B) lack of foreign trade
    (C) weak social structure
    (D) lack of strong political leaders
    (E) diverse geographical features

31. Buddhists believe that a state of grace or nirvana may be reached by

   (A) changing one's karma
   (B) following the moral duties of one's caste
   (C) being reincarnated as a Brahman
   (D) following the eightfold path
   (E) renouncing asceticism

32. What central feature of Hinduism did Buddhism reject?

   (A) union with the universal spirit as a major goal
   (B) use of missionaries to spread the religion
   (C) the caste system
   (D) the importance of ethical decision making
   (E) reincarnation

33. "He traveled throughout Syria, Palestine, Anatolia, and Greece, and found that many non-Jews were interested in the teachings of Christianity. He redirected his efforts toward these gentiles, and set up strong Christian communities all over the eastern Mediterranean."

   The quote above describes

   (A) Jesus
   (B) John
   (C) Peter
   (D) Mark
   (E) Paul

34. Which of the following is a significant difference between early Christianity and early Judaism?

   (A) Judaism was originally polytheistic, Christianity was not.
   (B) Christianity put more emphasis on missionary work, converting others to the religion.
   (C) The Roman Empire sought to eradicate Christianity but not Judaism.
   (D) Christianity did not accept the spiritual authority of the Torah, which expressed basic beliefs of Judaism.
   (E) In general, early believers in Judaism were more persecuted by polytheistic people than were early believers in Christianity.

35. Which of the following belief systems have their origins in China during the classical era (1000 BCE-500 CE)?

   I. Buddhism
   II. Daoism
   III. Legalism
   IV. Confucianism

   (A) I and IV only
   (B) I, II, and IV only
   (C) II and IV only
   (D) II, III, and IV only
   (E) I, II, III, and IV

UNIT ONE DBQ

Law Codes before 600 C.E.

Directions: The following question is based on the accompanying Documents 1-7. This question is designed to test your ability to work with and understand historical documents. Write an essay that:

- Has a relevant thesis and supports that thesis with evidence from the documents.
- Uses all or all but one of the documents.
- Analyzes the documents by grouping them in as many appropriate ways as possible. Does not simply summarize the documents individually.
- Takes into account both the sources of the documents and the authors' points of view.

You may refer to relevant historical information not mentioned in the documents.

Many societies had written law codes during the time periods before 600 C.E. Using the following documents, discuss BOTH the similarities and differences among written law codes before 600 C.E. In what ways do the codes reflect particular differences among various cultures, and in what ways do they reflect needs common to most societies of the era? What other documents might help you to better evaluate law codes before 600 C.E.?

Document 1

Source: *Code of Hammurabi*, 18th c. B.C.E.

[The purpose of the code is] to cause justice to prevail in the land, to destroy the wicked and the evil, and to prevent the strong from oppressing the weak,…to enlighten the land and to further the welfare of the people.

If his son is under age, and unable to administer his [deceased] father's affairs, then a third part of the field and garden shall be given to his mother, and his mother shall bring him up…

A captain, soldier, or official may not give his field, or garden, or house to his wife or his daughter; neither can they be given as payment for debt.

If a son has struck his father, his hands shall be cut off.

If a man has destroyed the eye of another free man, his own eye shall be destroyed.

If he has broken the bone of a free man, his bone shall be broken.

If he has destroyed the eye of a peasant, or broken a bone of a peasant, he shall pay one mina of silver.

Document 2

Source: The Book of Exodus, *The Ten Commandments*

I am the Lord thy God…Thou shalt have no other gods before Me…
Thou shalt not make unto thee a graven image…
Thou shalt not take the name of the Lord thy God in vain…
Remember the Sabbath day, to keep it holy…
Honor thy father and thy mother…
Thou shalt not murder…
Thou shalt not commit adultery…
Thou shalt not steal…
Thou shalt not bear false witness…
Thou shalt not covet…

Document 3

Source: *The Laws of Twelve Tables*, Roman Republic, 451 B.C.E.

Table III:
When a debt has been acknowledged...thirty days must be the legitimate time of grace. After that, the debtor may be arrested by laying on of hands. Bring him into court. If he does not satisfy the judgment...the creditor...may bind him either in stocks or in fetters....

Table IV:
Quickly kill...a dreadfully deformed child. If a father thrice surrender a son for sale, the son shall be free from the father.

Table V
Females shall remain in guardianship even when they have attained their majority.

Table VII
Should a tree on a neighbor's farm be bent crooked by a wind and lean over your farm, action may be taken for removal of that tree. It is permitted to gather up fruit falling down on another man's farm.

Table XI
Intermarriage shall not take place between plebeians and patricians.

Document 4

Source: *The Laws of Manu*, 2nd or 3rd c B.C.E. India

At night they [unclean jatis or castes] shall not walk about in villages and in towns. By day they may go about for the purpose of their work, distinguished by marks at the king's command, and they shall carry out the corpses of persons who have no relatives; that is a settled rule.
A man of low caste who through covetousness lives by the occupations of a higher one, the king shall deprive of his property and banish.
A wife, a son, and a slave, these three are declared to have no property; the wealth which they earn is acquired for him to whom they belong...
What was given before the nuptial fire, what was given on the bridal procession, what was given in token of love, and what was received from her brother, mother, or father, that is called the six-fold property of a woman.
Where women are honored, there the gods are pleased; but where they are not honored, no sacred rite yields reward..
Where the female relations live in grief, the family soon wholly perishes; but that family where they are not unhappy ever prospers.

Document 5

Source: Li Su, *On the Destruction of Books*, Qin Dynasty, 3rd c. B.C.E.

Your servant suggests that all books in the imperial archives, save the memoirs of Qin, be burned. All persons in the empire, except members of the Academy of Learned Scholars, in possession of the Book of Odes, the Book of History, and discourses of the hundred philosophers [including Confucius]' should take them to the local governors and have them burned. Those who dare to talk to each other about the Book of Ideas and the Book of History should be executed and their bodies exposed in the market place. Anyone referring to the past to criticize the present should, together with all members of his family, be put to death. Officials who fail to report cases that have come under their attention are equally guilty. After thirty days from the time of issuing the decree, those who have not destroyed their books are to be branded and sent to build the Great Wall. Books not to be destroyed will be those on medicine and pharmacy, agriculture and aboriculture [the cultivation of trees and shrubs]. People wishing to pursue learning should take the officials as their teachers.

Document 6

Source: Luke 2:1, *The New Testament*, 1st c B.C.E.-1st c. C.E.

And it came to pass in those days, that there went out a decree from Caesar Augustus, that all the world should be enrolled to be taxed.

Document 7

Source: *The Justinian Code*, Byzantine Empire, 6th c. C.E.

Slaves are in the power of masters, a power derived from the law of nations; for among all nations it may be remarked that masters have the power of life and death over their slaves, and that everything acquired by the slave is acquired for the master.

If the wheat of Titius is mixed with yours, when this takes place by mutual consent, the mixed heap belongs to you in common because each body, that is, each grain, which before was the property of one or other of you, has by your mutual consent been made your common property; but, if the intermixture were accidental, or made by Titius without your consent, the mixed wheat does not then belong to you both in common; because the grains still remain distinct, and retain their proper substance...if either of you keep the whole quantity of mixed wheat, the other has a real action [claim or suit] for the amount of wheat belonging to him, but it is in the province of the judge to estimate the quality of the wheat belonging to each.

No testing material on this page.

UNIT TWO

600-1450 C.E.

This second era is much shorter than the previous one, but during the years between 600 and 1450 C.E. many earlier trends continued to be reinforced, while some very important new patterns emerged that shaped all subsequent times.

QUESTIONS OF PERIODIZATION

Change over time occurs for many reasons, but three phenomena that tend to cause it are:

- **Mass migrations** – Whenever a significant number of people leave one area and migrate to another, change occurs for both the land that they left as well as their destination.
- **Imperial conquests** – If an empire (or later a country) deliberately conquers territory outside its borders, significant changes tend to follow for both the attackers and the attacked.
- **Cross-cultural trade and exchange** – Widespread contact among various areas of the world brings not only new goods but new ideas and customs to all areas involved.

During the classical era (about 1000 BCE to 600 CE), all of these phenomena occurred, as we saw in Unit I. With the fall of the three major classical civilizations, the stage was set for new trends that defined 600-1450 CE as another period with different migrations and conquests, and more developed trade patterns than before. Some major events and developments that characterized this era were:

- Older belief systems, such as Christianity, Hinduism, Confucianism, and Buddhism, came to become more important than political organizations in defining many areas of the world. Large religions covered huge areas of land, even though localized smaller religions remained in place.
- Two nomadic groups – the **Bedouins** and the **Mongols** – had a huge impact on the course of history during this era.
- A new religion – **Islam** – began in the 7th century and spread rapidly throughout the Middle East, Northern Africa, Europe, and Southeast Asia.
- Whereas Europe was not a major civilization area before 600 CE, by 1450 it was connected to major trade routes, and some of its kingdoms were beginning to assert world power.
- Major empires developed in both South America (the Inca) and Mesoamerica (the Maya and Aztec.)
- China grew to have hegemony over many other areas of Asia and became one of the largest and most prosperous empires of the time.

- Long distance trade continued to develop along previous routes, but the amount and complexity of trade and contact increased significantly.

This unit will investigate these major shifts and continuities by addressing several broad topics:

1) **The Islamic World** – Islam began in the Arabian peninsula in the 7th century CE, impacting political and economic structures, and shaping the development of arts, sciences and technology.

2) **Interregional networks and contacts** – Shifts in and expansion of trade and cultural exchange increased the power of China, connected Europe to other areas, and helped to spread the major religions. The Mongols first disrupted, then promoted, long-distance trade throughout Asia, Africa, and Europe.

3) **China's internal and external expansion** – During the Tang and Song Dynasties, China experienced an economic revolution and expanded its influence on surrounding areas. This era also saw China taken over by a powerful nomadic group (the Mongols), and then returned to Han Chinese under the Ming Dynasty.

4) **Developments in Europe** – European kingdoms grew from nomadic tribes that invaded the Roman Empire in the 5th century C.E. During this era, feudalism developed, and Christianity divided in two – the Catholic Church in the west and the Eastern Orthodox Church in the east. In both cases, the Church grew to have a great deal of political and economic power.

5) **Social, cultural, economic patterns in the Amerindian world** – Major civilizations emerged, building on the base of smaller, less powerful groups from the previous era. The Maya, Aztec, and Inca all came to control large amounts of territory and many other native groups.

6) **Demographic and environmental changes** – Urbanization continued, and major cities emerged in many parts of the world. Nomadic migrations during the era included the Aztecs, Mongols, Turks, Vikings, and Arabs. Long distance trade promoted the spread of disease, including the plague pandemics in the early fourteenth century.

THE ISLAMIC WORLD

Islam – the religion with the second largest number of supporters in the world today – started in the sparsely populated Arabian Peninsula among the Bedouins, a nomadic group that controlled trade routes across the desert. In the early 7th century, a few trade towns, such as Mecca and Medina, were centers for camel caravans that were a link in the long distance trade network that stretched from the Mediterranean to eastern China. Mecca was also the destination for religious pilgrims who traveled there to visit shrines to countless gods and spirits. In the center of the city was a simple house of worship called the **Ka'aba**, which contained among its many idols the **Black Stone**, believed to have been placed there by Abraham, the founder of Judaism. Jews and Christians inhabited the city, and they mixed with the majority who were polytheistic.

THE FOUNDING OF ISLAM

Islam was founded in Mecca by **Muhammad**, a trader and business manager for his wife, Khadijah, a wealthy businesswoman. Muhammad was interested in religion, and when he was about 40 he began visiting caves outside the city to find quiet places to meditate. According to Muslim belief, one night while he was meditating Muhammad heard the voice of the angel Gabriel, who told him that he was a messenger of God. Muhammad became convinced that he was the last of the prophets, and that the one true god, **Allah**, was speaking to him through Gabriel. He came back into the city to begin spreading the new religion, and he insisted that all other gods were false. His followers came to be called **Muslims**, or people who have submitted to the will of Allah.

Muhammad's ministry became controversial, partly because city leaders feared that Mecca would lose its position as a pilgrimage center if people accepted Muhammad's monotheism. In 622 C.E. he was forced to leave Mecca for fear of his life, and this famous flight to the city of Yathrib became known as the **hijrah**, and 622 became the official founding date for the new religion. In Yathrib he converted many to Islam, and he renamed the city **"Medina,"** or "city of the Prophet." He called the community the **umma**, a term that came to refer to the entire population of Muslim believers.

As Islam spread, Muhammad continued to draw the ire of Mecca's leadership, and he became an astute military leader in the hostilities that followed. In 630, the Prophet and 10,000 of his followers captured Mecca and destroyed the idols in the Ka'aba. He proclaimed the structure as the holy structure of Allah, and the Black Stone came to symbolize the replacement of polytheism by the faith in one god.

ISLAMIC BELIEFS AND PRACTICES

The Five Pillars of faith are five duties at the heart of the religion. These practices represent a Muslim's submission to the will of God.

- **Faith** – When a person converts to Islam, he or she recites the Declaration of Faith, "There is no God but Allah, and Muhammad is the Messenger of Allah." This phrase is repeated over and over in Muslim daily life.

- **Prayer** – Muslims must face the city of Mecca and pray five times a day. The prayer often takes place in **mosques** (Islamic holy houses), but Muslims may stop to pray anywhere. In cities and towns that are primarily Muslim, a *muezzin* calls people to prayer from a *minaret* tower for all to hear.

- **Alms** – All Muslims are expected to give money for the poor through a special religious tax called alms. Muhammad taught the responsibility to support the less fortunate.

- **Fasting** – During the Islamic holy month of **Ramadan**, Muslims fast from sunup to sundown. Only a simple meal is eaten at the end of the day that reminds Muslims that faith is more important than food and water.

- **Pilgrimage** – Muslims are expected to make a pilgrimage to Mecca at least once in their lifetime. This event, called the **hajj**, takes place once a year, and people arrive from all over the world in all kinds of conveyances to worship at the Ka'aba and several other holy sites nearby. All pilgrims wear an identical white garment to show their equality before Allah.

The single most important source of religious authority for Muslims is the **Qur'an**, the holy book believed to be the actual words of Allah. According to Islam, Allah expressed his will through the Angel Gabriel, who revealed it to Muhammad. After Muhammad's death these revelations were collected into a book, the Qur'an. Muhammad's life came to be seen as the best model for proper living, called the **Sunna**. Using the Qur'an and the Sunna for guidance, early followers developed a body of law known as **shari'a**, which regulated the family life, moral conduct, and business and community life of Muslims. Shari'a still is an important force in many Muslim countries today even if they have separate bodies of official national laws. In the early days of Islam, shari'a brought a sense of unity to all Muslims.

THE SPREAD OF ISLAM

Muhammad died in 632 CE, only ten years after the hijrah, but by that time, Islam had spread over much of the Arabian Peninsula. Since Muhammad's life represented the **"seal of the prophets"** (he was the last one), anyone that followed had to be a very different sort. The government set up was called a **caliphate**, ruled by a caliph (a title that means "successor" or "deputy") selected by the leaders of the umma. The first caliph was Abu-Bakr, one of Muhammad's close friends. He was followed by three successive caliphs who all had known the Prophet, and were "rightly guided" by the Qur'an and the memory of Muhammad. By the middle of the 8th century Muslim armies had conquered land from the Atlantic Ocean to the Indus River, and the caliphate stretched 6000 miles east to west.

Religious zeal certainly played an important role in the rapid spread of Islam during the 7th and 8th centuries C.E. However, several other factors help to explain the phenomenon:

- **Well-disciplined armies** – For the most part the Muslim commanders were able, war tactics were effective, and the armies were efficiently organized.

- **Weakness of the Byzantine and Persian Empires** – As the Islamic armies spread north, they were aided by the weakness of the empires they sought to conquer. Both the Byzantine and Persian Empires were weaker than they had been in previous times, and many of their subjects were willing to convert to the new religion.

- **Treatment of conquered peoples** – The Qur'an forbid forced conversions, so conquered people were allowed to retain their own religions. Muslims considered Christians and Jews to be superior to polytheistic people, not only because they were monotheistic, but also because they too adhered to a written religious code. As a result, Muslims called Christians and Jews **"people of the book"**. Many conquered people chose to convert to Islam, not only because of its appeal, but because as Muslims they did not have to pay a poll tax.

THE SUNNI-SHI'A SPLIT

The Arab tribes had fought with one another for centuries before the advent of Islam, and the religion failed to prevent serious splits from occurring in the caliphate. Each of the four caliphs was murdered by rivals, and the death of Muhammad's son-in-law **Ali** in 661 triggered a civil war. A family known as the **Umayyads** emerged to take control, but Ali's death sparked a fundamental division in the umma that has lasted over the centuries. The two main groups were:

- **Sunni** – In the interest of peace, most Muslims accepted the Umayyads' rule, believing that the caliph should continue to be selected by the leaders of the Muslim community. This group called themselves the Sunni, meaning "the followers of Muhammad's example."

- **Shi'a** – This group thought that the caliph should be a relative of the Prophet, and so they rejected the Umayyads' authority. **"Shi'a"** means "the party of Ali," and they sought revenge for Ali's death.

Even though the caliphate continued for many years, the split contributed to its decline as a political system. The caliphate combined political and religious authority into one huge empire, but it eventually split into many political parts. The areas that it conquered remained united by religion, but the tendency to fall apart politically has been a major feature of Muslim lands. Many other splits followed, including the formation of the **Sufi**, who reacted to the luxurious lives of the later caliphs by pursuing a life of poverty and devotion to a spiritual path. They shared many characteristics with other **ascetics**, such as Buddhist and Christian monks, with their emphasis on meditation and chanting.

THE CHANGING STATUS OF WOMEN

The patriarchal system characterized most early civilizations, and Arabia was no exception. However, women enjoyed rights not always given in other lands, such as inheriting property, divorcing husbands, and engaging in business ventures (like Muhammad's first wife, Khadijah.) The Qur'an emphasized equality of all people before Allah, and it outlawed female infanticide, and provided that dowries go directly to brides. However, for the most part, Islam reinforced male dominance. The Qur'an and the shari'a recognized descent through the male line, and strictly controlled the social and sexual lives of women to ensure the legitimacy of heirs. The Qur'an allowed men to follow Muhammad's example to take up to four wives, and women could have only one husband.

Muslims also adopted the long-standing custom of veiling women. Upper class women in Mesopotamia wore veils as early as the 13th century BCE, and the practice had spread to Persia and the eastern Mediterranean long before Muhammad lived. When Muslims conquered these lands, the custom remained intact, as well as the practice of women venturing outside the house only in the company of servants or chaperones.

ARTS, SCIENCES, AND TECHNOLOGIES

Because Islam was always a missionary religion, learned officials known as *ulama* ("people with religious knowledge") and *qadis* ("judges") helped to bridge cultural differences and spread Islamic values throughout the **dar al-Islam**, as Islamic lands came to be known. Formal educational institutions were established to help in this mission. By the 10th century CE, higher education schools known as *madrasas* had appeared, and by the 12th century they were well established. These institutions, often supported by the wealthy, attracted scholars from all over, and so we see a flowering of arts, sciences, and new technologies in Islamic areas in the 12th through 15th centuries.

When Persia became a part of the caliphate, the conquerors adapted much of the rich cultural heritage of that land. Muslims became acquainted, then, with the literary, artistic, philosophical, and scientific traditions of others. Persian was the principle language of literature, poetry, history, and political theory, and the verse of the *Rubaiyat* by Omar Khayyam is probably the most famous example. Although many of the stories of *The Arabian Nights* or *The Thousand and One Nights* were passed down orally from generation to generation, they were written down in Persian.

Islamic states in northern India also adapted mathematics from the people they conquered, using their Hindi numerals, which Europeans later called "Arabic numerals." The number system included a symbol for zero, a very important concept for basic calculations and multiplication. Muslims are generally credited with the development of mathematical thought, particularly algebra. Muslims also were interested in Greek philosophy, science, and medical writings. Some were especially involved in reconciling Plato's thoughts with the teachings of Islam. The greatest historian and geographer of the 14th century was **Ibn Khaldun**, a Moroccan who wrote a comprehensive history of the world. Another Islamic scholar, **Nasir al-Din**, studied and improved upon the cosmological model of Ptolemy, an ancient Greek astronomer. Nasir al-Din's model was almost certainly used by Nicholas Copernicus, a Polish monk and astronomer who is usually credited with developing the heliocentric model for the solar system.

INTERREGIONAL NETWORKS AND CONTACTS

Contacts among societies in the Middle East, the Indian subcontinent, and East Asia increased significantly between 600 and 1450 CE, and Africa and Europe became much more important links in the long-distance trade networks. Both the Indian Ocean Trade and the Silk Road were disrupted by major migrations during this period, but both recovered and eventually thrived. Europeans were first brought into the trade loop through cities like

Venice and Genoa on the Mediterranean, and the Trans-Saharan trade became more vigorous as major civilizations developed south of the Sahara.

Two major sea-trading routes – those of the Mediterranean Sea and the Indian Ocean – linked the newly created Muslim Empire together, and Arabic sailors came to dominate the trade. Muslims also were active in the Silk Road trade to India and China. To encourage the flow of trade, Muslim money changers set up banks throughout the caliphate so that merchants could easily trade with those at far distances. Cities along the trade routes became cosmopolitan mixtures of many religions and customs.

AFRICAN SOCIETIES AND EMPIRES

Until about 600 CE, most African societies based their economies on hunting and gathering or simple agriculture and herding. They centered their social and political organization around the family, and none had a centralized government. Beginning around 640, Islam spread into the northern part of the continent, bringing with it the unifying forces of religious practices and law, the shari'a. As Islam spread, many African rulers converted to the new religion, and centralized states began to form. The primary agents of trade, the Berbers of the Sahara, became Muslims, although they retained their identities and tribal loyalties. As a result, Islam mixed with native cultures to create a synthesis that took different forms in different places in northern Africa. This gradual, nonviolent spread of Islam was very conducive to trade, especially since people south of the Sahara had gold.

Between 600 and 1450 CE, two major empires emerged in West Africa, just south of the Sahara Desert:

- **Ghana** – By the 700s, a farming people called the Soninke had formed an empire that they called Ghana ("war chief") that was growing rich from taxing the goods that traders carried through their territory. Their most important asset was gold from the Niger River area that they traded for salt from the Sahara. The Arab and Berber traders also carried cloth, weapons, and manufactured goods from ports on the Mediterranean. Ghana's king had exclusive rights to the gold, and so controlled its supply to keep the price high. The king also commanded an impressive army, and so the empire thrived. Like the Africans along the Mediterranean, Ghana's rulers and elites converted to Islam, but most others retained their native religions.

- **Mali** – During the 11th century, the Almoravids, a Muslim group from northern Africa, conquered Ghana. By the 13th century, a new empire, called Mali, dominated West Africa. The empire began with Mande-speaking people south of Ghana, but it grew to be larger, more powerful, and richer than Ghana had been. Mali too based its wealth on gold. New deposits were found east of the Niger River, and African gold became a basic commodity in long distance trade. Mali's first great leader was **Sundiata**, whose life inspired an epic poem – *The Legend of Sundiata* – that was passed down from one generation to the next. He defeated kingdoms around Mali, and also proved to be an effective administrator. Perhaps even more famous was **Mansu Musa**, a 14th century ruler. He is best known for giving away so much gold as he traveled from Mali to Mecca for the hajj that he set off a major round of inflation, seriously affecting economies all along the long-distance trade routes. Mali's capital city, **Timbuktu**, became a world center of trade, education and sophistication.

Another major civilization developed in East Africa: **the Swahili city-states**. The people who lived in trade cities along the eastern coast of Africa provided a very important link for long-distance trade. The cities were not united politically, but they were well developed, with a great deal of cultural diversity and sophisticated architecture. The people were known collectively as the **Swahili**, based on the language that they spoke – a combination of Bantu and Arabic. Most were Muslims, and the sailors were renowned for their ability to maneuver their small boats through the Indian Ocean to India and other areas of the Middle East via the Red Sea and back again.

THE CHRISTIAN CRUSADES (LATE 11TH THROUGH 13TH CENTURIES C.E.)

Pope Urban II called for the Christian Crusades in 1095 with the urgent message that knights from western Europe must defend the Christian Middle East, especially the Holy Lands of the eastern Mediterranean, from Turkish Muslim invasions. The Eastern Orthodox Byzantine emperor called on Urban for help when Muslims were right outside Constantinople. What resulted over the next two centuries was not the recovery of the Middle East for Christianity, but many other unintended outcomes. By the late 13th century, the Crusades ended, with no permanent gains made for Christians. Indeed, Constantinople eventually was destined to be taken by Muslims in 1453 and renamed Istanbul.

Instead of bringing the victory that the knights sought, the Crusades had the ultimate consequence of bringing Europeans squarely into the major world trade circuits. The societies of the Middle East were much richer than European kingdoms were, and the knights encountered much more sophisticated cultures there. They brought home all kinds of trading goods from many parts of the world and stimulated a demand in Europe for foreign products, such as silk, spices, and gold. Two Italian cities – Venice and Genoa – took advantage of their geographic location to arrange for water transportation for knights across the Mediterranean to the Holy Lands. On the return voyages, they carried goods back to European markets, and both cities became quite wealthy from the trade. This wealth eventually became the basis for great cultural change in Europe, and by 1450, European kingdoms were poised for the eventual control of long-distance trade that they eventually gained during the 1450-1750 era.

THE IMPORTANCE OF THE MONGOLS

The Mongol invasions and conquests of the 13th century are arguably among the most influential set of events in world history. This nomadic group from Central Asia swept south and east, just as the Huns had done several centuries before. They conquered China, India, the Middle East, and the budding kingdom of Russia. If not for the fateful death of the Great Khan Ogadai, they might well have conquered Europe as well. As it is, the Mongols established and ruled the largest empire ever assembled in all of world history. Although their attacks at first disrupted the major trade routes, their rule eventually brought the *Pax Mongolica*, or a peace often compared to the *Pax Romana* established in ancient times across the Roman Empire.

THE RISE OF THE MONGOLS

The Mongols originated in the Central Aslian *steppes*, or dry grasslands. They were pastoralists, organized loosely into kinship groups called clans. Their movement almost certainly began as they sought new pastures for their herds, as had so many of their predecessors. Many historians believe that a severe drought caused the initial movement, and that the Mongol's superior ability as horsemen sustained their successes.

Around 1200 CE, a Mongol khan (clan leader) named **Temujin** unified the clans under his leadership. His acceptance of the title **Genghis Khan**, or "universal leader" tells us something of his ambitions for his empire. Over the next 21 years, he led the Mongols in conquering much of Asia. Although he didn't conquer China in his lifetime, he cleared the way for its eventual defeat by Mongol forces. His sons and grandsons continued the conquests until the empire eventually reached its impressive size. Genghis Khan is usually seen as one of the most talented military leaders in world history. He organized his warriors by the Chinese model into armies of 10,000, which were grouped into 1,000 man brigades, 100-man companies, and 10-man platoons. He ensured that all generals were either kinsmen or trusted friends, and they remained amazingly loyal to him. He used surprise tactics, like fake retreats and false leads, and developed sophisticated catapults and gunpowder charges.

The Mongols were finally stopped in Eurasia by the death of Ogodai, the son of Genghis Khan, who had become the Great Khan centered in Mongolia when his father died. At his death, all leaders from the empire went to the Mongol capital to select a replacement, and by the time this was accomplished, the invasion of Europe had lost its momentum. The Mongols were also contained in Islamic lands by the **Mamluk** armies of Egypt, who had been enslaved by the Abbasid Caliphate. These forces matched the Mongols in horsemanship and military skills, and defeated them in battle in 1260 before the Mongols could reach the Dardanelles strait. The Mongol leader Hulegu decided not to press for further expansion.

THE MONGOL ORGANIZATION

The Mongol invasions disrupted all major trade routes, but Genghis Khan's sons and grandsons organized the vast empire in such a way that the routes soon recovered. They formed four **Khanates**, or political organizations each ruled by a different relative, with the ruler of the original empire in Central Asia designated as the "Great Khan," or the one that followed in the steps of Genghis. Once the Mongols defeated an area, generally by brutal tactics, they were generally content to extract tribute (payments) from them, and often allowed conquered people to keep many of their customs. The Mongol khans were spread great distances apart, and they soon lost contact with one another. Most of them adopted many customs, even the religions, of the people they ruled. For example, the Il-khan that conquered the last caliphate in the Middle East eventually converted to Islam and was a great admirer of the sophisticated culture and advanced technologies of his subjects. So the Mongol Empire eventually split apart, and the Mongols themselves became assimilated into the cultures that they had "conquered."

TWO TRAVELLERS

Much of our knowledge of the world in the 13th and 14th century comes from two travelers, Ibn Battuta and Marco Polo, who widened knowledge of other cultures through writing about their journeys.

- **Marco Polo** – In the late 13th century, Marco Polo left his home in Venice, and eventually traveled for many years in China. He was accompanied by his father and uncle, who were merchants anxious to stimulate trade between Venice and points along the trade routes east. Polo met the Chinese ruler Kublai Khan (Genghis Khan's grandson), who was interested in his travel stories and convinced him to stay as an envoy to represent him in different parts of China. He served the khan for 17 years before returning home, where he was captured by Genoans at war with Venice. While in prison, he entertained his cellmates with stories about China. One prisoner compiled the stories into a book that became wildly popular in Europe, even though many did not believe that Polo's stories were true. Europeans could not believe that the fabulous places that Polo described could ever exist.

- **Ibn Battutu** – This famous traveler and prolific writer of the 14th century spent many years of his life visiting places within Islamic Empires. He was a Moroccan legal scholar who left his home for the first time to make a pilgrimage to Mecca. After his hajj was completed, he traveled through Mesopotamia and Persia, then sailed down the Red Sea and down the east African coast as far south as Kilwa. He later traveled to India, the Black Sea, Spain, Mali, and the great trading cities of Central Asia. He wrote about all of the places he visited, and compiled a detailed journal that has given historians a great deal of information about those places and their customs during the 14th century. A devout Muslim who generally expected fine hospitality, Ibn Battutu seldom kept his opinions to himself, and he commented freely on his approval or disapproval of the things that he saw.

Although few people traveled as much as Marco Polo and Ibn Battutu did, the large empires of the Mongols and other nomadic peoples provided a political foundation for the extensive cross-cultural interaction of the era.

CHINA'S HEGEMONY

Hegemony occurs when a civilization extends its political, economic, social, and cultural influence over others. For example, we may refer to the hegemony of the United States in the early 21st century, or the conflicting hegemony of the United States and Russia during the Cold War Era. In the time period between 600 and 1450 CE, it was impossible for one empire to dominate the entire globe, largely because distance and communication were so difficult. Both the Islamic caliphates and the Mongol Empire fell at least partly because their land space was too large to control effectively. So the best any empire could do was to establish regional hegemony. During this time period, China was the richest and most powerful of all, and extended its reach over most of Asia.

THE "GOLDEN ERA" OF THE TANG AND SONG

During the period after the fall of the Han Dynasty in the 3rd century C.E., China went into a time of chaos, following the established pattern of dynastic cycles. During the short-lived Sui Dynasty (589-618 C.E.), China began to restore centralized imperial rule. A great accomplishment was the building of the **Grand Canal**, one of the world's largest waterworks projects before the modern era. The canal was a series of manmade waterways that connected the major rivers and made it possible for China to increase the amount and variety of internal trade. When completed it was almost 1240 miles long, with roads running parallel to the canal on either side.

STRENGTHS OF THE TANG

In 618 a rebel leader seized China's capital, Xi'an, and proclaimed himself the emperor of the **Tang Dynasty**, an empire destined to last for almost three hundred years (till 907). Under the Tangs China regained strength and emerged as a powerful and prosperous society. Three major accomplishments of the Tang account for their long-lasting power:

- **A strong transportation and communications system** – The Grand Canal contributed to this accomplishment, but the Tang rulers also built and maintained an advanced road system, with inns, postal stations, and stables to service travelers along the way. People traveled both on foot and by horse, and the emperor used the roads to send messages by courier in order to keep in contact with his large empire.

- **The equal-field system** – The emperor had the power to allocate agricultural land to individuals and families, and the equal-field system was meant to ensure that land distribution was fair and equitable. Part of the emperor's motivation was to control the amount of land that went to powerful families, a problem that had caused strong challenges to the emperor's mandate during the Han Dynasty. The system worked until the 9th century, when influential families again came to accumulate much of the land.

- **A merit-based bureaucracy** – This system was well developed during the Han Dynasty, but the Tang made good use of it by recruiting government officials who were well educated, loyal, and efficient. Although powerful families used their resources to place relatives in government positions, most bureaucrats won their posts because of intellectual ability.

Tang China extended its hegemony by extracting **tribute** (gifts and money) from neighboring realms and people. China was often called "the Middle Kingdom," because its people saw their civilization at the center of all that paid it honor. The empire itself was far larger than any before it, following along the river valleys from Vietnam to the south and Manchuria to the north, and extending into parts of Tibet. In 668, the Tang overran Korea, and established a vassal kingdom called Silla.

RELIGIOUS ISSUES

Long before the Tang Dynasty was founded, Buddhism had made its way into China along the trade routes. By the pre-Tang era, Buddhist monasteries had so grown in influence that they held huge tracts of land and exerted political influence. Many rulers of the pre-Tang era, particularly those from nomadic origins, were devout Buddhists. Many variations of Buddhism existed, with **Mahayana Buddhism** prevailing, a major branch of the religion that allowed a great deal of variance in Buddha's original teachings. **Empress Wu** (690-705) was one of Buddhism's strongest supporters, contributing large sums of money to the monasteries and commissioning many Buddhist paintings and sculptures. By the mid-9th century, more than 50,000 monasteries existed in China.

Confucian and Daoist supporters took note of Buddhism's growing influence, and they soon came to challenge it. Part of the conflict between Confucianism and Buddhism was that in many ways they were opposite beliefs, even though they both condoned "right" behavior and thought. Confucianism emphasized duties owed to one's society, and placed its highest value on order, hierarchy, and obedience of superiors. Buddhism, on the other hand, encouraged its supporters to withdraw from society, and concentrate on personal meditation. Finally in the 9th century, Confucian scholar-bureaucrats conspired to convince the emperors to take lands away from the monasteries through the equal-field system. Under emperor Wuzong, thousands of monasteries were burned, and many monks and nuns were forced to abandon them and return to civilian life.

Not only was Buddhism weakened by these actions, but the Tang Dynasty lost overall power as well. However, Confucianism emerged as the central ideology of Chinese civilization and survived as such until the early 20th century.

THE FOUNDING OF THE SONG DYNASTY

During the 8th century, warlords began to challenge the Tang rulers, and even though the dynasty survived until 907 C.E., the political divisions encouraged nomadic groups to invade the fringes of the empire. Worsening economic conditions led to a succession of revolts in the 9th century, and for a few years China fell into chaos again. However, recovery came relatively quickly, and a military commander emerged in 960 to reunite China, beginning the **Song Dynasty**. The Song emperors did not emphasize the military as much as they did civil administration, industry, education, and the arts. As a result, the Song never established hegemony over as large an area as the Tang had, and political disunity was a constant threat as long as they held power. However, the Song presided over a "golden era" of Chinese civilization characterized by prosperity, sophistication, and creativity.

The Song vastly expanded the bureaucracy based on merit by sponsoring more candidates with more opportunities to learn Confucian philosophy, and by accepting more candidates for bureaucratic posts than the Sui and Tang.

PROBLEMS UNDER THE SONG

The Song created a more centralized government than ever before, but two problems plagued the empire and eventually brought about its fall:

- **Finances** – The expansion of the bureaucracy meant that government expenses skyrocketed. The government reacted by raising taxes, but peasants rose in two major rebellions in protest. Despite these warnings, bureaucrats refused to give up their powerful positions.

- **Military** – China had always needed a good military, partly because of constant threats of invasion by numerous nomadic groups. The Song military was led by scholar bureaucrats with little knowledge or real interest in directing armies. The **Jurchens**, a northern nomadic group with a strong military, conquered other nomads around them, overran northern China, and eventually capturing the Song capital. The Song were left with only the southern part of their empire that was eventually conquered by the Mongols in 1279 C.E.

ECONOMIC REVOLUTIONS OF THE TANG AND SONG DYNASTIES

Even though the Song military weakness eventually led to the dynasty's demise, it is notable for economic revolutions that led to Chinese hegemony during the era. China's economic growth in turn had implications for many other societies through the trade that it generated along the long-distance routes. The changes actually began during the Tang Dynasty and became even more significant during Song rule. Some characteristics of these economic revolutions are:

- **Increasing agricultural production** – Before this era, Chinese agriculture had been based on the production of wheat and barley raised in the north. The Tang conquest of southern China and Vietnam added a whole new capability for agriculture – the cultivation of rice. In Vietnam they made use of a new strain of **fast-ripening rice** that allowed the production of two crops per year. Agricultural techniques improved as well, with the use of the heavy iron plow in the north and water buffaloes in the south. The Tang also organized extensive irrigation systems, so that agricultural production was able to move outward from the rivers.

- **Increasing population** – China's population about 600 C.E. was about 45 million, but by 1200 (the Song Dynasty) it had risen to about 115 million. This growth occurred partly because of the agricultural revolution, but also because distribution of food improved with better transportation systems, such as the Grand Canal and the network of roads throughout the empire.

- **Urbanization** – The agricultural revolution also meant that established cities grew and new ones were created. With its population of perhaps 2,000,000, the Tang capital of Xi'an was probably the largest city in the world. The Song capital of Hangzhou was smaller, with about 1,000,000 residents, but it too was a cosmopolitan city with large markets, public theatres, restaurants, and craft shops. Many other Chinese cities had populations of more than 100,000. Because rice production was so successful and Silk Road and Indian Ocean trade was vigorous, other farmers could concentrate on specialty fruits and vegetables that were for sale in urban markets.

- **Technological innovations** – During Tang times craftsmen discovered techniques for producing porcelain that was lighter, thinner, more useful, and much more beautiful. Chinese porcelain was highly valued and traded to many other areas of the world, and came to be known broadly as *chinaware*. The Chinese also developed superior methods for producing iron and steel, and between the 9th and 12th centuries, iron production increased tenfold. The Tang and Song are best known for the new technologies they invented, such as gunpowder, movable type printing, and seafaring aids, such as the magnetic compass. Gunpowder was first used in bamboo flame throwers, and by the 11th century inventors had constructed crude bombs.

- **Financial inventions** – Because trade was so strong and copper became scarce, Chinese merchants developed paper money as an alternative to coins. Letters of credit called **"flying cash"** allowed merchants to deposit money in one location and have it available in another. The Chinese also used checks which allowed drawing funds deposited with bankers.

NEO-CONFUCIANISM

The conflict between Buddhism and Confucianism during the late Tang Dynasty eased under the Song, partly because of the development of **Neo-Confucianism**. Classical Confucians were concerned with practical issues of politics and morality, and their main goal was an ordered social and political structure. Neo-Confucians also became familiar with Buddhist beliefs, such as the nature of the soul and the individual's spiritual relationships. They came to refer to *li*, a concept that defined a spiritual presence similar to the universal spirit of both Hinduism and Buddhism. This new form of Confucianism was an important development because it reconciled Confucianism with Buddhism, and because it influenced philosophical thought in China, Korea, Vietnam, and Japan in all subsequent eras.

PATRIARCHAL SOCIAL STRUCTURES

As wealth and agricultural productivity increased, the patriarchal social structure of Chinese society also tightened. With family fortunes to preserve, elites insured the purity of their lines by further confining women to the home. The custom of **foot binding** became very popular among these families. Foot binding involved tightly wrapping young girls' feet so that natural growth was seriously impaired. The result was a tiny malformed foot with the toes curled under and the bones breaking in the process. The women generally could not walk except with canes. Peasants and middle class women did not bind their feet because it was impractical, but for elite women, the practice – like wearing veils in Islamic lands – indicated their subservience to their male guardians.

KUBLAI KHAN, THE YUAN DYNASTY, AND THE EARLY MING (1279-1450 C.E.)

The Mongols began to breach the Great Wall under Genghis Khan, but the southern Song was not conquered until his grandson, Kublai Khan captured the capital and set up a new capital in Beijing, which he called Khanbaluk, or "city of the Khan." This was the city that Marco Polo described to the world as the finest and richest in all the world. Under Kublai Khan, China was unified, and its borders grew significantly. Although Mongols replaced the top bureaucrats, many lower Confucian officials remained in place, and the Khan clearly respected Chinese customs and innovations. However, whereas the Song had emphasized cultural and organizational values, the Mongols were most adept in military affairs and conquest. Also, even though trade flourished during the Tang and Song era, merchants had a much lower status than scholars did. Kublai Khan and his successors put a great deal of effort into conquering more territory in Asia, and they elevated the status of merchants, actions deeply resented by the Confucian bureaucrats.

As borders expanded once again, the Yuan emperors experienced the old problem of empire – too few military to protect too many borders. The Mongols increased tributes and established **"tax farming"**, (a practice that gave middlemen the responsibility of collecting taxes), which led to corruption. The gap between the urban rich and the rural poor also grew, and a devastating plague spread though the population. All of these problems inspired conspiracy among the Confucian scholars, who led a revolt, toppled the Mongols, and established the **Ming Empire**.

The leader of the Ming revolt, **Zhu Yuan Zhang**, located the capital in Nanjing and made great efforts to reject the culture of the Mongols by closing off trade relations with Central Asia and the Middle East, and reasserting Confucian ideology. Thus the Ming set off a yo-yo effect of sorts in China that had been seen before, but became accentuated in the centuries that followed. China, a great civilization that was vitally connected to trade routes, shut herself off and turned to internal strengths. During this era, it was still possible because of great distances to other empires. China could choose to be left alone, and no one could do much about it, even if it limited long-distance trade profits. However, in subsequent eras this tendency to isolate itself would strip China of her hegemony and eventually lead to worldwide humiliation.

KOREA AND JAPAN

During the 7th century Tang armies conquered much of Korea, resulting in the Korean **Silla Dynasty**'s king recognizing the Tang emperor as his overlord. Tang forces withdrew from the peninsula, and even though Korea paid tribute to China, the Silla rulers were allowed to have a greatly deal of autonomy. Significantly, though, the tributary relationship resulted in a great deal of Chinese influence diffusing to Korea. The Silla built a new capital modeled on the Tang capital, Confucian schools were founded, and Buddhism sparked a great deal of popular interest. However, unlike China, Korea never developed a bureaucracy based on merit.

On the other hand, Chinese armies never invaded Japan, and even Kublai Khan's great forces could not overcome the treacherous straits that lie between Korea and Japan. The straits had isolated Japan since its beginnings, and its many islands and mountainous terrain led to separations among people who lived there. As a result, small states dominated by aristocratic clans developed, with agricultural communities developing wherever they were possible. Some Chinese influence, such as Confucianism, Buddhism, and Chinese writing characters diffused to Japan, but it remained unique in many ways. Two examples are:

- **Shintoism** – This native religion venerated ancestors, but also had a host of nature spirits and deities. Confucianism and Buddhism did not replace Shintoism, and it remained as an important religion in Japan.

- **Separation of imperial power from real political power** – Even though a Japanese emperor did emerge to rule the various clans, he served as a ceremonial figurehead and symbol of authority. The family that really ran things from 794 to 1188 were the **Fujiwaras** – who had military might that allowed them to manipulate the emperor. An important divergence from Chinese influence occurred during the late 11th century when the **Minamoto** clan seized power and installed their leader as the **shogun**, a military leader who ruled in place of the emperor.

The Japanese developed a system of **feudalism**, a political and economic system less developed than those of centralized empires, but more powerful than purely local government. Feudalism was accompanied by a set of political values that emphasized mutual ties, obligations, and loyalties. The Japanese elites – who came to be known as **daimyos** – found military talent in the samurai, professional warriors who swore loyalty to them. **Samurais** lived by a warrior's code – the **bushido** – that required them to commit suicide **(seppuku)** by disembowelment if they failed their masters.

DEVELOPMENTS IN EUROPE (500-1450 C.E.)

Until the 5th century most of the European continent was part of the Roman Empire. However, as the push from the Hun migrations from Central Europe caused other groups to move west as well, the Roman armies began to have problems in guarding their borders. As other weaknesses appeared that threatened the empire, Germanic groups such as the Goths, Ostrigoths, and Vandals began to take over, with Rome falling to the invasions in 476 C.E. Without the structure of the empire, the groups settled into areas of Europe and retained their own ways of life. The era from about 500 to 1000 C.E. is sometimes referred to as the "Dark Ages" in European history, partly because many aspects of the Roman civilization were lost, such as written language, advanced architectural and building techniques, complex government, and access to long-distance trade. For the most part, these early people of Europe could not read or write, and lived much as their nomadic ancestors had. In their isolation, they slowly cleared the forested areas for farming, but their greatest need was for protection. Dangers lay not only from animals in the forests, but also from other people that had settled in nearby areas. However, the need for protection grew to be most important when the **Vikings** from Scandinavia invaded many areas of Europe in the 8th and 9th centuries, followed by the **Magyars**, who came from the east in the late 9th century. In response, Europeans established feudalism, with many features similar to Japanese feudalism, but also with many differences.

European feudal institutions revolved around political and military relationships. The **lord**, a large landholder, provided his **vassals** with **fiefs**, or landholdings, in return for service. The most important service was military support, so these **knights** spent a great deal of time learning and practicing military techniques and horsemanship, as well as maintaining their fiefs. Vassals also supervised public works projects, and the administration of justice. The feudal political order developed into a complicated network of lord-vassal relationships, with lords having overlords, and overlords owing allegiance to kings. On these foundations early kingdoms, such as England and France, were built, but in other areas, such as modern-day Germany, the feudal organization remained highly decentralized.

COMPARATIVE FEUDALISM - JAPAN AND EUROPE		
	JAPAN	**EUROPE**
Similarities	System was grounded in political values that embraced all participants.	System was grounded in political values that embraced all participants.
	The idea of mutual ties and obligations was strong, with rituals and institutions that expressed them.	The idea of mutual ties and obligations was strong, with rituals and institutions that expressed them.
	Feudalism was highly militaristic, with values such as physical courage, personal or family alliances, loyalty, ritualized combat, and contempt for nonwarriors.	Feudalism was highly militaristic, with values such as physical courage, personal or family alliances, loyalty, ritualized combat, and contempt for nonwarriors.
Differences	Feudalistic ties relied on group and individual loyalties.	Feudalistic ties were sealed by negotiated contracts, with explicit assurances of the advantages of the arrangement.
	Legacy was a group consciousness in which collective decision-making teams were eventually linked to the state.	Legacy was the reliance on parliamentary institutions in which participants could discuss and defend legal interests against the central monarch.

THE DIVISION OF CHRISTENDOM

The Roman Empire was divided into two parts during the 4th century C.E. when imperial power shifted eastward from Rome to Byzantium. The emperor Constantine moved to the new center, and renamed the city Constantinople. As Christianity spread, it developed religious centers in both Rome and Constantinople, and as the two areas grew more politically independent, Christian practices and beliefs also split in different directions. Even though the church remained officially tied for many years after Rome fell in 476, in effect two different churches developed: the Eastern Orthodox Church in the east and the Roman Catholic Church in the west. The schism became official in 1054, when the Roman Pope and the Patriarch in Constantinople agreed that their religious differences could not be reconciled.

THE BYZANTINE EMPIRE

While the west was falling to the Germanic invasions in the 4th and 5th centuries C.E., the eastern empire remained intact, partly because it withstood fewer attacks. This Byzantine Empire survived for almost a millennium after the western empire collapsed. For a time, it was a powerful Christian Empire, but it came under pressure from Islamic Turkish people by the 11th century, and finally fell to the Ottoman Turks in 1453.

Caesaropapism

As the first Christian Emperor of Rome, Constantine claimed to have divine favor for his rule. He defined Christian practices and intervened in theological disputes. This policy came to be known as **"caesaropapism"**, whereby the emperor ruled as both secular lord and religious leader. This tendency to exalt Byzantine emperors as absolute rulers of both state and church was reinforced by the appearance of **Justinian** in the 6th century. He was an energetic, capable ruler with an energetic, capable wife called **Theodora**, a very religious Christian. Although they never resolved the many religious disputes that disrupted the empire, Justinian had many noteworthy accomplishments:

- **The building of the Hagia Sophia**, a magnificent domed church that still stands today as a Muslim mosque

- **Extension of the political boundaries of the empire** to regain most of the western territories again, only to be lost by later emperors

- **The development of the Justinian Code**, a law code that systemized Roman law going back to the Republic and continuing through the empire

Of the accomplishments listed, the Justinian Code is the emperor's most enduring legacy, since it became the basis of law in western Europe and eventually the United States.

The Decline of the Empire

Even Justinian could not revive the classical Roman Empire, and within 100 years of his death, large parts of the Byzantine Empire fell to Arab invaders. It thrived for a while as a smaller, more manageable entity, but by the late 11th century, the Seljuk Turks threatened Constantinople so that the Patriarch of the Eastern Orthodox Church called on Pope Urban II for help in defending the capital by Christian Crusaders.

THE CHURCH IN THE WEST

While political and economic decentralization characterized western Europe between 500 and 1000 C.E., the Catholic Church emerged as a unifying institution with great religious, political, and economic power. The time period is sometimes referred to as the "Age of Faith" because the church was so central to life in Europe.

The power of the church was promoted by an unlikely Germanic group known as the **Franks**. They controlled much of what is now France by the 5th century C.E. when their leader **Clovis** led his forces on a campaign that wiped out the remains of Roman authority a few years after Rome's fall in 476. Clovis converted to Christianity, under some pressure from his wife, and from then, the Franks' conquests were done in the name of Jesus. One of his descendants, **Charlemagne**, ruled a kingdom that spread across a huge part of Europe, including both modern day France and Germany. Charlemagne was able to rescue the Roman Pope from captivity, and the Pope returned the favor by crowning Charlemagne as the new emperor in 800 C.E., uniting church and state. Still, the Pope was the one controlling the crown, and the ceremony took place in Rome.

The Catholic Church established its influence in several ways:

- **Development of a church hierarchy** – The Pope in Rome came to be the head of the church, with cardinals that reported to him. Under the cardinals were archbishops, who governed bishops that were spread all over Europe. Individual priests lived in villages and towns and were supervised by the bishops.

- **Establishment of wandering ministries** – Not only did the church have priests attached to almost every village, but it also had wandering priests who represented its influence. Two orders were the **Franciscans**, known for their vows of poverty and ability to relate to peasants, and the **Dominicans**, a more scholarly order who ministered more to educational needs.

- **The establishment of monasteries** – Monasteries also spread all over Europe. These retreats from civilization were inhabited by **monks** who devoted their lives to study, worship, and hard work. **Convents** for nuns also were established, and both monasteries and convents served many vital functions:

    1) **Refuge for those in trouble** – The monasteries and convents were seen as safe havens that represented the protection that the church offered to people.
    2) **Communication to the central church hierarchy** – Abbots headed monasteries, and they served as another means of keeping church officials in touch with what was going on.
    3) **Centers of scholarship, education, and libraries** – Monks very often were the only people in Europe that could read and write, and they spent large amounts of time copying ancient manuscripts that otherwise might have been lost in the various invasions. Some monasteries eventually formed the first European universities that began their library collections with books the monks had copied.

THE MANORIAL SYSTEM

Feudalism generally defined the military and political relationships among kings, nobles, and knights, but **manorialism** describes the economic and political ties between landlords and their peasants. Most people were **serfs**, who farmed self-sufficient agricultural estates called manors. The manorial system had originated in the late Roman Empire as it helped people take care of basic economic needs as the empire weakened. Farming was difficult, although made easier by the introduction of the **moldboard plow** that allowed deeper turning of the soil.

Serfs had to give their lord part of their crops in return for grazing their animals on his land and milling their grain. They also did repairs to his castle and worked his land. They were not slaves, but few other options were open to them. The lord's castle and army in turn provided protection for the villages, and few dared to live outside the confines of the manor.

THE LATE MIDDLE AGES – 1000-1450 C.E.

The entire era in Europe between 500 and 1450 is also known as the "Middle Ages," a time between the fall of the Roman Empire and the revival of "civilization" starting with the European Renaissance in the early 15th century. Starting around 1000, Europe showed signs of revitalizing, largely because of the results of the Christian Crusades that put Europeans in touch with more sophisticated cultures to the east through the long-distance trade routes.

Before about 1300 Europe was populated by **serfs**, or peasants tied to lands owned by nobility, living in rural areas relatively isolated from others. No large cities existed yet, like the metropolises in China, the Middle East, and northern Africa. Many demographic changes took place that radically altered life in Europe:

- **The Agricultural Revolution** – Largely through contacts with others, Europeans learned and adapted agricultural techniques and inventions that greatly increased their crop production. They perfected the **three-field system**, in which they rotated crops, allowing a field to remain fallow every third year. They also used iron plows much better suited to the heavy soils of northern and western Europe. Watermills, horses, and horse harnesses (all in use in other areas of the world) contributed to farming efficiency.

- **Population increases** – With the increase in crop production came population growth, with more hands available to expand agriculture.

- **Revival of trade** – This revival started in Venice and Genoa, Italian cities that profited from trade during the Crusades. However, the growing population sparked demand for more products so that trade intensified town to town, and a new trade area developed in present-day northern France, Belgium, and the Netherlands.

- **Growth of towns/new towns** – The growing trade, crop production, and population stimulated villages to become towns, and the towns became centers for craftsmen, merchants, and specialized laborers.

- **Commercial Revolution** – Once European towns connected to the long-distance trade routes, they learned to use financial innovations developed elsewhere, like banks and bills of exchange.

- **Guilds** – Craftsmen formed **guilds**, or trade associations for their particular craft. These organizations came to be quite powerful, passing laws, levying taxes, and challenging powerful merchants. The guilds set standards for goods, regulated labor, and supervised apprentices as they learned the trade.

EARLY RUSSIA

For centuries before this era Indo-European people called the **Slavs** had lived in eastern European, very much in the paths of the east to west migrations that scattered them over the years. The Russians were one of these Slavic peoples who intermarried with the Viking invaders and began to organize a large state by the 10th century. The most important early city was **Kiev**, located in present-day Ukraine, which built up regular trade and contacts with Constantinople. They adopted the Eastern Orthodox religion, and established the Russian Orthodox Church. The princes of Kiev established firm control over the church, and they made use of the Byzantine legal codes put together by Justinian.

Russia, like the rest of Europe, was built on feudalistic ties, and over time the Kievan princes became less powerful than those that ruled Muscovy (Moscow), a province northeast of Kiev. When the Mongols invaded in the 13th century, the Muscovites cast their lot with the inevitable victors, serving the Mongols as collectors of tribute. The Mongols bestowed many favors, and Moscow grew in influence. Once Mongol power weakened, the princes saw their opportunity to rebel, and they seized the territory, calling their leader the "tsar," a derivative of the word "Caesar."

THE AMERINDIAN WORLD

Prior to 1492, the western and eastern hemispheres had very little contact with one another. Even though Christopher Columbus was certainly not the first to go from one hemisphere to the other, his voyage does represent the beginning of sustained contacts, a trend that was a major turning point in world history. However, during the period between 600 and 1450 C.E., large empires emerged in the Americas, just as they did in Europe, Africa, and Asia. One group – the **Maya** – adapted to the jungles of Central America and the Yucatan Peninsula. The two largest organized relatively late in the era: the **Aztecs** of Mesoamerica, and the **Inca** of South America.

THE MAYA

The Maya civilization flourished between 300 and 900 C.E., occupying present day southern Mexico, Guatemala, Belize, Honduras, and El Salvador. Early on, they were probably dominated by the mysterious people of **Teotihuacan**, a large city with several impressive temples that controlled central Mexico for many years. They developed agricultural techniques that allowed them to successfully raise crops in the tropics. At first they practiced slash and burn methods, but they learned to build terraces next to the numerous rivers designed to catch the rich alluvial soil. Their agriculturally based civilization thrived, and they eventually built more than eighty large ceremonial centers, as well as many smaller settlements.

THE AZTECS

Civilizations had long existed in what is now central Mexico before the appearance of the Aztecs. The **Olmecs** were there by 800 B.C.E., and many groups followed. During the 10th century a powerful group called the **Toltecs** established a capital at Tula, about 50 kilometers from modern Mexico City. The Toltecs came to control much of the area around them, but their civilization fell into decay by the end of the 12th century, just about the time that a new group, the Mexica, began to grow. They eventually became known as the Aztecs, a name meaning "the place of the seven legendary caves," or the place of their origins. The Aztecs migrated into the area and settled in an unusual place: an island in the middle of a swampland of Lake Texococo, a site that the Spanish would later build as Mexico City. There they established the great city of **Tenochtitlan**, and they expanded their empire by conquering nearby people and extracting tribute from them. By the middle of the 15th century, they dominated a huge area that extended almost coast to coast.

THE INCA

The Inca civilization developed during the 14th and 15th century on the base of older civilizations, such as the Chavin, Moche and Chimu. By the late 15th century, their empire stretched for almost 2500 miles along the Andes Mountain range from present-day Equador to Chile. Their capital was Cuzco, high in the mountains in Peru, and the city was connected to all parts of the empire by a complex system of roads and bridges. The term "Inca" was at first a title for the ruler of Cuzco, but it eventually referred to all people that spoke the native language, **Quechua**. Like the Chavin before them, the Inca lived on the narrow, dry seacoast to the west of the mountains and in the jungles to the east, but they centered their civilization in the mountain valleys of the Andes. Unlike the people of Mesoamerica, the South Americans made use of domesticated animals. Llamas and alpacas served the highlanders not only as pack animals on the roads, but they also provided wool, hides, and dung for fuel.

| COMPARATIVE AMERIDIAN CIVILIZATIONS ||||
PATTERNS	MAYA	AZTEC	INCA
Social	Priests had highest social status; warriors also highly valued War captives often became slaves (and sacrifices); mysterious demise of civilization about 900 C.E.	Rigidly hierarchical society, with a strong military elite who received land grants and tribute from commoners; large gap between rich and poor Priests also elite; learned complex calendars, presided over all important religious rituals Skilled craftsmen, merchants middle status Large number of slaves, mainly household servants Patriarchal society, but women received high honor for bearing warrior sons; women who died in childbirth equally honored to men who died in battle	Rigidly hierarchical society, with the Inca and his family having status of gods Main classes: rulers, aristocrats, priests, and peasants Military and administrative elite for large army and bureaucracy Small merchant class and fewer skilled craftsmen than Aztec; trade controlled by the government Carefully selected virgin women served the Inca and his family
Cultural	Religion central to civilization; cities were ceremonial centers with great temples; practiced human sacrifice to their many gods; Tikal main city with population of about 40,000; jaguar an important symbol Two elaborate calendars used for agriculture and for religious rituals Flexible and sophisticated writing that used both symbols and pictures Inherited Olmec ballgame, with losers executed and sacrificed	Religion central to civilization; cities were ceremonial centers with great temples decorated with gold; practiced human sacrifice to their many gods Principal gods – Tezcatlipoca ("the Smoking Mirror") and Quetzalcoatl ("the Feathered Serpent") Tenochtitlan – major city of 200,000 + large suburbs Inherited Olmec ballgame, with losers executed and sacrificed Elaborate calendar, writing system	Religion important, with Inti, the sun god, the major deity; Impressive temples, palaces, public buildings; used skillfully cut giant stones with no mortar decorated with gold Quechua native language, but no writing; use of a counting device, the quipu to keep elaborate records Elaborate road system, with two roads (one on the coast and one in the mountains) running the entire length of the empire Rich textiles, jewelry, and pottery made by general population

Economic	Agricultural based; built platforms to catch alluvial soil; main crop maize, but also cacao bean (source of chocolate) and cotton; no domesticated animals for work	Agricultural base; designed "floating gardens" of trapped soil to raise crops in swampy areas; raised maize, beans, squashes, tomatoes, peppers, and chiles; no domesticated animals for work Exacted extensive amount of tribute from conquered people; established significant trade with others in western hemisphere, including luxury goods such as jade, emeralds, jaguar skins, and sea shells	Agricultural and pastoral base; designed terraces in mountain valleys to raise crops; variety of crops, depending on elevation, included potatoes, maize, beans, peppers, chiles, coca leaves (stimulant), guinea pigs Large professional army Peasants owed compulsory labor to the state; women gave tribute through textiles, pottery, and jewelry
Political	Organized into city-states with no central government for the civilization; city of Chichen Itza dominated some other states; frequent fighting among city states; defeated ones became human sacrifices	Ruled by a central monarch in Tenochtitlan that did not have absolute power; council of powerful aristocrats made many decisions, including who the new ruler would be; winning wars and elaborate rituals increased legitimacy of rule No elaborate bureaucracy	Highly powerful centralized government, with the Inca (the ruler) believed to be a god; Inca theoretically owned all land; elaborate bureaucracy kept in touch with subjects; used quipu to keep extensive records Elaborate road system reinforced the Inca's power

DEMOGRAPHIC AND ENVIRONMENTAL CHANGES

The era from 600 to 1450 C.E. was a time when civilization spread geographically, covering many more parts of the world than previously. However, it was also a time of great migrations of people that had wide impacts on the people in settled areas. Arabs, Vikings, Turks, and Mongols all moved from one part of the globe to another, instigating change wherever they went.

- **Arabs** – The most significant effect of the Arab movement from the Arabian Peninsula was the spread of Islam. Arabs invaded, settled, and eventually ruled the Middle East, northern Africa, and southern Europe. Although the political structure of the caliphate did not survive, Islam held the areas together culturally as it mixed with native customs and religions. Despite the political disunity and the splits between Sunni and Shi'a, the Islamic World emerged as an entire cultural area during this era.

- **Vikings** – The Vikings swept into many parts of Europe – from Normandy, to Mediterranean areas to Russia – during the 8th and 9th centuries, looting and destroying communities, churches, and monasteries. Some settled and intermarried with natives, forming new groups such as the Normans and the Rus (Russians). However, a very important consequence of their invasions was the development of feudalism in Europe. The attacks convinced Europeans that protection was vital, and so they organized into a network of lords and vassals, that eventually built kingdoms with great armies ready to fight.

- **Turks** – The Turkish people were originally Indo-Europeans who migrated into the Middle East during various times of the era. The Seljuk Turks invaded the Byzantine Empire, sparking another great migration from Europe to the Middle East – the Crusaders. Seljuk Turks were indirectly responsible, then, for Europe's growing interest and involvement in long-distance trade. By the end of the era the Ottoman Turks were on the rise. They captured Constantinople and many other parts of Europe, and they gained control of trade on the Mediterranean. Turks even invaded India, forming the Delhi Sultanate, and introduced Islam to India with such force that the consequences reverberated though the rest of Indian history.

- **Mongols** – The Mongol conquests have been depicted as assaults by savage and barbarian people who brought nothing but death and destruction to the areas they attacked. Whereas no one can deny the brutality of the Mongols, their conquests had a much more varied impact on world history than has been acknowledged by many historians in the past. At the peak of their power, the *Pax Mongolica* meant that once-hostile people lived together in peace in areas where most religions were tolerated. From the Il-Khan in the Middle East to the Yuan Dynasty in China, Mongol rulers established order, and most importantly, provided the stage for intensified international contact. Protected by Mongol might, the trade routes carried new foods, inventions, and ideas from one civilization to the others, with nomadic people acting as intermediaries.

- **Bantu-speaking people** – Another important source of cultural diffusion during this era was the **Bantu Migration**, which took place in Africa. Bantu-speaking people originally lived in an area south of the Sahara, but probably because the desert was spreading southward, they began to migrate to better land. They spread south and east into many parts of Africa, and their language became a basis for the formation of many later languages. The Bantu Migration is generally believed to be a major source for **Africanity**, or a set of cultural characteristics (including language) that are commonly shared on the continent. Examples include music, the use of masks, and scarification (permanent beauty etchings on the skin).

CULTURAL DIFFUSION AND THE 14TH CENTURY PLAGUES

Cross-cultural exchanges had deadly consequences for many parts of the eastern hemisphere during the 14th century. As Eurasians traveled over long distances, they not only exchanged goods and ideas, but they unwittingly helped disease to spread as well. Since people who have had no previous exposure to a disease react to it much more seriously than those that have, the consequences were profound. The **bubonic plague** erupted in epidemics throughout most of Asia, Europe, and North Africa. Even though it abated in subsequent centuries, it broke out sporadically from place to place well into the seventeenth century.

The plague probably originated in southwestern China, where it had been incubating for centuries, but once long-distance trade began, it spread rapidly during the 14th century. The pathogen was spread by fleas that infested rats and eventually humans. Mongol military campaigns helped the plague spread throughout China, and merchants and travelers spread it to the west. By the 1340s it had spread to Black Sea ports and to Italian cities on the Mediterranean. From there, the plague spread rapidly throughout Europe as far as the British Isles.

Europeans referred to the plague as the **Black Death** because its victims developed black or purple swellings caused by buboes, internal hemorrhages that gave the plague its name. Once the plague hit a community, typically 60-70 percent of the population died, and in some cases, no one survived. Important results of the plague (other than individual death) are:

- **Decline in population** – In China decreasing population caused by the plague contributed to the decline of the Yuan Dynasty and lent support to the overthrow of Mongol control there. Europe's population dropped by about 25% during the 14th century. In Egypt population levels did not recover to pre-plague days probably until the 19th century.

- **Labor shortages** – The plague was no respecter of social class, and the affected areas lost craftsmen, artisans, merchants, religious officials, farmers, bureaucrats and rulers. In many areas farms fell into ruin, towns deteriorated, and trade almost came to a standstill. Labor shortages turned into social unrest, and rebellions popped up in many areas.

ENVIRONMENTAL CHANGES

The era from 600 to 1450 C.E. was not a period of massive environmental change. The most significant changes occurred because of population growth. The structures of civilization spread across sub-Saharan Africa, northern Europe, and Japan. As civilizations spread, agriculture claimed additional land, with some deforestation (especially in Europe) taking place. However, soil depletion around the Mediterranean was not nearly as great as it was during Ancient Roman times. The most severe effects were probably felt in Central America, where population density increased significantly. Small civilizations and nomadic groups that were easy on the environment were replaced by ever larger empires that claimed rain forests and other natural habitats.

The process of urbanization continued during this era, and cities grew larger and more numerous. As Islam spread, administrative centers appeared in the Middle East, and many grew into cities that attracted people to live under the protection they afforded. China especially during this era became urbanized, with the Tang and Song emperors building roads that connected cities to one another. Trade from the Silk Road and the Indian Ocean circuits enriched these cities, and great differences in status were accorded those that lived in urban vs. rural areas. Great cities grew up in the Americas, and towns in Europe grew to be the cities of Paris and London. However, agriculture still remained the primary occupation of people in civilizations around the world, so that large numbers still lived in rural areas.

IMPORTANT ISSUES: 600-1450 C.E.

During this era several major religions spread across large areas, creating cultural regions that unified based on their belief systems. As historians, we may speak of "Islamic lands" or "Christendom" or "Confucian Asia," and these terms are handy for comparisons. They may be used effectively to point out commonalities as well as differences. However, cultural areas are imperfect as units of analysis. Some problems include:

- **Imperfect boundaries between areas** – If you are comparing political units with definite boundaries, the geographic differences are clear. However, in using cultural labels, how do you categorize areas of mixed influence? For example, parts of the Middle East during this era had significant numbers of Muslims, Christians, and Jews, with a mixture of customs from all three religions. Southeast Asia, a crossroads area for trade, had virtually every religion imaginable.

- **Wide differences within the culture zones** – The areas are so broad that the categories often blur important cultural differences within. For example, Christendom's two parts were very different, and Christianity was interpreted in many ways. Muslims in Mali had only limited commonalities with Muslims in Central Asia.

Still, political boundaries do not provide perfect units to measure either. Boundaries often cut through cultural areas and represent artificial categories for analysis.

Change over time during this era was more characterized by modification, rather than innovation, with the notable exception of the Tang and Song economic revolutions. Nomadic groups during this time period probably reached their peak of influence on the course of world history. Whereas change emanated from both nomadic groups and civilized areas, the effects of the great migrations of the Arabs, Vikings, Turks, and Mongols during this era have been unmatched to the present day. However, little change occurred in other areas, such as gender and social class structures. Patriarchal families continued to be the norm, and social class distinctions that we saw in the river valley and classical civilizations tended to be drawn along the same lines: peasants v. aristocrats and rural v. urban. Elite women seem to have suffered the most, with ties to the home reinforced through practices such as veiling and footbinding. Although in these cases differences were accentuated, gender roles went through no basic structural changes. Long distance trade grew significantly, but it continued to follow the old routes established in the previous era. The western hemisphere still was not drawn into regular contact and communication. However, by 1450 the previously inconsequential Europeans were on the cusp of changing all of that, as worldwide trade began to develop in the 1450-1750 era.

UNIT TWO QUESTIONS

1. Which of the following is an example of an event or situation between 600 and 1450 C.E. that helps to distinguish it as a new period in world history?

    (A) The invasions of the Huns disrupted the former Roman Empire as they attacked from the northeast.
    (B) Christianity was spread around the eastern Mediterranean by Paul of Tarsus.
    (C) The Mongols invaded many areas of Eurasia and formed the largest empire in world history.
    (D) Buddhism entered China for the first time and for a time supplanted Confucianism.
    (E) Hinduism was established as the major religion on the Indian subcontinent.

2. The hijra (Muhammad's flight from Mecca to Medina in 622 C.E.) is an event that is central to Muslim beliefs because it

    (A) revealed the face of Allah to Muhammad
    (B) defined Jews and Christians as "People of the Book"
    (C) symbolically destroyed polytheistic beliefs in Arabia
    (D) weakened Byzantine rule throughout the region
    (E) established the umma, or the Muslim community

3. In the 9th century the Tang Dynasty was weakened by considerable conflict between

    (A) Buddhism and Shintoism
    (B) Shintoism and Hinduism
    (C) Confucianism and Hinduism
    (D) Buddhism and Confucianism
    (E) Buddhism and Hinduism

4. All of the following were characteristic of nomadic groups in the eras before 1450 C.E. EXCEPT:

    (A) Most were patriarchal, although women often had higher status than women in sedentary societies had.
    (B) Kinship ties generally determined social hierarchy and relationship.
    (C) Most of the themes of nomadic art centered on their animals
    (D) Nomadic societies almost never had positive influence on settled peoples.
    (E) Nomadic societies often traded with sedentary societies.

(Questions 5 and 6 are based on the following passage):

This civilization in Meso-America dominated all surrounding peoples during the 15th century. Their priests escorted captured warriors up the temple steps and tore out their hearts. In some ceremonies thousands of people died in this way. In this marathon of bloodshed, knife-wielding priests were known to collapse from exhaustion and had to be replaced with fresh executioners.

5. The civilization described above was the

   (A) Inca
   (B) Aztec
   (C) Chavin
   (D) Maya
   (E) Olmec

6. The main purpose of the ritual that the passage captures was to

   (A) please and satisfy the gods
   (B) make the crops grow
   (C) demonstrate the power of military victory
   (D) impress subjects with "theatre state" techniques
   (E) control the rapidly growing population

7. All of the following are part of the Five Pillars of Faith EXCEPT:

   (A) the Declaration of Faith
   (B) observation of fasting during the month of Ramadan.
   (C) right thought and right action
   (D) the pilgrimage, or *hajj*, to Mecca
   (E) prayer five times a day

8. All of the following groups invaded Europe between 400 and 1000 C.E. EXCEPT:

   (A) Huns
   (B) Mongols
   (C) Vikings
   (D) Magyars
   (E) Vandals

9. The early existence of "Africanity" can best be explained by the influence of

   (A) strong political leaders of most cultural groups
   (B) long distance trade that connected Africa to countries across the Indian Ocean
   (C) the spread of Christianity to all parts of Africa
   (D) the Bantu migrations
   (E) the Berber leadership in trade and iron metallurgy

10. "It is the imminent peril threatening you and all the faithful, which has brought us hither. From the confines of Jerusalem and the city of Constantinople a horrible tale has gone forth…"

    The above quote describes which of the following events?

    (A) the creation of the Eastern Roman Empire
    (B) the establishment of the Abbasid dynasty
    (C) the invasion of Europe by the Huns
    (D) the capture of the Holy Lands by the Seljuk Turks
    (E) the invasion of the Middle East by the Mongols

11. Bedouins were instrumental in spreading which of the following religions?

    (A) Buddhism throughout China
    (B) Christianity in Africa
    (C) Islam on the Arabian Peninsula
    (D) Presbyterianism in Scotland
    (E) Shintoism throughout Japan

(Questions 12 and 13 are based on the following photograph):

© AFP/Corbis

12. The scene represents a central event of a

    (A) Muslim hijra
    (B) commemoration of the Byzantine Empire in the Hagia Sophia
    (C) Muslim hajj
    (D) celebration of the Christian victories of the First Crusade
    (E) a reenactment of the Battle of the Camel

13. The center of attention in the scene is

    (A) a holy book
    (B) the political leader of the city that surrounds the event
    (C) the *sharia*
    (D) the Well of ZamZam
    (E) the Ka'aba

14. Which of the following is an accurate description of the Byzantine Empire?

    (A) It lasted a thousand years after the fall of Rome.
    (B) It was conquered by Charlemagne.
    (C) It conquered the Ottoman Turks.
    (D) It was established during the Age of Augustus Caesar.
    (E) It ended with the rise of Islam.

15. Which of the following most eased population pressure in Europe in the 14th century?

    (A) improved agricultural techniques
    (B) deaths caused by the Mongol invasions
    (C) deforestation
    (D) migration to the Holy Land
    (E) the Black Death

16. Most urban growth in western Europe after 1200 stemmed from

    (A) an influx of gold from Africa
    (B) the continuing growth of trade and manufacturing
    (C) an ambitious economic development plan designed by the pope
    (D) the clearing of new farmland
    (E) improvements in breeding techniques of farm animals

17. All of the following were significant technological advancements of the Chinese during the Song Dynasty EXCEPT:

    (A) gunpowder
    (B) the camel saddle
    (C) improvements in shipbuilding
    (D) moveable type
    (E) metallurgy: iron and steel working

18. The "Seal of the Prophet" reflects most directly a Muslim belief that

    (A) Muhammad is the last in a series of prophets sent by Allah with a message to humankind
    (B) Allah is the same spiritual force as the Jewish Jehovah
    (C) Islam will eventually supplant all other major religions in the world
    (D) The caliphs should always be chosen from among the descendants of Muhammad
    (E) Muhammad's nature is partly human and partly divine

(Questions 19 and 20 relate to the following quote):

"Their hulls were made of teak planks that were sewn together with cord made of coconut husks, and they were equipped with lateen sails that could be turned to catch the wind. Their pilots navigated by the stars at night and took advantage of monsoon winds to blow them to their ports."

19. The vessel referred to in the quote is called a

    (A) caravel
    (B) dhow
    (C) junk
    (D) canoe
    (E) trireme

20. The vessel was used most extensively in trade on the

    (A) Atlantic Ocean
    (B) Pacific Ocean
    (C) Indian Ocean
    (D) South China Sea
    (E) Mediterranean Sea

21. All of the following factors contributed to significant population increases in Tang/Song China EXCEPT:

    (A) development of fast-growing strains of rice
    (B) increased use of oxen and/or water buffalo in farming
    (C) new trade-based prosperity in the cities
    (D) improvements in plows and other agricultural tools
    (E) Buddhist disapproval of birth control practices

22. In the period between 500 and 1000 C.E., all of the following statements accurately compare the eastern and western parts of what had been the Roman Empire EXCEPT:

    (A) Christians in both areas were largely under the control of the Pope.
    (B) In general the civilizations of the east were more advanced economically and culturally than were those of the west.
    (C) The east kept more aspects of the old Roman civilization intact than did the west.
    (D) Civilizations in the east generally were more directly involved in world trade routes.
    (E) Political organizations in the west were generally more fragmented than they were in the east.

23. Which of the following is Justinian's most significant long-term accomplishment?

    (A) He united Christians by helping to solve religious disputes.
    (B) He reconquered much of the territory that the old Roman Empire once controlled.
    (C) He rebuilt Rome and restored it to its former glory.
    (D) He established monotheism firmly in the east by banishing all forms of polytheism.
    (E) He systematized the Roman legal code.

24. How did Neo-Confucianism differ from the older version of Confucianism?

    (A) It put less emphasis on the authority of the eldest male in the family.
    (B) It broadened the concept of "*li*" to recognize the existence of an overall cosmic order.
    (C) Although it kept women in subservient roles, it allowed them more rights and freedoms than they had in previous times.
    (D) It was much less tolerant of competing belief systems, including Buddhism, Daoism, and Legalism.
    (E) It put less emphasis on the importance of maintaining harmony and balance in society.

25. What was the most important issue that caused the original split between Sunni and Shi'ite Muslims?

    (A) whether or not Islam should emphasize conversion and expansion
    (B) whether or not Islamic law and secular law should be blended into one legal code
    (C) whether caliphs should be chosen from Muhammad's family or from the leadership of the umma
    (D) where Muhammad should be buried: Mecca or Medina
    (E) whether or not women should be allowed to have leadership roles in the umma

26. What major public work was first constructed during the Sui Dynasty?

    (A) the Great Wall
    (B) a sewage system in Chang'an
    (C) the first palace in Beijing
    (D) the Grand Canal
    (E) an aqueduct system that brought water to all major Chinese cities

27. Which civilization split political leadership between ceremonial and real policy making powers in the era before and after 1000 C.E.?

   (A) China
   (B) Korea
   (C) Vietnam
   (D) India
   (E) Japan

28. The establishment of the Mongol Empire had all of the following consequences EXCEPT:

   (A) the reopening and extension of the Silk Road
   (B) the strengthening of maritime trade in the South China Sea
   (C) the diffusion of gunpowder technology
   (D) the demand for European products such as wool, porcelain, sugar, spices, and coffee
   (E) the rise of the autocracy in Russia

29. Which of the following was a major result of the Christian Crusades?

   (A) Christian Europe forged an alliance with Il Khan (khanate in the Middle East).
   (B) The Holy Land was freed from Muslim control.
   (C) The pope achieved power at the expense of kings.
   (D) Commercial towns like Venice declined in influence and power.
   (E) Europeans were introduced to new technology and cultures.

30. Which of the following became the tsars of Russia after the Mongols were driven out?

   (A) the princes of Kiev
   (B) the princes of Novgorod
   (C) the princes of Moscow
   (D) the khans of the Golden Horde
   (E) the priests of the Aryans

31. When the Mongols came to Chinese territory in the 1220s, they found

   (A) a unified empire that fiercely resisted attack.
   (B) a much smaller Song Dynasty that had lost much of their territory to other empires
   (C) an unsophisticated culture in decline from attacks by the Xiongnu
   (D) the Chinese had fled south to Annam
   (E) a foreign emperor already ruling a seriously weakened China

32. What were the two major sources of stability during the "Dark Ages" (500-1000) in Europe?

   (A) protection by Roman officials and the Orthodox Church
   (B) Roman law and the Catholic Church
   (C) feudalism and the Catholic Church
   (D) centralized government and the barter system
   (E) profits from trade and protection by the Vikings

33. Japanese and European feudalism were similar in all of the following ways EXCEPT:

   (A) The system was grounded in political values that embraced all participants.
   (B) The idea of mutual ties and obligations was strong.
   (C) Feudalism was highly militaristic.
   (D) Rituals and institutions reinforced feudalism.
   (E) Feudalistic ties were sealed by negotiated contracts.

34. Which of the following phenomena are highly likely to lead to "big changes" in world history?

   I. mass migrations
   II. imperial conquests
   III. cross-cultural trade and exchange

   (A) I only
   (B) II only
   (C) I and III only
   (D) II and III only
   (E) I, II and III

35. What conflict within Chinese culture was triggered by the overthrow of the Yuan Empire?

   (A) equal distribution of wealth v. prosperity of a merchant class
   (B) aggressive warfare v. genteel city sophistication
   (C) Buddhism v. Confucianism
   (D) isolation and nationalism v. contact with other civilizations and trade
   (E) national v. provincial identities

COMPARATIVE ESSAY

Directions: You are to answer the following question. You should spend 5 minutes organizing or outlining your essay. Write an essay that:

- Has a relevant thesis and supports that thesis with appropriate historical evidence
- Addresses all parts of the question
- Makes direct, relevant comparisons

"Modernity" is a frequently used concept for evaluating civilizations. Compare characteristics of the Inca Empire with those of the Aztec Empire in terms of modernity. Was one empire more "modern" than the other? Provide evidence for your answer, and in your evidence, include your definition of "modernity."

No testing material on this page.

UNIT THREE

1450-1750 C.E.

In the previous era (600-1450 C.E.), sometimes called the post-classical period, we explored the rise of new civilizations in both hemispheres, the spread of major religions that created cultural areas for analysis, and an expansion of long-distance trade to include European and African kingdoms. However, no sustained contact occurred between the eastern and western hemisphere. During the time period between 1450 and 1750 C.E., the two hemispheres were linked and for the first time in world history, long-distance trade became truly worldwide.

QUESTIONS OF PERIODIZATION

This era includes only 300 years, but some profound and long-lasting changes occurred. Characteristics of the time between 1450 and 1750 include:

1) **The globe was encompassed** – For the first time, the western hemisphere came into continued contact with the eastern hemisphere. Technological innovations, strengthened political organization, and economic prosperity all contributed to this change that completely altered world trade patterns.

2) **Sea-based trade rose in proportion to land-based trade** – Technological advancements and willingness of political leaders to invest in it meant that sea-based trade became much more important. As a result, old land-based empires lost relative power to the new sea-based powers.

3) **European kingdoms emerged that gained world power** – The relative power and prosperity of Europe increased dramatically during this time in comparison to empires in the longer-established civilization areas. However, Europe did not entirely eclipse powerful empires in Southwest Asia, Africa, and East Asia.

4) **The relative power of nomadic groups declined** – Nomads continued to play an important role in trade and cultural diffusion, and they continued to threaten the borders of the large land-based empires. However, their power dwindled as travel and trade by water became more important.

5) **Labor systems were transformed** – The acquisition of colonies in North and South America led to major changes in labor systems. After many Amerindians died from disease transmitted by contact with Europeans, a vigorous slave trade from Africa began and continued throughout most of the era. Slave labor became very important all over the Americas. Other labor systems, such as the mita and encomienda in South America, were adapted by the Spanish and Portuguese from previous native traditions.

6) **"Gunpowder Empires" emerged in the Middle East and Asia** – Empires in older civilization areas gained new strength from new technologies in weaponry. Basing their new power on "gunpowder," they still suffered from the old issues that had plagued land-based empires for centuries: defense of borders, communication within the empire, and maintenance of an army adequate to defend the large territory. By the end of the era, many were less powerful than the new sea-based kingdoms of Europe.

MAJOR DEVELOPMENTS – 1450-1750 C.E.

We will investigate the broad, important characteristics of this time period outlined above by studying these major topics:

- **Changes in trade, technology, and global interactions** – The Atlantic Ocean trade eventually led to the crossing of the Pacific Ocean. New maritime technologies made these interactions possible, and global trade patterns changed dramatically.

- **Major maritime and Gunpowder Empires** – Major maritime powers include Portugal, Spain, France, and England, and major Gunpowder Empires were the Ottoman, Ming and Qing China, the Mughal, Russia, Tokugawa, Songhay (Songhai), and Benin.

- **Slave systems and slave trade** – This was the era for the most extensive slave systems and slave trade, with the new European colonies in the Americas relying on slavery very heavily. The slave trade was an important link in the Atlantic Ocean trade.

- **Demographic and environmental changes** – The new trade patterns greatly altered habitats for plants and animals and resulted in changes in human diet and activities as well. Major migrations across the Atlantic Ocean also altered demographic patterns profoundly.

- **Cultural and intellectual development** – This era also was shaped by the European Renaissance, Protestant Reformation, and Enlightenment. Neo-Confucianism grew in influence in China, and new art forms developed in the Mughal Empire in India.

CHANGES IN TRADE, TECHNOLOGY, AND GLOBAL INTERACTIONS

The 14th century brought demographic collapse to much of the eastern hemisphere with the spread of the bubonic plague. During the 15th century, as areas began to recover and rebuild their societies, they also sought to revive the network of long-distance trade that had been so devastated by the disease. The two areas that worked most actively to rebuild trade were China and Europe.

MING CHINA AND THE OUTSIDE WORLD

When the Ming drove the Mongols out, they were intent on restoring the glory of Han China, and they turned first to restoring China's internal trade and political administration. Even though the Ming emperors were wary of foreigners, they allowed foreign merchants to trade in Quanzhou and Guangzhou, ports that were closely supervised by the government. China had too long prospered from trade to give it up completely, and foreigners eagerly sought silk, porcelain and manufactured goods, in exchange for spices, cotton fabrics, gems, and pearls.

In order to restore Chinese hegemony in Asia, Emperor Yongle sponsored seven naval expeditions commanded by Admiral **Zheng He**, whose voyages took place between 1405 and 1433. He was a Muslim from southwestern China who rose through the administrative ranks to become a trusted advisor of the emperor. For each journey he launched a fleet of vessels like the world had never seen before. The Chinese junks were huge with nine masts, by far the largest ships ever launched up until that point in history. They were far larger than the ships that Christopher Columbus was to sail only a few decades later. Altogether the ships traveled the Chinese seas to Southeast Asia, and on across the Indian Ocean to India, the Middle East, and Africa. Throughout his travels he dispensed lavish gifts, and he also dealt harshly with pirates and political leaders that tried to defy Chinese might. He returned to China with presents from his hosts and stories that awed the Chinese, especially Emperor Yongle. Zheng He's most famous gifts were destined for the imperial zoo – zebras and giraffes from Africa that drew crowds of amazed people who had never seen such animals before.

The main purposes of the voyage were twofold: to convince other civilizations that China had indeed regained their power and to reinstitute tribute from people that no longer gave it. The latter did not bring any income to China, mainly because the cost of the voyages and gifts was more than any revenue they stimulated.

Zheng He's voyages were halted in the 1430s when Emperor Yongle died. Confucian bureaucrats, who had little desire to increase China's interactions with other civilizations, gained control of the court and the new emperor, and refused to continue to finance the voyages. According to the new court, the money was needed to better protect the empire from its age-old problem: nomadic invasions from the west. The voyages and the Ming reaction to them provide good evidence for the pattern that was setting in: the impulse to trade and contact others v. the tendency to turn inward for fear of the negative effects on the Han Chinese.

EUROPEAN EXPLORATIONS

Across the globe, as the mid-15th century approached, kingdoms in another area were ready to venture to the open seas with motivations very different from those of the Chinese:

- **Profit from commercial operations** – Geographically, Europe was on the outskirts of the established trade routes. The impractical nature of overland travel for Europeans was confirmed by the fact that the first European trade cities – Venice and Genoa – made their fortunes by sea travel. And so the Europeans set out to make their fortunes via water transportation.

- **Spread of Christianity** – True to its roots, Christianity had remained over the centuries a missionary religion. The Catholic Church took this responsibility seriously, and as a result, Europe was overwhelmingly Catholic by 1450. Once they began traveling to other lands, they aggressively promoted the spread of the Christian faith, so that their missionary motives were often as strong as their desire for profits.

Portuguese Exploration

Portugal was the first European kingdom to explore other lands seriously. One reason was its geographic location on the Atlantic Ocean, with a long seacoast with good harbors. Another took the form of an often underrated historical figure, **Prince Henry the Navigator**. He wanted to increase Portugal's maritime influence and profits, and he also wanted to spread Christianity. From Portugal his ships ventured to the Strait of Gibraltar, where they seized the Muslim city of Ceuta, allowing Christian ships to travel safely between the Atlantic and the Mediterranean. Next Portuguese mariners explored nearby islands, and eventually made their way down the coast of Western Africa.

Henry's influence was so great mainly because he started a school for navigators that trained some of the most famous and skilled mariners of the day. Two of his students solved an ancient mystery: Where is the southern tip of Africa? In 1488 Bartolomeu Dias had sailed around the Cape of Good Hope and returned to Portugal with the news. A few years later Vasco da Gama rounded the Cape, found the southern Swahili cities, and hired a Muslim guide that helped him to sail all the way to India. These voyages – though the ships traveled no further than those of Zheng He – were the beginnings of sustained European sea travel that eventually led to Europe's rise to power.

For most of the 16th century, the Portuguese dominated the Indian Ocean trade. How did they capture this old sea route that had been shared by Arabs, Persians, Indians, and Southeast Asians? The most important single answer is technological: they had superior weapons. Their ships were armed with cannons that they used so skillfully that their relatively small ships could overpower almost any other type of vessel. The Portuguese were intent on converting all that they met to Christianity, although they often did more harm than good, infuriating the natives by burning down mosques and/or forcing conversions.

Early Spanish Expeditions

Since the Portuguese dominated the Indian Ocean trade, other European kingdoms looked for other routes to the east, where they sought to capture some of the trade that so filled Portuguese pockets. Spain was one of the first to seek an alternate route when Queen Isabella and King Ferdinand sponsored the voyages of Italian sailor **Christopher Columbus**. Using maps devised by the Greek geographer Ptolemy, Columbus believed that the voyage west was possibly shorter than the Portuguese route from Europe around the tip of Africa and east. Ptolemy's maps were wrong, since they assumed that the circumference of the early was only 16,000 miles (as opposed to the actual 25,000), and Columbus of course landed in the Americas, "discovering" the new hemisphere for Europeans. He returned to Spain without the trade goods that he expected to find from the east, but he convinced the Spanish monarchs that he had landed in the islands off the Asian coast. On his subsequent voyages he explored more areas, but he never reached the mainland, nor did he ever publicly acknowledge that he had failed in his mission – finding a new route to Asia.

THE CONQUEST OF THE AMERICAS

What Diaz, da Gama, Columbus, and other early European explorers did do was unwittingly start an entirely new era of world trade and cross-cultural exchange. Europeans conquered and claimed the territories and greatly increased their prosperity and power, and Christianity spread to a whole new hemisphere. Portugal and Spain even presumed to divide the world in two by seeking the Pope's blessing on the **Treaty of Tordesillas**, which drew a line north and south through the Atlantic, giving Portugal the lands east and Spain the lands west. Portugal actually lost in the long run because the lands that they "received" were already claimed by empires that did not recognize the Portuguese claims.

During the 16th century the Portuguese slowly faded as a power while Spain claimed and kept more and more land in the western hemisphere. In 1519 a Spanish expedition led by **Hernan Cortes** marched to the Aztec capital of Tenochtitlan and defeated the great empire with only a few hundred soldiers. How? Two weapons helped a great deal – guns and disease. Gunpowder technology revolutionized the world during the 1450-1750 era, and the Amerindian Empires were among its first victims. Disease also made a big difference. Shortly after the Spanish arrived in Tenochtitlan, a smallpox epidemic broke out in the city that killed or incapacitated the Aztec army. A few years later **Francisco Pizarro** attacked and defeated the Inca. With the fall of those two empires the Spanish gained virtual control of Mesoamerica and South America, with the exception of Brazil, which fell on the Portuguese side of the line set by the Treaty of Tordesillas.

THE WORLD ENCOMPASSED

One event symbolizes, if not encapsulates, the accomplishments of the Europeans: the voyage of **Ferdinand Magellan** between 1519 and 1522. Magellan found the southern tip of South America and sailed west across the Pacific. He eventually made it to the islands off the coast of Asia, sailed through the Indian Ocean, around the tip of Africa, and home to Spain. Ironically, Magellan didn't make the entire voyage because he was killed in the Philippines, and only one of his ships actually made it all the way home. What he proved did not provide any particular financial gain. Instead, Magellan discovered just how wide the Pacific Ocean is and how impractical Columbus' earlier hunch really was. However, his voyage was the first to go around the world, and it symbolized the first union of the hemispheres and the resulting worldwide contacts that have characterized world history since 1522.

THE FRENCH AND ENGLISH IN NORTH AMERICA

The French and English did not arrive in the Americas until the 17th century, but when they did, they claimed much of North America in areas that the Spanish did not go. The French explored and settled the St. Lawrence River area through Canada, as well as the Mississippi River valley south all the way to its mouth in the Gulf of Mexico. The English settled along the eastern seacoast in North America. Although the three great powers were destined to eventually clash over land claims, most conflicts did not occur until the 18th century. Virtually all explorers sought sea routes to Asia that they hoped would be shorter than the circuit that Magellan took. The English differed from most others in that they allowed great trading companies to control their colonization. These companies encouraged people to settle in the New World, so that the English colonies became quite heavily populated by the end of the 17th century.

THE GREAT CIRCUIT AND THE COLUMBIAN EXCHANGE

The trade routes that appeared during this era in the Atlantic Ocean were collectively known as the **Great Circuit**. The routes connected four continents: North America, South America, Europe, and Africa, and they linked directly to the old water trade routes established in previous eras. The Atlantic routes were generally circular and complex, with most ships making several stops along the way on at least two of the continents, but sometimes more. These huge circuits represent the most significant change in long-distance trade since its earliest days.

The cross-cultural exchange that developed along the Great Circuit is known as the Columbian Exchange, giving credit to the man that unwittingly started the whole thing. The **Columbian Exchange** included a huge number of products that changed diets and work habits around the world. Generally, the goods traded according to this pattern:

- **Europe to the Americas** – horses, cows, pigs, wheat, barley, sugar cane, melons, grapes

- **Africa (includes Asian products) to the Americas** – bananas, coconut palms, coffee, sugar cane, goats, chickens

- **The Americas to Europe and Africa** – corn, potatoes, tomatoes, sweet potatoes, pumpkins, squash, beans, pineapples, peppers, tobacco, chocolate

As a result of the new trade routes, the variety in many people's diet increased and resulted in better nutrition and health. Disease also was transferred with the most devastating effects on the Amerindian populations. They had no immunities to diseases that people of the eastern hemisphere had built up resistance to, such as measles, diphtheria, typhus, influenza, malaria, and yellow fever. Estimates vary, but all historians agree that the devastation cannot be overstated. Generally only one major disease that originated in the Americas traveled the other direction – syphilis.

TECHNOLOGY AND THE MARITIME REVOLUTION

The new trade patterns could never have been established without some very important technological inventions, most of which Europeans adapted from other cultures:

- **Guns and gunpowder** – Although the Chinese invented explosives, Europeans adapted them for guns. European metalwork advanced to the point that smiths were able to forge the first guns and cannons. Their accuracy was limited, but their power as weapons was awesome by the standards of the time. Guns and gunpowder allowed European explorers to intimidate and defeat virtually any foe.

- **New ship technology** – The European ships were not nearly as large as the Chinese junks, but their deep drafts and round hulls made them well suited for travel on the Atlantic Ocean.

- **The compass** – This technology was copied from the Arabs, who had earlier learned it from the Chinese. The compass pointed north, an important indication for ships traveling east to west.

- **The astrolabe** – An invention of the Arabs, the astrolabe allowed a sea captain to tell how far north or south his ship was from the equator.

- **Cartography** – European explorers recorded the new territories on maps, and the art of accurate mapmaking progressed significantly. One new map style created was the **Mercator Projection** that distorted land size seriously in extreme northern and southern areas. However, the projection was relatively accurate for the middle ranges, and those were the routes that navigators were following.

MAJOR EMPIRES: 1450-1750

Political developments during this era saw the greatest changes in European governments, and by extension the government structures that they set up in the New World. New Gunpowder Empires emerged in other parts of the world, and in most cases, their rulers governed absolutely, as did most of the rulers in Europe.

THE POLITICAL AND SOCIAL TRANSFORMATION OF EUROPE

In 1450, the kingdoms in Europe were governed by rulers with only a tentative grasp of political power. They were fragmented and the political structures were still held together by feudal ties. Instead of uniting Europeans, their growing control of the new Atlantic system deepened the divisions among them. During the 16th century, the growing wealth of Spain tilted power toward the **Habsburg** family that ruled many lands in Europe, including Spain. By the end of the century, England and France were on the rise, and the rivalries among the countries were intense.

CENTRALIZATION OF GOVERNMENT

During this era between 1450 and 1750 some of the old feudal kings amassed enough power to allow their kingdoms to sponsor the expensive sea voyages necessary for colonization in the New World. Three powerful countries that emerged were Spain, England, and France. In all three cases these monarchs curbed the power of the nobility and built strong centralized regimes.

The new monarchs came up with new means of financing their ambitions, such as imposing taxes, fines, and fees, and amassing large armies too powerful for individual nobles to match. The English king Henry VIII received a big windfall by confiscating the wealth of Catholic monasteries when he officially separated the English church from Rome. English kings also contained the power of the nobility by subjecting them to royal justice through the developing judicial system.

Spanish Imperial Attempts

Spain's newfound wealth in the 16th and 17th century was based largely on trade, and the vital link that their American colonies played in world circuits. A good example is provided by the famous **Manila Galleons** that for 250 years traveled back and forth across the Pacific Ocean between Manila in the Philippines and Acapulco on the west coast of Mexico. The galleons were vast and well armed, and they took Asian luxury goods to Mexico, and returned with their hulls full of gold and silver. Most of the precious metals made their way into China, an inducement that convinced the Ming emperors to keep trade with outsiders alive. Meanwhile, some of the Asian silks and porcelain stayed in Mexico for use by the Spanish viceroys and other elites, but most of the goods went overland by Mexico to ships that carried them to Spain and other European markets. The Spanish rulers almost turned this wealth into domination of Europe, but not quite.

The Habsburgs were a family that not only ruled Spain but large parts of the **Holy Roman Empire** that covered most of central Europe, as well as territory that is now the Netherlands and Belgium. Charles V, grandson of Ferdinand and Isabella, for a time ruled it all. However, he was unable to coordinate the fragmented territories, with their various kings, princes, dukes, and bishops that still thought in feudalistic terms. Moreover, Charles had to defend his eastern territories from the growing **Ottoman Empire**. Under the Ottoman's great ruler, **Suleiman the Magnificent**, the Muslim army advanced all the way to the eastern European city of Vienna. There, in the fateful **Siege of Vienna** in 1529 Charles defeated the Ottomans and so protected Europe from further invasions. However, the Ottoman threat continued for years, and they exacted a heavy toll on Charles' empires. So overstretched did he feel that he abdicated his throne and divided his lands between his brother Ferdinand, who received the Holy Roman Empire, and his son, **Philip II**, who became king of Spain.

Philip proved to be an able successor to his father, but he had many of the same problems. This time the Ottoman threat came from the Mediterranean, and even though Philip defeated them at the Battle of Lepanto, the Ottomans still dominated many of the lands that bordered the sea. Perhaps his most famous defeat was at the hands of **Elizabeth I** of England, where his supposedly invincible **Spanish Armada** was demolished by the small but quick English "seadogs." However, despite these setbacks, the Spanish still held great wealth and power at the end of the 16th century, and were envied by the other European countries, especially England, France, and the Netherlands.

Absolutism v. Constitutionalism

Most of the newly powerful European states, including Spain and France, developed into **absolute monarchies**, or governments in which the king held all power. Absolutism was reinforced by the belief in **divine right**, or the god-given authority to rule. According to divine right theory, kings were not gods but served as "God's lieutenants upon earth." In these countries, no one else had the right to share policymaking powers with the king, not even the nobility.

In France absolutism was shaped by **Cardinal Richelieu**, the chief minister to King Louis XIII in the early 17th century. He undermined the power of the nobility by burning their castles and crushing attempts to conspire against the king. He also built a large bureaucracy capable of collecting taxes efficiently and serving as the "eyes and ears" of the king. The most famous of the absolute French rulers was **Louis XIV**, who ruled for 72 years, finally dying in 1715. He designated himself the "Sun King," the magnetic center of all around him, and his often repeated, "L'etat c'est moi" (I am the state) expresses his unshakable belief in his absolute authority. He contained the nobles by inviting them to his huge, ornate palace at Versailles, where they were welcome to stay as long as they liked. Many stayed for long periods of time, enjoying the sumptuous life of unending banquets, hunting, dancing, and gossip circuits. Meanwhile, the nobles were away from their castles, unable to start any rebellions, and completely under the thumb of their clever king.

Other countries followed the French model, although generally less successfully. Rulers in Austria, Prussia, and Russia built huge palaces and sought to increase central control. Both Prussia and Russia had developed into formidable powers by 1750.

Elsewhere, in England and the Netherlands, a different government model was developing. Neither had a written constitution, but they both allowed limitations to be placed on the ruler's power. In England the nobility demanded and received the right to counsel with the king before he imposed new taxes, starting with William the Conqueror in the 11th century. The limitations were famously encapsulated in the **Magna Carta** of 1215, a document that listed the rights of nobility. From this right to counsel developed a **"parliament"** (literally a place to talk things over) that came to blows with King Charles I in the 1640s in the English Civil War. Parliament won this war, and even though the institution of the monarchy was eventually retained, it marks the turning point of power toward a limited, or **"constitutional" government**. In both England and the Netherlands, wealthy merchants were allowed to participate in government, partly because their continuing prosperity was vital to the states.

Whether they developed into absolute or constitutional monarchies, centralization of government in Europe was a vital step in building state power from the medieval feudalism. Without it, colonization, and eventually the building of vast, worldwide empires, would have been impossible.

CHANGES IN SOCIAL AND GENDER STRUCTURES

With the growth of trade, European towns grew, and by 1700 Europe had large cities. Paris and London both had over 500,000 people, Amsterdam had about 200,000, and twenty other cities had populations over 60,000. Life in these cities was vastly different than before, and their existence affected people who lived elsewhere, in villages and towns. Some of the changes are:

- **The rise of the bourgeoisie** – Whereas the social structure in medieval Europe was split into two classes (nobility and serfs), increasing trade and business created a new class that the French called the **bourgeoisie**, meaning "town dwellers." Over time the bourgeoisie came to have more wealth than the nobles, since they often formed mutually beneficial alliances with monarchs anxious to increase state revenues.

- **Growth in the gap between the rich and the poor** – By the late 16th century, the rising wealth of the bourgeoisie created a growing gap between the rich and the poor. The poor were not only the rural peasants, but they also lived in cities as craftsmen, peddlers, and beggars.

- **Changes in marriage arrangements** – Most marriages in the rest of the world were still arranged by families, but the custom of young men and women choosing their own spouses started in early modern Europe. This change was partly due to separations between generations that occurred when younger people moved to towns, but also to the growing trend toward later marriages. Craftworkers and the poor had to delay marriages while they served as apprentices or built their dowries, and bourgeois men delayed marriage in order to finish their educations. The need for education was growing because of the demands for business success. For example, participation in long-distance trade often meant learning new languages and/or acquiring legal expertise. Since people were older when they married, they tended to be more independent from their parents.

COLONIAL MODELS

The governments that European nations set up in their colonies in the New World reflected their own governments back home. Both Spain and Portugal, who followed the absolutist model, set up expensive, controlling bureaucracies that they tried to rule directly. Both also had as major goals the conversion of natives to the Catholic Church. In contrast, the English principle of the limited monarchy allowed some independence for colonial governments. The English also had less interest in converting natives to Christianity than they did in building prosperous, money-generating colonies. The French were unable to establish few colonial governments with wide control, partly because they found wealth in trading furs. Animal trapping required that men move up and down rivers, and they were unable to set up cities, except in New Orleans in the south, and Quebec in the north.

COLONIAL POLITICAL AND SOCIAL STRUCTURES		
	Political Structures	**Social Structures**
Spain	Both the Spanish and the Portuguese kings appointed **viceroys**, or personal representatives, to rule in the king's name. Spain set up a **Council of the Indies**, whose members remained in Spain, as a supervisory office to pass laws. Advisory councils were then set up within each viceroyalty, which divided according to region. Difficulty in communication caused viceroys and councils to have a great deal of independence. Large bureaucracies developed in urban areas, such as Mexico City.	Almost complete subjugation of Amerindians, placed at bottom of social structure. A hierarchical class system emerged. Peninsulares (Europeans born in Spain) had the highest status, and creoles (Europeans born in the Americas) were second. In the middle were mestizos (blend of European and Amerindian) and mulattoes (blend of European and African), and at the bottom were full blood natives and Africans. Slavery common, also used encomienda and mita labor systems.
England	No elaborate bureaucracy like Spanish/Portuguese. Individual colonies allowed to set up their own structures, with most of them setting up representative bodies like the British Parliament. British government formed partnerships with trading companies, and was most interested in profits. Practice of "salutary neglect" until mid-18th century allowed colonies to run many of their own affairs.	Less successful at subjugating Amerindians, who were generally more friendly to the French. Colonies were more diverse than the Spanish, with South Carolina's social structure the most hierarchical and Massachusetts the least. Mixing of races (European, Amerindian, African) blurred social distinctions, but still had divisions. Slavery common, especially in the agricultural southern colonies.

THE GUNPOWDER EMPIRES

In contrast to the sea-based empires developing in Europe, land-based empires remained the dominant political form in other parts of the eastern hemisphere. The era between 1450 and 1750 saw the appearance of several land-based empires who built their power on the use of gunpowder: the Ottomans and the Safavids in Southwest Asia, the Mughals in India, the Ming and Qing in China, and the new Russian Empire. All had huge land armies armed with guns. These empires developed relatively independently from western influence, and to some extent they counterbalanced the growth of European power and colonization.

An important consequence of the appearance of the Gunpowder Empires was their conquest of most nomadic groups. Since the nomads had less access to guns, the empires were finally able to conquer and subjugate them. In many areas direct relations among states or merchant groups replaced nomadic intermediaries for international contact. For example, European kings invited diplomats from other countries to join their courts, and China also received foreign representatives.

THE MUSLIM EMPIRES

In the previous era, the political power of Muslim lands had been crushed by Mongol invasions in the 13th century and those of **Timur**, a central Asian of Mongol descent, in the 14th century. Three new empires – the Ottoman, the Safavid, and the Mughal – rose between 1450 and 1750, and collectively they supported a new flowering of Islamic civilization. However, competition between them also led to important political divisions and military clashes. All three originated in the Turkic nomadic cultures of the central Asian steppe, and they all had absolute monarchs who modeled their courts on those of earlier Islamic dynasties.

COMPARATIVE MUSLIM EMPIRES				
	Geographic Characteristics	**Political and Military**	**Economic and Social**	**Religious and Cultural**
Ottoman Empire	It developed from modern-day Turkey. At its height, it encompassed lands around the southern and eastern Mediterranean, Constantinople, the Red Sea, the Tigris and Euphrates Rivers, and eastern Europe.	Great army of mounted and foot soldiers; made use of Janissaries, Balkan Christians captured as boys who became skilled soldiers and bureaucrats Ruled by a sultan, an absolute ruler aided by strong bureaucracy, who often were army officers; top official was the "grand vizier"; Suleiman the Magnificent most famous ruler Great navy, as well	More sustained trade than the other empires, partly due to control of the Dardanelles, Black Sea, Mediterranean Sea More equality for women, with some trading in real estate	Most were Sunni Muslim, although a diversity of religions, including Christians Culturally diverse, largely due to trade connections and diversity of lands governed Important merchant class Constantinople highly sophisticated, cosmopolitan city
Safavid Empire	Developed east of the Ottomans, encompassing land space that is now modern Iran	Belief in the "Hidden Imam," a descendent of Ali that would return to rule; ruler is stand-in until then Strong army equipped with firearms; no navy	Marginal trade, inland capital Rigidly patriarchal, with few freedoms for women	Most were Shi'a Muslims, forced conversion by Ismail, 16th century ruler; deep chasms between Shi'a and Sunni felt here Less diversity of people
Mughal Empire	Mughal land included that of modern day Pakistan and Afghanistan, as well as the northern part of the Indian subcontinent	Strong military that attacked from the west Muslim rulers with centralized power; expensive war meant that high taxes were necessary. Muslim authority over rebellious Hindu population Most famous ruler was Akbar, who married a Hindu, tried to reconcile the faiths	Limited trade, inland capital Land grant system based on military service; conflicted with previous regional ruler claims	Muslim rulers over Hindu population' tensions from the beginning New faith – Sikhism, a blend of Islam and Hinduism; became militant after guru beheaded by Mughal ruler

Although each of the Muslim Empires had their own special problems, they faced some similar ones that eventually led to their decline.

- **Inadequate transportation and communication systems** – Although they had the necessary military technology to control their empires, transporting it to where it was needed was another issue. The larger they grew, the more difficult it was for the infrastructure to be adequate for the task.

- **Unruly warrior elites and inadequate bureaucracies** – The military leaders knew their importance to the state, and they often operated quite independently of the government. Even in the Ottoman Empire, where the bureaucracy was the strongest, the sultan eventually lost control of the Janissaries, who rebelled against him when their constant demands went unfulfilled.

- **The rise of European rivals** – Ultimately, the Europeans benefited more from the gunpowder revolution than the Muslim Empires. European countries were smaller, both in population and land space, and so mobilization of their human and natural resources was easier. They were also in such strong competition with one another that the Europeans were spurred on to try new technologies and reforms.

THE MING AND EARLY QING DYNASTIES IN CHINA

The Ming Emperors continued to rule China until the mid-1600s, but the dynasty was in decline for many years before that. Although its cultural brilliance and economic achievements continued until about 1600, China had some of the same problems that the Muslim empires had: borders difficult to guard, armies expensive to maintain, and transportation and communication issues. Some particular factors that weakened Ming China included:

- **Climatic change** – A broad change of climate swept from Europe to China during the 1600s, with the weather turning much colder. This change seriously affected agriculture and health, and also contributed to serious famine across China. These conditions led frustrated peasants to frequent rebellion.

- **Nomadic invasions** – The 1500s saw the reemergence of the Mongols as a regional power, this time with the help and support of Tibet. In gratitude, the Mongols bestowed the Tibetan leader with the title of **dalai lama**, or "universal teacher" of Tibetan Buddhism. The Japanese also attacked Korea, a Chinese tributary state, requiring Ming armies to defend the area.

- **Pirates** – As sea-based trade became more and more important, the number of **pirates** also increased in the Chinese seas, just as they did in the Americas. Pirates were both Chinese and Japanese, and they lay in wait for ships going in and out of Chinese ports.

- **Decline of the Silk Road** – After so many centuries, the famed Silk Road trade finally fell into decline during this era. New technologies and European control meant that more and more trade was conducted by water, and land-based trade decreased.

- **Inept rulers** – The last emperors lived in luxury in the Forbidden City, and had little to do with governing the empire. For example, the last emperor was so disengaged that he did not know that he was under attack until the enemy literally were climbing over the palace walls.

The Early Qing Dynasty

The Ming Dynasty was finally overthrown in 1644 by the **Manchus**, a northern power that had previously helped Ming emperors fight the Mongols and Japanese. The Manchus turned on the Ming once they discovered how weak the empire was, and they called themselves the **Qing** ("pure") **Empire** because they saw themselves as restoring China to glory. However, the Manchu were seen by some as not being truly "Chinese" because they were northern people from the outside, just as the Mongols had been almost four centuries before.

The Qing Dynasty was to rule China until 1911, and in the years before 1750, the empire was very strong. The emperors ruled under many of the same precepts that China had always had, such as the mandate of heaven, which they saw as justification for their takeover. The Manchu did keep their ethnic identity, forbidding intermarriage between Manchus and Chinese. They also outlawed the Chinese from learning the Manchurian language, and they required Chinese men to shave their heads and grow long **queues** at the back of their heads as a sign of submission.

Despite the problems that China faced as a land-based Gunpowder Empire, the early Qing Dynasty – until the late 18th century – ruled over a "golden age" of Chinese civilization. Two of its early emperors had long and prosperous reigns: **Kangxi** (1661-1722) and **Qianlong** (1736-1795). Kangxi was an enlightened, brilliant ruler whose many talents illustrate the era. He was a Confucian scholar, poet, and supporter of education, but he was also a conquering warrior who understood the importance of military might. China was so prosperous in these early Qing days that Qianlong cancelled taxes on several occasions because the government simply didn't need the money.

Chinese Contact with Europeans

East-west contacts between China and Europe intensified during the early Qing Dynasty. One type of contact – Christian missionaries from the west – had probably come to China as early as the 7th century, but the plague and the collapse of the Yuan Dynasty had all but stopped the interchange. Contact revived during the 16th century when the **Jesuits** first began arriving in China. The Jesuit priests were an order of the Catholic Church that specialized in international missionary work. One of the early Jesuits, **Matteo Ricci**, very much impressed the Chinese, who admired his education, brilliance, and respect for Chinese customs and accomplishments. The Jesuits dazzled their hosts with European science and technology. For example, they were able to use their math skills to correct Chinese calendars that up until then had miscalculated solar eclipses. They prepared maps of the world, and charmed the Chinese with gadgets (like chiming clocks), and the emperors saw to it that Jesuits had a special place in their courts. However, they had limited success in converting people to Christianity. After the Pope condemned what he called "ancestry worship," Kangxi ordered the end to Jesuit ministries.

The Jesuits did inspire trade demands as word about the riches and sophistication of Qing China got back to Europe. Chinese products – tea, porcelain, silk, wallpaper, and decorative items – became quite fashionable among the European elite, and Kangxi was commonly seen by Europeans as a great philosopher king. The Chinese reacted by opening the southern port of Canton to Europeans, but again, the Middle Kingdom was very wary of foreign contact, and so they closely supervised the trade.

TOKUGAWA JAPAN

A "gunpowder empire" emerged in Japan, unusual in the sense that Japan was not land-based. The Japanese **daimyos**, or regional lords, had operated fairly independently from the shoguns before the early 17th century, when these military, feudalistic leaders were unified under one powerful family, the **Tokugawa**. The emperor was still honored as the ceremonial leader, as reflected in the name given to the Tokugawa government – the **bakufu**, or the tent government that temporarily replaced the emperor. The tent government eventually settled in Edo (modern Tokyo), and ruled their independent subjects by instituting **alternate attendance**, the practice of daimyos spending every other year at the Tokugawa shogun's court. This requirement meant that daimyos had limited time to focus on building armies back home, and they also had to maintain expensive second homes in Edo.

The Tokugawa shoguns had less patience with Christian missionaries from the west than the Chinese did. Their aversion to Europeans was based partly on their observation of the Spanish conquest of the Philippines, a fate that they did not want to share. They also worried that Europeans might conspire with the daimyos to destroy Tokugawa control. In the 1630s the shogunate literally "closed Japan," by forbidding all Japanese from going abroad and expelling all Europeans from Japan. They carefully controlled trade with other Asians, and European traders could come no closer than nearby islands. These policies were strictly enforced as far as the shoguns were able to, although daimyos on far islands were difficult to control.

THE RUSSIAN EMPIRE

By the time of the golden age of the Qing Dynasty, the Russian Empire had expanded all the way from its origins in Eurasia east to the Pacific coast. There they came into border conflicts with the Chinese, but they also shared the problem of attack by Mongols and other nomadic people of Central Asia. However, Russian tsar **Peter the Great**, who ruled Russia during the late 17th and early 18th centuries, cast his eyes in the other direction toward Europe for guidance in strengthening his growing empire. Russia's early days had been shaped by the Byzantine Empire, and when the Byzantine's power faded, so did that of the early Russian tsars. Before Peter's rule, Russians had had almost no contact with Western

Europe, and their lack of access to warm water ports crippled their ability to participate in the Maritime Revolution. The feudalistic political and economic structure meant that tsars had trouble containing the **boyars**, or Russian nobility, who often plotted against them. Partly because of this threat, the tsars practiced absolutism, with the power of the tsar backed by divine right granted by the Russian Orthodox Church. Peter's Russia was a vast, cold empire with almost no infrastructure – no navy, a limited army, very few decent roads, and few warm water ports.

Peter hoped to strengthen his country by westernizing it. As a boy he frequently visited the "German suburb" of Moscow, the place where all foreigners were forced to live, apart from Russians. Peter was intrigued with their maritime talk and with the sea-faring instruments they showed him. As a young man he took the first of several trips to Europe, where he studied shipbuilding and other western technologies, as well as governing styles and social customs. He returned to Russia convinced that the empire could only become powerful by imitating western successes, and he instituted a number of reforms that revolutionized it:

- **Military reform** – He built the army by offering better pay and also drafted peasants for service as professional soldiers. He created a navy by importing western engineers and craftsmen to build ships and shipyards, and other experts to teach naval tactics to recruits. Of course, his Gunpowder Empire developed better weapons and military skills.

- **Building the infrastructure** – The army was useless without roads and communications, so Peter organized peasants to work on roads and do other service for the government.

- **Expansion of territory** – The navy was useless without warm water ports, and Peter gained Russian territory along the Baltic Sea by defeating the powerful Swedish military. He tried to capture access to the Black Sea, but he was soundly defeated by the Ottomans who controlled the area.

- **Reorganization of the bureaucracy** – In order to pay for his improvements, the government had to have the ability to effectively tax its citizens. The bureaucracy had been controlled by the boyars, but Peter replaced them with merit based employees by creating the **Table of Ranks**, eventually doing away with titles of nobility.

- **Relocation of the capital** – Peter moved his court from Moscow to a new location on the Baltic Sea, his "Window on the West" that he called St. Petersburg. The city was built from scratch out of a swampy area, where it had a great harbor for the navy. Its architecture was European, of course.

When Peter died, he left a transformed Russia, an empire that a later ruler, Catherine the Great, would further strengthen. But he also left behind a new dynamic in Russian society – the conflicting tendencies toward westernization mixed with the traditions of the Slavs to turn inward and preserve their own traditions.

AFRICAN KINGDOMS

In 1450 Africa was a diverse continent with a blend of large civilizations, city-states, rural villages, and hunter and gatherer societies. Many people in the north, Subsaharan and eastern coastline areas were Muslim, but many native religions remained quite strong.

The largest and most organized empire of Africa from the middle of the 15th century until the late 16th century was **Songhay** (Songhai) in northwest Africa in areas that had been controlled by the earlier Kingdom of Mali. The empire was organized under **Sunni Ali**, a leader who brought the important trading cities of Timbuktu and Jenne under his control. He developed a centralized government with governors to oversee provinces, as well as an army and navy to protect trade. Songhay was prosperous, its cities boasted beautiful public buildings, and Islam was strongly supported by the elite. But Songhay did not have guns, and that was their downfall. In 1591 a Moroccan army opened their muskets on the Songhay forces, and they were defeated.

The 16th century also saw the destruction of most of the Swahili city-states. Vasco da Gama had noticed them when he passed through on his way to India, and within a few years the Portuguese had aimed their cannons at all the cities, and either captured them or burned them to the ground.

The fate of the **Kingdom of Kongo** was an early sign of what contact with Europe was to bring to Africa. Kongo was on the Atlantic Ocean in central Africa, and it developed into a centralized state during the 14th century. The Portuguese set up a trading relationship with them in the late 15th century and converted the Kongo kings to Christianity. From the beginning, the Portuguese traded textiles, weapons, advisors, and craftsmen for gold, silver, ivory and especially slaves.

THE SLAVE TRADE AND SLAVE SYSTEMS

The Portuguese brought a few slaves home from Africa, but found that they were impractical for use in Europe with its small, family-based farms and town life. However, it soon was clear how slavery could be readily adopted in the Americas. Like the overwhelming majority of preindustrial societies, African kingdoms practiced slavery, and when Europeans offered to trade their goods for slaves, African traders accommodated them. As a general rule, African slave hunters would capture Africans, usually from other groups than their own, and transport them to trading posts along the coast for European ships to carry to the New World. However, despite the fact that slavery already existed in Africa, the Atlantic trade interacted with and transformed these earlier aspects of slavery.

THE AFRICAN SLAVE TRADE

Before the Atlantic slave trade began, slavery took many forms in Africa, ranging from peasants trying to work off debts to those that were treated as "chattel," or property. The Atlantic trade emphasized the latter, and profits from the trade allowed slaveholders both in Africa and the Americas to intensify the level of exploitation of labor. African slaves were traded to two areas of the world: the Western Hemisphere and Islamic lands in the Middle East and India.

TRADE TO MUSLIM LANDS

Fewer slaves crossed the Sahara than crossed the Atlantic, but the numbers were substantial. Whereas most slaves that went to the Americas were male, most of those destined for the Middle East and India were female. These women either became a part of a wealthy individual's **harem**, or collection of wives and concubines that filled his household. The wives were not slaves, and their children had higher status than those of the concubines. The African women were almost always granted the lower status as concubines. Other slaves in the Islamic lands were males who were often bought to fight in the large Gunpowder Empire armies.

TRADE TO THE AMERICAS

The major reason that slave labor was practical in the Americas was that so many of the Amerindians who probably would have done the work had died. The economic challenge was to get workers to the New World in as cost effective way as possible. The Spanish and Portuguese expeditions were government ventures, but the success of the Atlantic economy during the 17th and 18th centuries was based on private enterprise. The economic system of **mercantilism** was developed most effectively by the British and the Dutch, with private companies under charter from the governments carrying out the trade. Mercantilism's main goal was to benefit the mother country by trading goods to accumulate precious metals, that enriched the country. The African slave trade was an important part of mercantile trade. The Great Circuit trade went something like this:

1) The first leg from Europe carried hardware, guns, and Indian cotton to Africa.
2) The second leg was the notorious **Middle Passage** that carried African slaves to the New World. Slaves were packed as tightly as possible in the ships, often under very inhumane conditions.
3) The last leg carried plantation goods from the colonies back to Europe.

The theory was that on every leg the ships carried goods from a place where they were abundant to a place where they were scarce. The profits could be enormous, but shipwrecks, slave deaths, and piracy could turn profit into loss. A subset of the Great Circuit trade was the **Triangular Trade** that carried rum from New England to West Africa, slaves to the West Indies, and molasses and rum back to New England.

LABOR SYSTEMS IN THE AMERICAS

The Spanish were most interested in finding gold and silver in the Americas, and so early on they began mining for it. In areas where no precious metals existed, they set up plantations to raise crops from bananas to sugar cane. They first tried these labor systems:

- **Mita** – The Inca had made extensive use of the **mita** system, a sort of labor tax to support elites and the elderly. Generally, an adult male had to spend 1/7 of his time working for the Inca, a few months at a time. When his obligation to the state was complete, he would return home until his service time came up again. The Spanish adopted this system, particularly for their silver mines in Bolivia and surrounding areas. The problem was that so many natives died, that the Spanish kept having to increase the time spent in the mines that it became impractical. Finally, the work in the mines was so grueling that few Indians were left to do the work.

- **Encomienda** – This system was used primarily for agricultural work. Natives in an area were placed under the authority of *encomenderos*, or Spanish bosses, who could extract labor and tribute according to the needs of the area. Again, this system only lasted during the 16th century because so many natives died.

In North America the English colonies had varying bases for their economies. In the north, farms were small and family run, and city-based trade was important. In the south the soil and climate were better suited for large farms, and so a plantation system developed. A labor system used both in North America and the Caribbean was **indentured servitude**, in which an employer would pay the passage of a person to the New World in return for several years of labor. After the debt was paid in years worked, the servant would be free. This system was limited in its usefulness, especially in the Caribbean where indentured servant eventually refused to go because of the harsh working conditions on the sugar plantations.

EARLY SLAVE SYSTEMS IN THE SOUTH AMERICA AND THE CARIBBEAN

Before 1650 most slaves were destined either for the sugar plantations in Brazil and mainland Spanish colonies, but during the second half of the 17th century, more and more went to the Caribbean. Sugar cane was not native to the areas, but once imported, it grew well and resulted in great profit. The strong demand for sugar in Europe was complemented by the trade with China for tea. Perhaps most stereotypically, the English teatime depended on a regular supply of these products. Sugar plantations required large investments of capital because the cane had to be processed within a few hours of when it was cut in order to extract the sugary syrup. So each plantation not only had vast fields of sugar cane, but also had a mill and processing plant. Many slaves were needed for the work, which was hot and grueling.

The demand was greater for male slaves than for females because of the nature of the work, so the sex ratio was such that family life was impossible for most. Disease among slaves was particularly problematic in the Caribbean and Brazil, with many dying from dysentery caused by contaminated water and malaria. As a result, slave populations in these areas did not experience a natural growth, and so had to be replaced by more through the slave trade.

EARLY SLAVE SYSTEMS IN NORTH AMERICA

Sugar plantations were among the first to appear in North America as well, mainly in the warm, humid lowlands of present-day Louisiana. However, in the mid-1600s tobacco smoking became fashionable in England, and so tobacco plantations rose in the tidelands of Virginia. North American climates were generally healthier than those in the Caribbean, so slaves in North America did experience a natural increase, requiring fewer new slaves for trade. However, as plantations spread across the South, and eventually began raising other crops, such as cotton, the slave trade remained vigorous.

WHICH CAME FIRST: RACISM OR SLAVERY?

This question is one that historians like to ask, but they seldom agree on the answer. Still, it is an important question to consider in thinking about how significant changes occur in world history. Slavery is an institution as old as civilization itself. We see examples of slavery in ancient river valley and classical societies, and most subsequent civilizations at least make some use of slaves. However, an intriguing fact is that slavery increased dramatically between 1450 and 1750 C.E. Much of the increase occurred in the New World, but we also see slavery intensify in the Middle East and Africa, where female slaves were often either servants or concubines, male children eunuchs, and adult males served in armies. Although slaves came from other places, most of the slave trade came out of Africa. Why did this phenomenon happen?

One answer is that it was mainly **racism**, or the belief that one race of people is inferior to another. If one assumes racial superiority, then it follows that slavery is justified because the inferior race is actually considered to be subhuman. In the 16th century, when Europeans first encountered Africans, they interpreted African ways of life as inferior to those in Europe, and so didn't think of enslavement as being immoral. Another version argues that everyone is **ethnocentric**, or believes that their ways of life are superior to others, and so any contact with different races brings out this natural human characteristic.

An opposite approach is to think of the main motivation for slavery as economic. Forcing someone to work for you brings an economic benefit. Civilizations throughout history have built their power on the backs of slaves. The 1450-1750 phenomenon occurred because European colonizers were looking for ways to make their colonies profitable, and slavery was one of the solutions. Once people were captured, transported, and put to work in the New World, racism came about in order to justify the way that these human beings were treated. So, the slave traders and holders came to say things like, "They're not really human anyway," or "They can't survive on their own because they can't think for themselves." Instead of racism causing slavery, slavery caused racism.

What do you think? Take your pick:

DID RACISM CAUSE SLAVERY, OR DID SLAVERY CAUSE RACISM?	
Arguments for racism causes slavery:	**Arguments for slavery causes racism:**
All people are ethnocentric; they assume that their race is superior to others; slavery and the slave trade resulted.	The Great Circuit was set up for profits. In thinking about what Africans had that was needed in the New World, slave labor was an obvious answer.
The cultures in Africa were very different from those Europeans had seen before; enslaving people that seemed so inferior did that appear to be immoral to them.	The Europeans took advantage of the fact that Africans already practiced slavery. There was no need to capture them themselves. It was easy to arrange trade at posts along the Atlantic, a good way to make money.
How do you explain why Africans were specially victimized? Couldn't they have enslaved other Europeans, or people elsewhere in the world? There had to be racism.	Europe was on the rise, and the slave trade was a good way to assert their growing power. Trading slaves from Africa was a sign to all the world that Europeans were now dominant.
The missionary nature of Christianity assumed it to be a superior religion. Otherwise, why convert people? This assumption led to racism, or the belief that the cultures were inferior in other ways than religious beliefs.	Once slaves went to work, they usually outnumbered their masters, a situation that invited uprisings, attempts to break free. This fear of being outnumbered caused the masters to be racist, imagining their captives to be evil schemers intent on killing them.
The harsh treatment of slaves on the trans-Atlantic crossing proves that traders did not really think of them as human. Racism caused the treatment.	Treatment on ships was economically motivated. Packing in as many as possible with little to eat meant that profits would be greater. Racism only justified the treatment.
Africans did capture other Africans, but they were ethnocentric, too, because they usually enslaved people from other groups; Europeans did the same thing.	The economic reality was that Africans were in control in Africa. They too wanted profits, and so responded to European demand.
The treatment of slaves as chattel (things to be sold) can only be seen as racism, since Europeans did not think about enslaving one another.	Europeans used economic incentives, such as selling guns, liquor, and tobacco, to convince the Africans to trade slaves. Slaves were simply the most lucrative product that Africans had.

DEMOGRAPHIC AND ENVIRONMENTAL CHANGES

Demographic changes between 1450 and 1750 were significant. Some major population shifts included:

- **A rise in the population of Europe** – Europe's population had been decimated by the 14th century plague epidemic, so during the 15th and 16th centuries population levels were growing to match previous levels. Even though population pressure is not a good explanation for the movement of Europeans across to the New World, a long-term population expansion can be seen. For example, in 1000 C.E., Europe had an estimated 36 million people. In 1700 the population had grown to 120 million, the largest percentage increase of any of the continents.

- **A decrease in the population of the Americas** – This trend may run counter to common knowledge, but it does reflect the decimation of Amerindian populations by their encounters with Europeans. For example, in the late 15th century North America had almost 4 fi million people, Mexico had more than 21 million, the Caribbean and Central America each had almost 6 million, and South America (Andes and Lowlands) had almost 30 million. By 1700 the entire western hemisphere had only 13 million, a decrease from 67 million or so in 1500. Even though Europeans had settled in both North and South America by 1700, their numbers were too few to make an overall demographic difference.

- **No overall population decrease occurred in Africa** – Again, counter to common belief, the slave trade did not decimate the populations of Africa. By 1700 Africa had more than 60 million people, almost doubling their population in 1000. To be sure, some areas of Africa did reflect huge population losses, and logically those were places where the slave trade was most vigorous. Because the Atlantic trade was so much larger than the Saharan trade, areas most affected were along Africa's west coast, such as the Gold Coast and Slave Coast to the north, the Bight of Biafra in the middle, and Angola in the south.

Between 1000 and 1700 C.E., the populations of Asia – including the Middle East, Indian, and East Asia – more than doubled to a total of about 415 million. Clearly, overall world population grew, and the majority of people by the end of the time period still lived in the Middle East and Asia.

The Columbian Exchange almost certainly caused some environmental changes that help to explain the population trends listed above. For example, maize and cassava (a nutritious plant used in modern day tapioca) were transported by Portuguese ships from Brazil to Angola in southwest Africa. Angolans cultivated the crops, which adapted very well to their land. Some historians believe that this exchange provided the base for the population increase that followed, despite the fact that many Angolans were captured and deported to the New World as slaves. Likewise, the Andean potato eventually became the staple for poor people in Europe, sustaining population growth despite the number of people that began to migrate to the New World.

Major environmental changes occurred in the New World in two major ways:

- **Soil exhaustion** – Plantations in the Americas tended to rely on single crops, a process that depletes the soil of nutrients, and since land was plentiful, often the planters just moved on to clear more land. For example, in the Caribbean, instead of rotating sugar with other crops, planters found it more profitable to clear new lands when yields began to decline. Eventually, they moved on to other islands.

- **Deforestation** – The Spanish first cut down forests in the Caribbean to make pastures for the cattle they brought, and deforestation accelerated when more areas were cleared for plantations. In North America, shipbuilding in the northern English colonies took its toll of forests. In all of the Americas, the forests near the coasts were the first to go, so that deforestation was significant in many areas by 1750.

Deforestation was also taking place in Europe during this period. Timber was needed for ships, buildings, wagons, barrels, and many other items. Wood shortages were made worse by the **Little Ice Age** that began in Europe during the 1590s. People burned wood to keep warm, and by the mid-17th century, forests were growing scarce and wood prices skyrocketed. This wood shortage encouraged the use of coal for fuel, and since England had coal in great supply, deforestation almost certainly helped their economy grow. However, deforestation had many negative effects, especially on the poor.

The Little Ice Age spread as far as China, where it caused hardship that led people to rebellion and discontent, a condition that contributed to the mid-17th century demise of Ming China.

CULTURAL AND INTELLECTUAL DEVELOPMENTS

Any study of the transformation of Europe in the era between 1450-1750 would be incomplete without considering the influence of vast cultural and intellectual changes that began in the Italian city-states before 1450. Trade stimulated by the Crusades had made several of the city-states wealthy, such as Venice, Genoa, and Florence. Wealthy families, such as the **Medici** in Florence, became **patrons** of the arts, encouraging and supporting such geniuses as **Leonardo da Vinci** and **Michelangelo**. Some of the biggest supporters of Renaissance art and sculpture were the Catholic Popes, who commissioned work for the Vatican and St. Peter's cathedral in Rome. The era also saw a revival of interest in reading, writing, architecture, and philosophy. Without the patrons' wealth, the **Italian Renaissance** would have been impossible, but it almost certainly was stimulated by contact with the more sophisticated civilizations of the Middle East and South and East Asia.

The Renaissance, or "rebirth" was characterized by an attempt to revive the values of the classical civilizations of the Mediterranean, Greece and Rome. Although most of the major Renaissance figures did not actively defy the church, they put emphasis on other aspects of life than the religious. An important philosophical influence restored from ancient civilizations was **humanism**, which focused on the accomplishments, characteristics, and capabilities of humans, not of God. Humanism is reflected in Renaissance art, with newly skilled artists showing individual differences in faces and beautiful examples of human physiques. The Renaissance spread from Italy north, and by the 16th century had inspired new art styles in the Netherlands and Germany, as well as such literary geniuses as **William Shakespeare** in England. The importance of the European Renaissance goes far beyond art and literature because it encouraged people to think in different ways than they had before, a quality that Europeans would need as they ventured in science, technology, and eventually across the Atlantic to the Americas.

THE SCIENTIFIC REVOLUTION

The revival of interest in Greek and Roman influences also stimulated developments in math and science. The mathematical traditions that governed the conception of the universe were based in Greek mathematics that had been preserved and built upon by scientists in Muslim lands, such as Nasir al-Din in the 13th century. The Catholic Church endorsed the views of Ptolemy, the Greek philosopher and astronomer who constructed a **geocentric** theory where all planets, the moon, and the sun revolved around the earth. Using calculations from al-Din, a Polish monk and mathematician, **Nicholas Copernicus**, concluded that the geocentric theory did not make sense. Instead, his data indicated that the earth and all the other planets rotated around the sun, a conclusion that he did not share widely, for fear of retaliation from the church. In fact, his heliocentric theory was not published until after his death in 1543.

The scientist that really got into trouble over the heliocentric theory was Italian **Galileo Galilei**, who strengthened and improved Copernicus' theory. Other scientists, such as **Johannes Kepler**, had demonstrated that planets moved in elliptical orbits, and Galileo confirmed those theories as well. Perhaps most famously, he built a telescope that allowed him to observe the phenomena directly, recording details of heavenly bodies that the ancients could never have known about. Galileo's theories were published in *The Starry Messenger* in 1610, a highly controversial book criticized by other scientists, as well as officials of the church. Galileo made the mistake of making fun of people that disagreed with him, and he was arrested and put on trial, eventually recanting his theory publicly in order to save his own life.

Perhaps the greatest scientist of the era was **Isaac Newton** (1642-1727), an English mathematician whose genius shaped many modern fields of science. He formulated the set of mathematical laws for the force of gravity, made discoveries regarding the nature of light, and built on earlier Indian and Arab ideas for algebra. Newton did not challenge the authority of the Catholic Church, but he did prove that the Greeks and Romans were mistaken in some of their theories, and that fact encouraged others to question traditions that had not been challenged before.

THE PROTESTANT REFORMATION

The Catholic Church had been a very important societal force in medieval Europe. Not only had people's lives revolved around religion, but the church had actively defined many other aspects of society, including politics, art, and science. During the era from 1450 to 1750 the church lost significant power in almost every way. Not only were scientists and literary writers beginning to challenge the church, but the Pope's political power was compromised as centralization of government gave more authority to kings. Starting in the early 16th century, the church's religious authority was seriously weakened by the **Protestant Reformation**, a movement led by **Martin Luther**, a German priest who believed that the church was seriously flawed.

The Catholic Church was very rich by the early 1500s. Popes were often from Italian merchant families, and their wealth was bolstered by the many lands that church officials claimed all over Europe. Their land ownership in turn led to great political power that many kings deeply resented. Martin Luther, a priest and teacher at the University of Wittenberg, was troubled by all of these trends, especially as he compared the situation to the modest beginnings of Christianity and his interpretation of the teachings of Jesus. His doubts were provoked by a priest named Tetzel.

Luther placed a great deal of emphasis on the importance of faith, the glue that he believed formed the bond between Christians and God. According to his own writings, his most important revelation was that faith and actions cannot be separated. A true believer will naturally do good works, so the two are intertwined. He believed that the church practice of accepting **indulgences** directly contradicted this basic building block of true Christianity. Indulgences were payments to the church that insured eternal salvation, or life after death in heaven. For example, in 1519, when Luther openly challenged the religious authority of the church, the Pope was conducting an indulgence campaign to raise money for a new basilica for St. Peter's Church in Rome. Tetzel was the priest collecting indulgences in Wittenberg, who so enraged Luther with his blatant selling of indulgences for promises of salvation that he wrote and openly displayed the *95 Theses*, which listed 95 problems with church practices. With this action, Luther did what no priest had dared to do before – openly defy the authority of the church.

The developments after Luther's posting of the *95 Theses* indicate just how dramatically times were changing in Europe. Luther was excommunicated from the church, but he managed to hide from them throughout his long life with the help of many German princes. His writings were widely accepted in Germany, where **Protestantism**, as the protest movement came to be called, took firm root. Other Protestant groups sprang up in France, and from there found new vitality in Geneva, Switzerland, where **John Calvin** started yet another branch of Protestantism called **Calvinism**. Calvinism was carried to Scotland by one of Calvin's admirers, John Knox, and from there it made its way into England. Another blow to the church came when King **Henry VIII** of England separated religious institutions in his kingdom from the church when the Pope refused to grant him an annulment from his first wife, Catherine of Aragon.

By the end of the 16th century, large parts of Europe, particularly in Germany and Britain, were no longer under the authority of the Catholic Church. The church responded with its own internal reformation, but the result was a Europe deeply divided between Protestants and Catholics, a dynamic that fed the already intense competition among European nations.

THE IMPORTANCE OF THE PRINTING PRESS

Johannes Gutenberg, a printer from Mainz Germany, contributed greatly to the rapid spread of Protestantism. He died in 1468, many years before the Reformation began, but without his construction of a workable printing press around 1450, Luther's word almost certainly never would have gotten out. In 1454 he printed his famous **Gutenberg Bible** with moveable type, and the book inspired early Renaissance writers, such as Erasmus, to use the technology to print their own works. By 1550 at least 10 million printed works were circulating around Europe from presses in hundreds of towns. Guttenberg did not invent moveable type or the printing press. Both the Chinese and Koreans had used them in earlier years, and they too had spread literacy in Asia by printing books and making them accessible to more people. In Europe the device appeared as a critical invention at a critical time in European history. Without it the Renaissance, the Scientific Revolution, the Protestant Reformation, and ultimately the Maritime Revolution would not have been possible.

THE EARLY EUROPEAN ENLIGHTENMENT

During the 17th century, the Scientific Revolution began to be applied to social and political areas of life, a movement known as the **Enlightenment**. Enlightenment philosophers believed that human reason that discovered laws of science could also discover the laws that governed social and political behavior. The movement was also inspired by the Reformation, which had challenged and revised accepted religious thought, and by contact with political and social philosophies from other parts of the world.

In England the English Civil War shaped political thought. The king was decapitated, and political authority fell to Parliament, causing English political philosopher **John Locke** to reconsider the nature of government. In his famous *Second Treatise of Civil Government*, he argued that rulers get their right to rule not from the heavens, but from the consent of the governed. His philosophy laid the basis for **rule of law**, not by the whim of the monarch, an idea that was far from new. However, he added that if monarchs overstepped the law, citizens not only had the right, but the duty to rebel. His philosophy influenced thinkers in the late 1700s, who in turn inspired democratic revolutions in many places, including North America and France.

CULTURAL AND INTELLECTUAL LIFE IN CHINA

The Ming and early Qing emperors of this era continued to look to Chinese traditions to strengthen cultural and intellectual life. Neo-Confucianism, which had first emerged as a powerful philosophy during the Song era, was very strong, and numerous Confucian schools were founded by the emperors to reinforce its beliefs. The civil service exams were maintained, and other Chinese philosophy, literature and history were compiled during this time. For example, Emperor Kangxi compiled a *Collection of Books* that he had printed and distributed throughout China, reflecting the influence of the printing press in Asia as well as in Europe. Emperor Qinglong's *Complete Library of the Four Treasures* was too large to print, but he had seven manuscript copies placed in different libraries around China.

The printing press also made popular novels available, which were read by literate businessmen. Confucian scholars looked down on popular novels, but their appearance indicates the spread of literacy beyond the bureaucratic elite. Perhaps the most famous of these books was *Journey to the West*, an account of the journey of famous Buddhist monk Xuanzang to India to retrieve the Buddhist canon, thus bringing Buddhism to China. The novel featured a magical monkey who was Xuanzang's traveling companion, a character who became one of the most celebrated in Chinese literature.

PATRONAGE IN THE ISLAMIC EMPIRES

Just as wealth in the Italian city-states prompted patronage of the arts, so it did in the Islamic Empires as well. The emperors competed to attract the best scholars, literary writers, artists, and architects to their courts. The Ottoman sultans built beautiful palaces and mosques, with the most famous religious complex built by Suleyman the Magnificent called **Suleymaniye**, a blend of Islamic and Byzantine architectural features. The Safavid capital, Isfahan, was considered to be one of the most architecturally beautiful in all the world, with its monumental entryways, large courtyards, and intricate decoration.

Perhaps the most famous monument in Islamic lands was the **Taj Mahal**, built by Mughal Emperor Shah Jahan, who dedicated the white marble mosque and tomb to the memory of his wife. He planned to build a similar mausoleum out of black marble for himself, but he was deposed by his son and spent the rest of his life in prison, where he supposedly could see his wife's tomb through a small window with the help of a mirror.

By 1750 the world was a much different one than had existed in 1450. This era saw the rise of Europe, though scholars debate just how much power Europeans actually had in the world economy. They dominated the New World, which was connected by regular, sustained contact to the eastern hemisphere during this time. They also controlled much of the African slave trade, but it is important to note that no European had ventured far into the interior of the continent by 1750. They were still dependent on African kingdoms to bring the slaves to the trading posts, and Europeans had not set up significant colonies in Africa, except at the very southern tip, Capetown near the Cape of Good Hope. This situation would change dramatically during the following era.

Great empires continued to form in East Asia, the Middle East, and India, as the technological invention of gunpowder allowed them to conquer the nomadic groups that had challenged their authority for centuries. However, land-based empires clearly lost power in proportion to sea-faring powers, as world trade routes connected the western hemisphere to the east. These increased contacts were to have important consequences for people all over the world in the period from 1750-1914.

Reference:

Population statistics in Unit Three modified from Dennis H. Wrong, ed., *Population and Society* (1977); William M. Deneven, *the Native Populations of the Americas* in 1492 (1976), 289-292.

UNIT THREE QUESTIONS

(Questions 1 and 2 are based on the following quote):

"In contrast to the sea-based empires developing in Europe, land-based empires remained as important political forces between 1450-1750. All had huge land armies. These empires developed relatively independently from western influence, and to some extent they counterbalanced the growth of European power and colonization."

1. The empires described in the quote above built their power most directly on

   (A) the mandate of heaven
   (B) the technology of gunpowder
   (C) control of Silk Road trade
   (D) parliamentary principles
   (E) the development of new breeds of horses and camels

2. The quote accurately describes all of the following empires EXCEPT

   (A) Han China
   (B) Ottoman Empire
   (C) Safavid Empire
   (D) Mughal Empire
   (E) Russian Empire

3. Sikhism is accurately defined as a religion that

   (A) was native to Japan, but shared similar beliefs to Daoism
   (B) flourished primarily in Southeast Asia
   (C) originated in the Ottoman Empire as another major split in Islam
   (D) originated in India, with a blend of Muslim and Hindu beliefs
   (E) developed in Central America as a protest to Spanish-imposed Christianity

4. Which of the following decisions by the Portuguese most directly affected the Arab African cities of the east coast of Africa?

   (A) to trade only from coastal centers
   (B) to monopolize the Indian Ocean trade
   (C) to set up an African trading network that included the interior trade routes of the Sahara
   (D) to allow Christian missionaries to evangelize in the cities of the east coast
   (E) to start a navigators' school in Portugal

5. All of the following are common problems that the Muslim Empires of 1450-1750 shared EXCEPT:

   (A) Sunni-controlled governments whose power was seriously challenged by a Shi'a minority
   (B) inadequate transportation and systems for their armies
   (C) unruly warrior elites that challenged the government
   (D) inadequate bureaucracies that could not adequately govern or keep in touch with citizens
   (E) the rise of European rivals who ultimately built stronger militaries than they did

6. Which of the following European powers established hegemony over the Indian Ocean trade during the 16th century?

   (A) Dutch
   (B) English
   (C) Spanish
   (D) Portuguese
   (E) French

7. A dividing line drawn by the Pope to separate Portuguese and Spanish claims was established through the

   (A) Edict of Nantes
   (B) Treaty of Westphalia
   (C) Treaty of Tordesillas
   (D) Treaty of Paris
   (E) Council of Trent

8. By the 16th century the center of commercial activity for Europeans had shifted from the Mediterranean to the

   (A) Black Sea
   (B) Baltic Sea
   (C) Pacific Ocean
   (D) Indian Ocean
   (E) Atlantic Ocean

(Questions 9 and 10 are based on the following picture)

© AKG Images

9. Whose beard is being cut in the picture above?

   (A) a French army officer during the French and Indian War
   (B) a German mercenary during the American Revolution
   (C) a Russian boyar during the reign of Peter the Great
   (D) an Ottoman vizier by an English conqueror
   (E) a Spanish naval officer during the conquest of his Armada

10. What is the main reason that the individual's beard is being cut?

   (A) to make him comply with an official order intended to make his country modernize
   (B) to make him pay homage to a conquering ruler
   (C) at his request, to enable him to be named by his ruler as a member of the highest elite group
   (D) as a requirement for all men who fight in the military
   (E) as part of a sanitation measure in major ports of call along long-distance trading routes

1450-1750 C.E. Unit Three 115

11. The successful return of Magellan's ship *Victoria* to Spain in 1522 signaled that

   (A) the Spanish were not to be the dominant force in the Americas
   (B) Europeans were now positioned to make themselves masters of the oceans
   (C) the English would come to dominate territories around the world
   (D) Spain was now able to dominate trade with Asia
   (E) Spain would soon eclipse England as the most powerful European power

12. The Portuguese were able to assert control over the Indian Ocean trade because

   (A) they took over Aden, the city that centrally controlled most of the trade
   (B) the constant warfare in the region allowed the disruption of traditional trade systems
   (C) Portuguese trade goods were vastly superior to anything found in the region
   (D) the people they traded with were naïve and easily taken advantage of
   (E) their ships and weapons were militarily superior to the lightly armed merchant dhows

13. All of the following factors contributed to the success of the Spanish in quickly creating a vast empire in the Americas EXCEPT:

   (A) The Spanish assembled a large army that quickly overran the Western Hemisphere.
   (B) The long isolation of the Americas made its inhabitants vulnerable to European diseases.
   (C) The Spanish had superior military technology.
   (D) They were motivated by their desire to convert the natives to Christianity.
   (E) Only two empires – great distances apart – were strong enough to militarily challenge the Spanish.

14. The Renaissance philosophy of humanism emphasizes the importance of

   (A) religious rather than secular teachings
   (B) the accomplishments and capabilities of individual human beings
   (C) trade as the primary method of building wealth
   (D) technological innovations
   (E) the Muslim influence on the development of European thought

(Question 15 and 16 are based on the following photograph):

IndiaWorld.com

15. The main reason that this building was constructed between 1632 and 1649 was to serve as

    (A) a place of worship for people of many faiths
    (B) a palace for the ruler
    (C) a mausoleum for the ruler's dead wife
    (D) an administrative building for the government
    (E) a center of long-distance trade

16. The building was constructed in a place ruled by the

    (A) Russian tsar
    (B) Ottoman sultan
    (C) Gupta emperor
    (D) Mongol khan
    (E) Mughal emperor

17. Which of the following was an important reason why the Ming Empire weakened and fell by the mid-1600s?

    (A) A serious change of climate made southern China too hot to raise rice.
    (B) The bulk of the Silk Road trade was captured and controlled by the Muslim Empires.
    (C) The Portuguese and English were successful in capturing several of their southern ports.
    (D) The Mongols regained power and resumed their attacks from the north and west.
    (E) The last, but strongest, Ming ruler was killed by the Japanese.

18. What was the main reason that the Edo court practiced alternate attendance?

    (A) to contain the influence of Christian missionaries
    (B) to ensure the samurais' loyalty to the emperor
    (C) to evaluate military preparedness
    (D) to show deference to their overlords, the Chinese Qing family
    (E) to ensure that the daimyos would be unable to overthrow the shogun

19. What was the main purpose of Zheng He's voyages?

    (A) to prove the seaworthiness of the Chinese ships
    (B) to search for a passage to the Americas
    (C) to defeat the pirates of Malacca so that sea travel would once again be safe
    (D) to extend China's influence by bearing gifts and exacting tribute
    (E) to visit Mecca and Muhammad's grave

20. All of the following are reasons why discovery voyages ceased after Zheng He's death EXCEPT:

    (A) The sponsoring emperor also died.
    (B) Confucian court officials resisted cross-cultural contacts and trade.
    (C) Court officials did not believe that Chinese sailors were sufficiently skilled to voyage any further than they did.
    (D) War broke out in the Western provinces, so the government needed to spend money there.
    (E) Court officials criticized Zheng He's voyages for not being profitable.

21. Which of the following most clearly differentiates the period from 1450 to 1750 from earlier periods?

    (A) decline of manorialism in western Europe
    (B) the rise of the Seljuk Turks as a world power
    (C) the inclusion of the Americas in the global trade network
    (D) the opening of Japan to trade with the West
    (E) the replacement of Romanesque architecture with the Gothic style in western Europe

22. By the end of the period from 1450 to 1750 the governments of Great Britain and France had which of the following characteristics in common?

    (A) Both nations were constitutional monarchies.
    (B) The power to levy taxes was controlled by the monarch in both nations.
    (C) Neither nation had wide class differences.
    (D) Both nations were absolute monarchies.
    (E) Both nations had strong centralized governments

23. "We have seen that kings take the place of God, who is the true father of the human species. We have also seen that the first idea of power which exists among men is that of the paternal power; and that kings are modeled on fathers."

    The above definition of kingship BEST fits the monarch of which of the following countries between 1450 and 1750?

    (A) England
    (B) Ireland
    (C) Germany
    (D) Italy
    (E) France

24. The immediate reason for Luther's protest against the Catholic Church was

    (A) the church's practice of excommunication
    (B) the church's ban on usury
    (C) the Papal refusal to permit Luther to marry
    (D) church-sponsored sale of indulgences
    (E) his support for German nationalism

25. Which of the following expresses Martin Luther's main philosophical disagreement with the Roman Catholic Church?

    (A) He did not believe in infant baptism, a common practice of the church.
    (B) He believed that the clergy were not well qualified to serve the church because their main concern was getting rich.
    (C) He believed that the Church equated good works with salvation, and ignored the importance of faith.
    (D) He disagreed with the church's position that during communion the bread and wine literally changed into the body and blood of Jesus.
    (E) He believed in predestination, and the church condemned this belief.

26. The Spanish Armada's defeat signaled the

    (A) decline of Spain's military dominance in Europe
    (B) beginning of Spain's global dominance
    (C) end of the era of European naval power
    (D) success of the Muslim invasion of western Europe
    (E) rise of French military dominance in Europe

27. The Copernican universe at first found more critics than supporters largely because

   (A) Copernicus was wrong
   (B) it directly challenged popular beliefs
   (C) Copernicus could not prove his theories empirically
   (D) people did not trust his data because it came from Islamic scholars
   (E) it challenged the intellectual synthesis of classical and biblical authorities.

28. Which of the following best describes the historical significance of the early modern period (1450-1750) in Europe?

   (A) It was an era when the lives of ordinary Europeans improved significantly.
   (B) In this era, women made much progress in gaining equality with men.
   (C) Most European governments shifted from absolutism to constitutional monarchies.
   (D) The balance of world power shifted from other areas of the world to European countries.
   (E) Populations decreased, allowing standards of living to improve for those that survived.

29. Coercive labor systems were predominant in all of the following areas of the New World between 1450 and 1750 EXCEPT:

   (A) the southern English colonies
   (B) the northern English colonies
   (C) the Caribbean
   (D) Portuguese Brazil
   (E) Spanish colonies of Central and South America

30. Which of the following groups had the highest social status in New Spain?

   (A) peninsulares
   (B) creoles
   (C) mestizos
   (D) mulattoes
   (E) Amerindians

31. What was the "Middle Passage"?

 (A) mid-priced tickets for the middle classes for passage from Europe to the Americas
 (B) the route across the Central American isthmus that connected the gold and silver routes from Peru on the Pacific side to the Atlantic Ocean
 (C) the trade route from the Caribbean to New England that carried molasses and sugar
 (D) the trade route from Africa to the Americas where ships carried mainly slaves
 (E) the route from European countries to the West African coast

32. Which of the following were products native to the New World that contributed the most to the Columbian Exchange?

 (A) chocolate and bananas
 (B) potatoes and corn (maize)
 (C) horses and cows
 (D) sugar and molasses
 (E) wheat and rice

33. Why were women more in demand than men in the trans-Saharan slave trade?

 (A) Women made better house servants than men did.
 (B) Women were sold along with their children, so buyers got more slaves for their money.
 (C) The slaves were destined to become concubines in lands that practiced polygamy.
 (D) The women were less likely to die on the long trek across the desert to ports on the Mediterranean.
 (E) The men were more likely to run away from their masters than the women.

34. Slave systems became much more prevalent in the New World during the 17th and early 18th century primarily as a result of the production of

 (A) tobacco
 (B) cotton
 (C) gold and silver
 (D) corn
 (E) sugar

35. In which area(s) of the New World did slaves experience a natural increase (more births than deaths) during the 18th century?

   I. North America
   II. Caribbean
   III. Brazil

(A) I only
(B) I and II only
(C) II and III only
(D) I and III only
(E) I, II, and III

CHANGE OVER TIME ESSAY

Directions: You are to answer the following question. You should spend 5 minutes organizing or outlining your essay. Write an essay that:

- Has a relevant thesis and supports that thesis with appropriate historical evidence.
- Addresses all parts of the question.
- Uses historical context to show change over time and/or continuities.

Describe and analyze the cultural, economic, and political impact of Christianity on ONE of the following regions between 600 and 1750 C.E. Be sure to discuss continuities as well as changes.

    East Asia
    Europe

UNIT FOUR

1750-1914

The era between 1750 and 1914 C.E. was one of clear European hegemony. In the previous era (1450 to 1750 C.E.), Europeans had tilted the balance of world power away from Asia, where powerful civilizations had existed since ancient times. However, despite growing European influence based on sea trade and colonization, major land-based empires in Asia still influenced long-distance trade and shaped political and economic conditions around them. In this era, Europe not only dominated the western hemisphere, as it had in the last, but it came to control the eastern hemisphere as well. How did they do it? Part of the answer lies in a set of discoveries and happenings that together constitute an important "Marker Event" – the Industrial Revolution. Another set of philosophical and political events were equally important – the establishment of democracy as a major element of a new type of political organization – the "nation."

QUESTIONS OF PERIODIZATION

Very important characteristics that distinguish 1750-1914 from previous eras in world history include:

- **European dominance of long-distance trade** – Whether by "unequal treaties" or colonization, sea-based trade gave European countries control of all major trade circuits in the world.

- **"Have" and "have not" countries created by Industrialization** – The Industrial Revolution gave huge economic and political advantages to countries where it occurs over countries that remained primarily agricultural.

- **Inequalities among regions increase due to imperialism** – Industrialized countries set out to form overseas empires, sometimes through colonization and other times by economic and/or political domination.

- **Political revolutions inspired by democracy and desire for independence** – These revolutions continue to the present, but "seed" revolutions that put new democratic forms of government in place occurred during this era. The "nation" emerged as a new type of political organization.

We will analyze these important characteristics of the period by examining these topics:

- **Changes in global commerce, communications, and technology** – Patterns of world trade and contact changed as the Industrial Revolution revolutionized communications and commerce. Distances became shorter as the Suez and Panama Canals cut new channels for travel, and new technology meant that ships were faster than before. Railroads revived land travel.

- **Demographic and environmental changes** – Huge numbers of people migrated to the Americas from Europe and Asia, so that population in the western hemisphere grew dramatically. The slave trade ended, and so did forced migrations from Africa to the New World. Industrialization had a huge impact on the environment, as demands for new fuels came about and cities dominated the landscape in industrialized countries. Industrialization also increased the demand for raw materials from less industrialized countries, altering natural landscapes further.

- **Changes in social and gender structures** – Serf and slave systems became less common, but the gap between the rich and poor grew in industrialized countries. We will explore the controversy regarding changes in women's roles in response to industrialization. Did women's status improve, or did gender inequality grow?

- **Political revolutions and independence movements; new political ideas** – Absolutism was challenged in many parts of the globe, and democracy took root as a result of economic and social change and Enlightenment philosophies that began in the 17th century. "Nations" arose as political entities that inspired nationalism and movements of political reform.

- **Rise of western dominance** – The definition of "west" remained centered in Europe, but expanded to include the United States and Australia. Western dominance reached not only economic and political areas, but extended to social, cultural, and artistic realms as well.

Although coercive labor systems as such declined during this era, new questions of equality and justice emerged as west came to dominate east, and the gap between the rich and poor grew larger, particularly in the most prosperous countries.

CHANGES IN GLOBAL COMMERCE, COMMUNICATIONS, AND TECHNOLOGY

By 1750 international trade and communications were nothing new. During the 1450-1750 era Europeans had set up colonies in the Americas so that for the first time in world history the western and eastern hemispheres were in constant contact with one another. However, after 1750 the pace of trade picked up dramatically, fed by a series of economic and technological transformations collectively known as the **Industrial Revolution**.

THE INDUSTRIAL REVOLUTION

Remember that to be called a Marker Event in world history, a development should qualify in three ways:

- It must cross national or cultural borders, affecting many civilizations.
- Later changes or developments in history must be at least partially traced to this event or series of events.
- It must have impact in other areas. For example, if it is a technological change, it must impact some other major areas, like government, belief systems, social classes, or the economy.

Like the Neolithic Revolution that occurred 10,000 years before it, the Industrial Revolution qualifies as a Marker Event according to all of the above criteria. It brought about such sweeping changes that it virtually transformed the world, even areas in which industrialization did not occur. The concept seems simple – invent and perfect machinery to help make human labor more efficient – but that's part of its importance. The change was so basic that it could not help but affect all areas of people's lives in every part of the globe.

The Industrial Revolution began in England in the late 18th century, and spread during the 19th century to Belgium, Germany, Northern France, the United States, and Japan. Almost all areas of the world felt the effects of the Industrial Revolution because it divided the world into "have" and "have not" countries, with many of the latter being controlled by the former. England's lead in the Industrial Revolution translated into economic prowess and political power that allowed colonization of other lands, eventually building a worldwide British Empire.

WHY BRITAIN?

The Industrial Revolution helped England greatly increase its output of manufactured goods by substituting hand labor with machine labor. Economic growth in Britain was fueled by a number of factors:

- **An Agricultural Revolution** – The Industrial Revolution would not have been possible without a series of improvements in agriculture in England. Beginning in the early1700s, wealthy landowners began to enlarge their farms through **enclosure**, or fencing or hedging large blocks of land for experiments with new techniques of farming. These scientific farmers improved **crop rotation** methods, which carefully controlled nutrients in the soil. They bred better livestock, and invented new machines, such as Jethro Tull's **seed drill** that more effectively planted seeds. The larger the farms and the better the production the fewer farmers were needed. Farmers pushed out of their jobs by enclosure either became tenant farmers or they moved to cities. Better nutrition boosted England's population, creating the first necessary component for the Industrial Revolution: labor.

- **A technological revolution** – England also was the first to experience a technological revolution, a series of inventions built on the principles of mass production, mechanization, and interchangeable parts. Josiah Wedgwood developed a mold for pottery that replaced the potters wheel, making mass production of dishes possible. Many experimented with machinery to speed up human labor, and interchangeable parts meant that machines were more practical and easier to repair.

- **Natural resources** – Britain had large and accessible supplies of coal and iron – two of the most important raw materials used to produce the goods for the early Industrial Revolution. Also available was water power to fuel the new machines, harbors for its merchant ships, and rivers for inland transportation.

- **Economic strength** – During the previous era, Britain had already built many of the economic practices and structures necessary for economic expansion, as well as a middle class (the bourgeoisie) that had experience with trading and manufacturing goods. Banks were well established, and they provided loans for businessmen to invest in new machinery and expand their operations.

- **Political stability** – Britain's political development during this period was fairly stable, with no major internal upheavals occurring. Although Britain took part in many wars during the 1700s, none of them took place on British soil, and its citizens did not seriously question the government's authority. By 1750 Parliament's power far exceeded that of the king, and its members passed laws that protected business and helped expansion.

NEW INVENTIONS

The earliest transformation of the Industrial Revolution was Britain's textile industry. In 1750 Britain already exported wool, linen, and cotton cloth, and the profits of cloth merchants were boosted by speeding up the process by which spinners and weavers made cloth. One invention led to another since none were useful if any part of the process was slower than the others. Some key inventions were:

- **The flying shuttle** – John Kay's invention carried threads of yarn back and forth when the weaver pulled a handle, greatly increasing the weavers' productivity.

- **The spinning jenny** – James Hargreaves' invention allowed one spinner to work eight threads at a time, increasing the output of spinners, allowing them to keep up with the weavers. Hargreaves named the machine for his daughter.

- **The water frame** – Richard Arkwright's invention replaced the hand-driven spinning jenny with one powered by water power, increasing spinning productivity even more.

- **The spinning mule** – In 1779, Samuel Crompton combined features of the spinning jenny and the water frame to produce the spinning mule. It made thread that was stronger, finer, and more consistent than that made by earlier machines. He followed this invention with the **power loom** that sped up the weaving process to match the new spinners.

These machines were bulky and expensive, so spinning and weaving could no longer be done at home. Wealthy textile merchants set up the machines in **factories**, and had the workers come to these places to do their work. At first the factories were set up near rivers and streams for water power, but other inventions later made this unnecessary. Before the late 1700s Britain's demand for cotton was met by India, but they increasingly came to depend on the American south, where plantation production was speeded by Eli Whitney's invention of the **cotton gin**, a machine that efficiently separated the cotton fiber from the seed. By 1810 southern plantations used slave labor to produce 85 million pounds of cotton, up from 1.5 million in 1790.

TRANSPORTATION IMPROVEMENTS

Once the textile industry began its exponential growth, transportation of raw materials to factories and manufactured goods to customers had to be worked out. New inventions in transportation spurred the Industrial Revolution further. A key invention was the **steam engine** that was perfected by James Watt in the late 1790s. Although steam power had been used before, Watt invented ways to make it practical and efficient to use for both water and land transportation.

Perhaps the most revolutionary use of steam energy was the railroad engine, which drove English industry after 1820. The first long-distance rail line from the coastal city of Liverpool to inland Manchester was an immediate success upon its completion in 1830, and within a few decades, most British cities were connected by rail. Railroads revolutionized life in Britain in several ways:

1) Railroads gave manufacturers a cheap way to transport materials and finished products.
2) The railroad boom created hundreds of thousands of new jobs for both railroad workers and miners.
3) The railroad industry spawned new industries and inventions and increased the productivity of others. For example, agricultural products could be transported farther without spoiling, so farmers benefited from the railroads.
4) Railroads transported people, allowing them to work in cities far away from their homes and travel to resort areas for leisure.

THE SPREAD OF THE INDUSTRIAL REVOLUTION

The Industrial Revolution occurred only in Britain for about 50 years, but it eventually spread to other countries in Europe, the United States, Russia, and Japan. British entrepreneurs and government officials forbade the export of machinery, manufacturing techniques, and skilled workers to other countries but the technologies spread by luring British experts with lucrative offers, and even smuggling secrets into other countries. By the mid-19th century industrialization had spread to France, Germany, Belgium, and the United States.

The earliest center of industrial production in continental Europe was Belgium, where coal, iron, textile, glass, and armaments production flourished. By 1830 French firms had employed many skilled British workers to help establish the textile industry, and railroad lines began to appear across Western Europe. Germany was a little later in developing industry, mainly because no centralized government existed there yet, and a great deal of political unrest made industrialization difficult. However, after the 1840s German coal and iron production skyrocketed, and by the 1850s an extensive rail network was under construction. After German political unification in 1871, the new empire rivaled England in terms of industrial production.

Industrialization began in the United States by the 1820s, delayed until the country had enough laborers and money to invest in business. Both came from Europe, where overpopulation and political revolutions sent immigrants to the United States to seek their fortunes. The American Civil War (1861-1865) delayed further immigration until the 1870s, but it spurred the need for industrial war products, all the way from soldiers' uniforms to guns to railroads for troop transport. Once the war was over, cross-country railroads were built which allowed more people to claim parts of vast inland America and to reach the west coast. The United States had abundant natural resources – land, water, coal and iron ore – and after the great wave of immigration from Europe and Asia in the late 19th century – it also had the labor.

During the late 1800s, industrialization spread to Russia and Japan, in both cases by government initiatives. In Russia the tsarist government encouraged the construction of railroads to link places within the vast reaches of the empire. The most impressive one was the Trans-Siberian line constructed between 1891 and 1904, linking Moscow to Vladivostock on the Pacific Ocean. The railroads also gave Russians access to the empire's many coal and iron deposits, and by 1900 Russia ranked fourth in the world in steel production. The Japanese government also pushed industrialization, hiring thousands of foreign experts to instruct Japanese workers and managers in the late 1800s. Railroads were constructed, mines were opened, a banking system was organized, and industries were started that produced ships, armaments, silk, cotton, chemicals, and glass. By 1900 Japan was the most industrialized land in Asia, and was set to become a 20th century power.

CHANGES IN PATTERNS OF WORLD TRADE

Industrialization greatly increased the economic, military, and political strength of the societies that embraced it. By and large, the countries that benefited from industrialization were the ones that had the necessary components of land, labor and capital, and often government support. However, even though many other countries tried to industrialize, few had much success. For example, India tried to develop jute and steel industries, but the entrepreneurs failed because they had no government support and little investment capital. An international division of labor resulted: people in industrialized countries produced manufactured products, and people in less industrialized countries produced the raw materials necessary for that production. Industrial England, for example, needed cotton, so turned to India, Egypt, and the American South to produce it for them. In many cases this division of labor led to colonization of the non-industrialized areas. As industrialization increased, more iron and coal were needed, as well as other fibers for the textile industry, and the British Empire grew rapidly in order to meet these demands.

Many countries in Latin America, sub-Saharan Africa, south Asia, and southeast Asia became highly dependent on one cash crop, such as sugar, cotton, and rubber. This practice earned Latin American countries the nickname of "Banana Republics." Such economies were very vulnerable to any change in the international market. Foreign investors owned and controlled the plantations that produced these crops, and most of the profits went to them. Very little of the profits actually improved the living conditions for people that lived in those areas, and since they had little money to spend, a market economy could not develop.

Despite the inequalities, the division of labor between people in countries that produced raw materials and those that produced manufactured goods increased the total volume of world trade. In turn, this increased volume led to better technology, which reinforced and fed the trade. Sea travel became much more efficient, with journeys that had once taken months or years reduced to days or weeks. By 1914 two great canals shortened sea journeys by thousands of miles. The Suez Canal built by the British and French in the 1850s linked the Mediterranean Sea to the Red Sea, making it no longer necessary to go around the tip of Africa to get from Europe to Asia by sea. The Panama Canal, completed in 1913, did a similar thing in the western hemisphere, cutting a swath through Central America that encouraged trade and transportation between the Atlantic and Pacific Oceans.

DEMOGRAPHIC AND ENVIRONMENTAL CHANGES

The Industrial Revolution significantly changed population patterns, migrations, and environments. In industrialized nations people moved to the areas around factories to work there, cities grew, and as a result an overall migration from rural to urban areas took place. This movement was facilitated by the growth of railroads and improvement of other forms of transportation. This era also saw migrations on a large scale from Europe and Asia into the Americas, so that the overall population of the western hemisphere increased. However, this movement did not translate into a decrease of population in the eastern hemisphere. Particularly in Europe, the Agricultural Revolution improved nutrition, especially as the potato (transported from the New World in the previous era) became a main diet staple for European peasants.

THE END OF THE ATLANTIC SLAVE TRADE AND SLAVERY

Even as we may debate whether slavery and the slave trade came about because of racism or economic benefit, we may argue about why both ended during this era. From the beginning, as the Atlantic slave trade enriched some Africans and many Europeans, it became a topic of fierce debate in Europe, Africa, and the Americas in the late 18th century. The American and French revolutions stimulated these discussions, since both emphasized liberty, equality, and justice, topics that fed a strong **abolitionist movement**. Because most slaves were not allowed to learn to read and write, most outspoken abolitionists were free whites in England and North America. However, Africans themselves took up the struggle to abolish slavery and the slave trade, rising in frequent slave revolts in the 18th and 19th centuries that made slavery an expensive and dangerous business. Probably the most famous African spokespersons was **Olaudah Equiano**, a west African who published an autobiography in 1789 that recounted his experiences as a slave in Africa and the New World. He later gained his freedom, learned to read and write, and became active in the abolitionist movement. Many people read his works, heard him speak, and were influenced to oppose slavery.

Despite the importance of the abolitionist movement, economic forces also contributed to the end of slavery and the slave trade. Plantations and the slave labor that supported them remained in place as long as they were profitable. In the Caribbean, a revolution, led by **Toussaint L'Ouverture** resulted in the liberation of slaves in Haiti and the creation of the first black free state in the Americas. However, the revolution was so violent that it sparked fear among plantation owners and colonial governments throughout the Caribbean. In the late 18th century, a rapid increase in Caribbean sugar production led to declining prices, and yet prices for slaves remained high and even increased.

Even as plantations experienced these difficulties, profits from the emerging manufacturing industries were increasing, so investors shifted their money to these new endeavors. Investors discovered that wage labor in factories was cheaper than slave labor on plantations because the owners were not responsible for food and shelter. Entrepreneurs began to see Africa as a place to get raw materials for industry, not just slaves.

THE END OF THE SLAVE TRADE

Most European countries and the United States had abolished the slave trade before the mid-19th century: Britain in 1807, the United States in 1808, France in 1814, the Netherlands in 1817, and Spain in 1845. Ardent abolitionists in Britain pressured the government to send patrol ships to the west coast of Africa to conduct search and seizure operations for ships that violated the ban. The last documented ship that carried slaves on the Middle Passage arrived in Cuba in 1867.

THE END OF SLAVERY

The institution of slavery continued in most places in the Americas long after the slave trade was abolished, with the British abolishing slavery in their colonies in 1833. The French abolished slavery in 1848, the same year that their last king was overthrown by a democratic government. The United States abolished slavery in 1865 when the North won a bitter Civil War that had divided the southern slave-holding states from the northern non-slavery states. The last country to abolish slavery in the Americas was Brazil, where the institution was weakened by a law that allowed slaves to fight in the army in exchange for freedom. Army leaders resisted demands that they capture and return runaway slaves, and slavery was abolished in 1888, without a war.

IMMIGRATION TO THE AMERICAS

Various immigration patterns arose to replace the slave trade. Asian and European immigrants came to seek opportunities in the Americas from Canada in the north to Argentina in the south. Some were attracted to discoveries of gold and silver in western North America and Canada, including many who made their way west from the eastern United States. However, European and Asian migrants who became workers in factories, railroad construction sites, and plantations outnumbered those who were gold prospectors.

By the mid 19th century European migrants began crossing the Atlantic to fill the factories in the eastern United States. Increasing rents and indebtedness drove farmers from Ireland, Scotland, Germany and Scandinavia to North America, settling in the Ohio and Mississippi River Valleys in search of land. The potato famine forced many Irish peasants to make the journey, and political revolutions caused many Germans to flee the wrath of the government when their causes failed. By the late 19th and early 20th centuries, most immigrants to North America were from southern and eastern Europe, fleeing famine, poverty, and discrimination in their countries of origin.

While migrants to the United States came to fill jobs in the developing industrial society, those who went to Latin America mostly worked on agricultural plantations. About 4 million Italians came to Argentina in the 1880s and 1890s, and others went to Brazil, where the government paid the voyage over for Italian migrants who came to work on coffee plantations after slavery was abolished. Others came from Asia, with more than 15,000 indentured laborers from China working in sugarcane fields in Cuba during the 19th century. Chinese and Japanese laborers came to Peru where they worked on cotton plantations, in mines, and on railroad lines.

THE DEMOGRAPHIC TRANSITION

This era saw a basic change in the population structures of industrialized countries. Large families had always been welcome in agricultural societies because the more people a family had, the more land they were able to work. Children's work was generally worth more than it costs to take care of them. However, in the west, including the United States, the birth rate declined to historically low levels in the 19th century. This **demographic transition** from high birth rates to low reflected the facts that child labor was being replaced by machines and that children were not as useful as they were in agricultural societies. Instead, as life styles changed in urban settings, it became difficult to support large families, both in terms of supporting them with salaries from industrial jobs and in housing them in crowded conditions in the cities. High birth rates continued elsewhere in the world, so the West's percentage of total world population began to slip by 1900 even as its world power peaked.

ENVIRONMENTAL CHANGES

Wilderness areas in Europe were virtually gone by 1750, with almost every piece of land used by farmers or townspeople. However, the process continued during this era, and deforestation became the most serious problem. Americans transformed their lands even more rapidly as people moved west, clearing forests for farms and then moving on when the soil was depleted. The cultivation of cotton was especially harmful. Planters cut down forests, grew cotton for a few years, moved west, and abandoned the land to scrub pines.

Surprisingly, industrialization actually relieved environmental depletion in Britain because raw materials once grown on British soil – like wool and grain – were replaced by coal and iron found underground. Iron replaced wood in many building structures, including ships, so that deforestation slowed.

The most dramatic environmental changes in industrialized countries occurred in the towns. Never before had towns grown so fast, and major cities formed. London grew from about 500,000 inhabitants in 1700 to more than 2 million by 1850, with the largest population a city had ever had in world history. Cities in the middle industrial belt of Britain, such as Liverpool and Manchester grew rapidly during this period as well. New York City in the United States reached about 600,000 in 1850.

CHANGES IN SOCIAL AND GENDER STRUCTURE

Industrialization also transformed social and gender structures in countries where it developed, although it is not entirely clear as to whether the "gender gap" narrowed or widened. By and large industrialization widened the gap between the rich and the poor by creating opportunities for businessmen to be far richer than the upper classes in an agricultural society ever could be. Although they were free, not forced, laborers, the wages for factory workers were very low, and many suffered as much if not more poverty than they had as rural peasants.

WORKING CONDITIONS

Industrialization offered new opportunities to people with important skills, such as carpentry, metallurgy, and machine operations. Some enterprising people became engineers or opened their own businesses, but for the vast majority of those who left their farming roots to find their fortunes in the cities, life was full of disappointments. Most industrial jobs were boring, repetitive, and poorly paid. Workdays were long with few breaks, and workers performed one simple task over and over with little sense of accomplishment. Unlike even the poorest farmer or craftsman, factory workers had no control over tools, jobs, or working hours. Factory workers could do very little about their predicament until the latter part of the period, when labor unions formed and helped to provoke the moral conscience of some middle class people. Until then, workers who dared to go on strike – like the unmarried girls at the Lowell mills in Massachusetts – were simply replaced by other workers from the abundant supply of labor.

FAMILY LIFE

Because machinery had to be placed in a large, centrally located place, workers had to go to factories to perform their work, a major change in lifestyles from those in agricultural societies. In previous days all family members did most of their work on the farm, which meant that the family stayed together most of the time. Division of labor meant that they did different types of work, mostly split by gender and age, but the endeavor was a collective one. Even in the early days of commercialization, "piece work" was generally done by people at home, and then delivered to the merchant or businessman. Now people left their homes for hours at a time, often leaving very early and not returning till very late. Usually both husband and wife worked away from home, and for most of this period, so did children. Family life was never the same again.

In the early days of industrialization, the main occupation of working women was domestic servitude. If they had small children, they usually tried to find work they could do at home, such as laundry, sewing, or taking in lodgers. However, even with both parents working, wages were so low that most families found it difficult to make ends meet. Most industrialists encouraged workers to bring their children along with them to the factories because children usually could do the work, too, and they were quite cheap.

CHANGES IN SOCIAL CLASSES

A major social change brought about by the Industrial Revolution was the development of a relatively large middle class, or "bourgeoisie" in industrialized countries. This class had been growing in Europe since medieval days when wealth was based on land, and most people were peasants. With the advent of industrialization, wealth was increasingly based on money and success in business enterprises, although the status of inherited titles of nobility based on land ownership remained in place. However, land had never produced such riches as did business enterprises of this era, and so members of the bourgeoisie were the wealthiest people around.

However, most members of the middle class were not wealthy, owning small businesses or serving as managers or administrators in large businesses. They generally had comfortable lifestyles, and many were concerned with respectability, or the demonstration that they were of a higher social class than factory workers were. They valued the hard work, ambition, and individual responsibility that had led to their own success, and many believed that the lower classes only had themselves to blame for their failures. This attitude generally extended not to just the urban poor, but to people who still farmed in rural areas.

The urban poor were often at the mercy of **business cycles** – swings between economic hard times to recovery and growth. Factory workers were laid off from their jobs during hard times, making their lives even more difficult. With this recurrent unemployment came public behaviors, such as drunkenness and fighting, that appalled the middle class, who stressed sobriety, thrift, industriousness, and responsibility.

Social class distinctions were reinforced by **Social Darwinism**, a philosophy by Englishman Herbert Spencer. He argued that human society operates by a system of natural selection, whereby individuals and ways of life automatically gravitate to their proper station. According to Social Darwinists, poverty was a "natural condition" for inferior individuals.

GENDER ROLES AND INEQUALITY

Changes in gender roles generally fell along class lines, with relationships between men and women of the middle class being very different from those in the lower classes.

LOWER CLASS MEN AND WOMEN

Factory workers often resisted the work discipline and pressures imposed by their middle class bosses. They worked long hours in unfulfilling jobs, but their leisure time interests fed the popularity of two sports: European soccer and American baseball. They also did less respectable things, like socializing at bars and pubs, staging dog or chicken fights, and participating in other activities that middle class men disdained.

Meanwhile, most of their wives were working, most commonly as domestic servants for middle class households, jobs that they usually preferred to factory work. Young women in rural areas often came to cities or suburban areas to work as house servants. They often sent some of their wages home to support their families in the country, and some saved dowry money. Others saved to support ambitions to become clerks or secretaries, jobs increasingly filled by women, but supervised by men.

MIDDLE CLASS MEN AND WOMEN

When production moved outside the home, men who became owners or managers of factories gained status. Industrial work kept the economy moving, and it was valued more than the domestic chores traditionally carried out by women. Men's wages supported the families, since they usually were the ones who made their comfortable life styles possible. The work ethic of the middle class infiltrated leisure time as well. Many were intent on self-improvement, reading books or attending lectures on business or culture. Many factory owners and managers stressed the importance of church attendance for all, hoping that factory workers could be persuaded to adopt middle-class values of respectability.

Middle class women generally did not work outside of the home, partly because men came to see stay-at-home wives as a symbol of their success. What followed was a **"cult of domesticity"** that justified removing women from the work place. Instead, they filled their lives with the care of children and the operation of their homes. Since most middle-class women had servants, they spent time supervising them, but they also had to do fewer household chores themselves.

Historians disagree in their answers to the question of whether or not gender inequality grew because of industrialization. Gender roles were generally fixed in agricultural societies, and if the lives of working class people in industrial societies are examined, it is difficult to see that any significant changes in the gender gap took place at all. However, middle class gender roles provide the real basis for the argument. On the one hand, some argue that women were forced out of many areas of meaningful work, isolated in their homes to obsess about issues of marginal importance. On the farm, their work was "women's work," but they were an integral part of the central enterprise of their time: agriculture. Their work in raising children was vital to the economy, but industrialization rendered children superfluous as well, whose only role was to grow up safely enough to fill their adult gender-related duties. On the other hand, the **"cult of domesticity"** included a sort of idolizing of women that made them responsible for moral values and standards. Women were seen as stable and pure, the vision of what kept their men devoted to the tasks of running the economy. Women as standard-setters, then, became the important force in shaping children to value respectability, lead moral lives, and be responsible for their own behaviors. Without women filling this important role, the entire social structure that supported industrialized power would collapse. And who could wish for more power than that?

NEW POLITICAL IDEAS AND MOVEMENTS

In 1750 only England and the Netherlands had constitutional monarchies, governments that limited the powers of the king or ruler. All the other kingdoms of Europe, as well as the Muslim Empires and China, practiced absolutism. Absolutist rulers benefited from the tendency for governments to centralize between 1450 and 1750 because it extended the power they had over their subjects. Most of the rulers reinforced their powers by claiming special authority for the supernatural, whether it be the mandate of heaven as practiced in China, or divine right as European kings declared. Between 1750 and 1914, absolute rulers almost everywhere lost power, and the rule of law became a much more important political principle.

One of the most important political concepts to arise from the era was the "nation-state," a union often characterized by a common language, shared historical experiences and institutions, and similar cultural traditions, including religion at both the elite and popular levels. As a result, political loyalties were no longer so determined by one's attitudes toward a particular king or noble but by a more abstract attachment to a "nation."

FORCES FOR POLITICAL CHANGE

As the Industrial Revolution began in England, the economic changes were accompanied by demands for political changes that spread to many other areas of the world by the end of the 19th century. Two important forces behind the change were:

- **The influence of the Enlightenment** – The 1700s are sometimes referred to as the "Age of Enlightenment," because philosophical and political ideas began to seriously question the assumptions of absolute governments. The Enlightenment began in Europe, and was a part of the changes associated with the Renaissance, the Scientific Revolution, and the Protestant Reformation, all taking place between 1450 and 1750. The Enlightenment invited people to use their "reason" using the same humanistic approach of Renaissance times. People can figure things out, and they can come up with better governments and societies. In the 1600s John Locke wrote that a ruler's authority is based on the will of the people. He also spoke of a **social contract** that gave subjects the right to overthrow the ruler if he ruled badly. French *philosophes*, such as Voltaire and Jean-Jacques Rousseau spread the new ideas to France, where they began uproar in a land that epitomized absolutism.

- **New wealth of the bourgeoisie** – Ongoing commercialization of the economy meant that the middle class grew in size and wealth, but not necessarily in political power. These self-made men questioned the idea that aristocrats alone should hold the highest political offices. Most could read and write, and found Enlightenment philosophy appealing in its questioning of absolute power. They sought political power to match the economic power that they had gained.

REVOLUTIONS

A combination of economic, intellectual, and social changes started a wave of revolutions in the late 1700s that continued into the first half of the 19th century. They started in North America and France, and spread into other parts of Europe and to Latin America.

THE AMERICAN REVOLUTION

Ironically, the first revolution inspired by the new political thought that originated in England began in the North American colonies and was directed at England. It began when American colonists resisted Britain's attempt to impose new taxes and trade controls on the colonies after the French and Indian War ended in 1763. Many also resented Britain's attempts to control the movement west. "Taxation without representation" turned British political theory on its ear, but it became a major theme as the rebellion spread from Massachusetts throughout the rest of the colonies. Colonial leaders set up a new government and issued the Declaration of Independence in 1776. The British sent forces to put the rebellion down, but the fighting continued for several years until the newly created United States eventually won. The United States Constitution that followed was based on enlightenment principles, with three branches of government that check and balance one another. Although initially only a few had the right to vote and slavery was not abolished, the government became a model for revolutions to come.

THE FRENCH REVOLUTION

A very different situation existed in France. No established nobility existed in the United States, so when independence was achieved, the new nation had no old social and political structure to throw off. In contrast, the Revolution in France was a civil war, a rising against the *Ancien Regime*, or the old kingdom that had risen over centuries. The king, of course, had absolute power, but the nobility and clergy had many privileges that no one else had. Social classes were divided into three estates: First was the clergy, Second the nobility, and the Third Estate was everyone else. On the eve of the Revolution in 1789, about 97% of the population of France was thrown into the **Third Estate**, although they held only about 5% of the land. They also paid 100% of the taxes.

Part of the problem was that the growing class of the bourgeoisie had no political privileges. They read Enlightenment *philosophes*, they saw what happened in the American Revolution, and they resented paying all the taxes. Many saw the old political and social structure as out of date and the nobles as silly and vain, undeserving of the privileges they had.

The French Revolution began when King Louis XVI called the **Estates-General**, or the old parliamentary structure, together for the first time in 160 years. He did so only because the country was in financial crisis brought on by too many wars for power and an extravagant court life at Versailles Palace. Many problems converged to create the Revolution: the nobles' refusal to pay taxes, bourgeoisie resentment of the king, Louis XVI's incompetence, and a series of bad harvests for the peasants. The bourgeoisie seized control of the proceedings and declared the creation of the **National Assembly**, a legislative body that still exists in France today. They wrote the **Declaration of the Rights of Man and the Citizen**, modeled after the American Declaration of Independence, and they set about to write a Constitution for France.

The years after the revolution began were turbulent ones that saw the king beheaded and the government taken over by the **Jacobins**, a radical group that sought equality through executing those that disagreed with the government. **The Reign of Terror** lasted for about two years, with thousands of people guillotined and thousands more fleeing the country. The Jacobin leaders themselves were eventually guillotined; the country teetered for several years in disarray, and finally was swept up by Napoleon Bonaparte as he claimed French glory in battle. Democracy did not come easily in France.

CONSERVATIVE REACTION TO REVOLUTION

Napoleon Bonaparte, of minor nobility from the island of Corsica, rose through the ranks of the French military during a time of chaos. He seized the French Government at a time when no one else could control it. He promised stability and conquest, and by 1812 the French Empire dominated Europe to the borders of Russia. His invasion of Russia was unsuccessful, done in by cold winters, long supply lines, and Tsar Alexander I's burn and retreat method that left French armies without food. Finally, an alliance of European countries led by Britain defeated Napoleon in 1815 at Waterloo in modern day Belgium. Although Napoleon was defeated and exiled, other countries were horrified by what had happened in France: a revolution, the beheading of a king, a terrorizing egalitarian government, and finally a demagogue who attacked all of Europe. To conservative Europe, France was a problem that had to be contained before their ideas and actions spread to the rest of the continent.

The allies that had defeated Napoleon met at Vienna in 1815 to reach a peace settlement that would make further revolutions impossible. The **Congress of Vienna** was controlled by the representatives of three nations: Britain, Austria, and Russia. Each country wanted something different. The British wanted to destroy the French war machine, Russia wanted to establish an alliance based on Christianity, and Austria wanted a return to absolutism. They reached an agreement based on restoring the **balance of power** in Europe, or the principle that no one country should ever dominate the others. Rather, the power should be balanced among all the major countries. France actually came out rather well in the proceedings, due in large part to the talents of their representative, Tallyrand. However, the Congress restricted France with these major decisions:

- Monarchies – including the monarchy in France – were restored in countries that Napoleon had conquered.
- France was "ringed" with strong countries by its borders to keep its military in check.
- The **Concert of Europe** was formed, an organization of European states meant to maintain the balance of power.

THE SPREAD OF REVOLUTION AND NEW POLITICAL IDEAS

No matter how the Congress of Vienna tried to stem the tide of revolution, it did not work in the long run. France was to wobble back and forth between monarchy and republican government for thirty more years, and then was ruled by Napoleon III (Bonaparte's nephew) until 1871, when finally a parliamentary government emerged. And other countries in Europe, as well as colonies in Latin America, had heard "the shot heard round the world," and the true impact of the revolutionary political ideas began to be felt.

REVOLUTIONS IN LATIN AMERICA

From North America and France, revolutionary enthusiasm spread throughout the Caribbean and Spanish and Portuguese America. In contrast to the leaders of the War for Independence for the United States, most of the early revolutions in Latin America began with subordinated Amerindians and blacks. Even before the French Revolution, Andean Indians, led by Tupac Amaru, besieged the ancient capital of Cuzco and nearly conquered the Spanish army. The Creole elite responded by breaking the ties to Spain and Portugal, but establishing governments under their control. Freedom, then, was interpreted to mean liberty for the property-owning classes. Only in the French colony of Saint Domingue (Haiti) did slaves carry out a successful insurrection.

The rebellion in 1791 led to several years of civil war in Haiti, even though French abolished slavery in 1793. When Napoleon came to power, he sent an army to tame the forces led by **Toussaint L'Ouverture**, a former slave. However, Napoleon's army was decimated by guerrilla fighters and yellow fever, and even though Toussaint died in a French jail, Haiti declared its independence in 1804.

Other revolutions in Latin America were led by political and social elites, although some of them had important populist elements.

- **Brazil** – Portugal's royal family fled to Brazil when Napoleon's troops stormed the Iberian Peninsula. The presence of the royal family dampened revolutionary fervor, especially since the king instituted reforms in administration, agriculture, and manufacturing. He also established schools, hospitals, and a library. The king returned to Portugal in 1821, after Napoleon's threat was over, leaving Brazil in the hands of his son Pedro. Under pressure from Brazilian elites, Pedro declared Brazil's independence, and he signed a charter establishing a constitutional monarchy that lasted until the late 19th century when Pedro II was overthrown by republicans.

- **Mexico** – **Father Miguel Hidalgo** led Mexico's rebellion that eventually led to independence in 1821. He was a Catholic priest who sympathized with the plight of the Amerindian peasants and was executed for leading a rebellion against the colonial government. The Creole elite then took up the drive for independence that was won under the leadership of **Agustin de Iturbide**, a conservative military commander. However, Father Hidalgo's cause greatly influenced Mexico's political atmosphere, as his populist ideas were taken up by others who led the people in revolt against the Creoles. Two famous populist leaders were **Emiliano Zapata** and **Pancho Villa**, who like Father Hidalgo were executed by the government. Mexico was not to work out this tension between elite and peasants until well into the 20th century.

- **Spanish South America** – Colonial elite – landholders, merchants, and military – also led Spanish colonies in South America in rebellion against Spain. The term **"junta"** came to be used for these local governments who wanted to overthrow colonial powers. Two junta centers in South America were:

1. **Caracas, Venezuela** – At first, laborers and slaves did not support this Creole-led junta. However, they were convinced to join the independence movement by **Simon de Bolivar**, a charismatic military leader with a vision of forging "Gran Columbia," an independent, giant empire in the northern part of South America. He defeated the Spanish, but did not achieve his dream of empire. Instead, regional differences caused the newly independent lands to split into several countries.

2. **Buenos Aires, Argentina** – Another charismatic military leader – **Jose de San Martin** – led armies for independence from the southern part of the continent. His combined Chilean/Argentine forces joined with Bolivar in Peru, where they helped the northern areas to defeat the Spanish. Martin's areas, like those led by Bolivar, also split along regional differences.

All in all, constitutional experiments in North America were more successful than those in South America. Though South Americans gained independence from colonial governments during the 19th century, their governments remained authoritarian and no effective legislatures were created to share the power with political leaders. Why this difference?

| COMPARATIVE CONSTITUTIONAL EXPERIMENTS – NORTH AMERICA AND SOUTH AMERICA ||
NORTH AMERICA	**SOUTH AMERICA**
Mother country had parliamentary government, so colonial governments had a constitutional model	Mother country governed by absolute monarch; colonial governments had authoritarian model
Colonies had previous experience with popular politics; had their own governments that often operated independently from British control	Colonies had no experience with popular politics; colonial governments led by authoritarian Creoles
Military leaders were popular and sometimes became Presidents (Washington, Jackson), but they did not try to take over the government as military leaders; constitutional principle that military would be subordinate to the government	Had difficulty subduing the power of military leaders; set in place the tradition of military juntas taking over governments
American Revolution occurred in the 1770s; vulnerable new nation emerged at an economically advantageous time, when the world economy was expanding	Latin American Revolutions occurred during the early 1800s, a time when the world economy was contracting, a less advantageous time for new nations

The differences in political backgrounds of the two continents led to some very different consequences. For the United States (and eventually Canada), it meant that relatively democratic governments left entrepreneurs open to the Industrial Revolution, which, after all, started in their mother country. For Latin America, it meant that their governments were less supportive and/or more removed from the economic transformations of the Industrial Revolutions, and stable democratic governments and economic prosperity would be a long time in coming.

IDEOLOGICAL CONSEQUENCES OF REVOLUTIONS

The Enlightenment philosophy that inspired revolutions in the United States, France, and Latin America brought about lasting changes in western political ideology, with some people reacting against the chaos that revolutions brought, and others inspired by the values of democracy, liberty, equality, and justice. Three contrasting ideologies may be seen by the early 1800s:

- **Conservatism** – People who supported this philosophy at first advocated return to absolute monarchy, but came to accept constitutional monarchy by the mid-1800s. Generally, conservatives disapproved of the revolutions of the era, particularly the French Revolution with all the violence and chaos that it brought.

- **Liberalism** – Liberals supported a republican democracy, or a government with an elected legislature who represented the people in political decision-making. These representatives were generally from the elite, but were selected (usually by vote) from a popular base of citizens. Emphasis was generally on liberty or freedom from oppression, rather than on equality.

- **Radicalism** – Radicals advocated drastic changes in government and emphasized equality more than liberty. Their philosophies varied, but they were most concerned with narrowing the gap between elites and the general population. The Jacobins during the French Revolution and Marxism that appeared in the mid 19th century were variations of this ideological family.

REFORM MOVEMENTS

The political values supported by revolutions were embraced by some who saw them as applying to all people, including women and former slaves. Values of liberty, equality, and democracy had profound implications for change within societies that had always accepted hierarchical social classes and gender roles. Reform movements sprouted up as different people put different interpretations on what these new political and social values actually meant.

Women's Rights

Advocates of women's rights were particularly active in Britain, France, and North America. **Mary Wollstonecraft**, an English writer, was one of the first to argue that women possessed all the rights that Locke had granted to men, including education and participation in political life. Many French women assumed that they would be granted equal rights after the revolution. However, it did not bring the right to vote or play major roles in public affairs. Since gender roles did not change in the immediate aftermath of revolution, social reformers pressed for women's rights in North America and Europe. Americans like Elizabeth Cady Stanton and **Susan B. Anthony** in the United States decided to concentrate their efforts on **suffrage**, or the right to vote. A resolution passed at Seneca Falls, New York, in 1848, emphasized women's rights to suffrage, as well as to education, professional occupations, and political office. Their movement did not receive popular support, however, until the 20th century, but their activism laid a foundation for large-scale social change later.

The Limits of the Abolitionist Movement

Although slavery was abolished in Europe and North America by the late 19th century, blacks did not realize equality within the time period. Although former slaves were guaranteed the right to vote in the late 1860s in the United States, they were effectively barred from political participation by state and local legislation called **Jim Crow laws**. Blacks all over the Americas tended to have the least desirable jobs, limited educational opportunities, and lower social status than whites.

Conservative Reactions to Reform

During the late 1800s two systems of related political thought emerged among conservatives to justify inequalities:

- **Scientific racism** – This idea system became popular among conservative thinkers in industrialized societies. It used scientific reasoning and evidence to prove its premise that blacks are physiologically and mentally inferior to whites. The theory generally constructed three main "races" in the world – Caucasian, Mongoloid, and Negroid – and built its arguments that basic differences existed among them that made Negroids inherently inferior to Caucasians. Scientific racism, then, justified the inferior positions that blacks had in the society and the economy.

- **Social Darwinism** – This philosophy justified not racial differences, but differences between the rich and the poor. It used Darwin's theory of **natural selection** (living things that are better adapted to the environment survive, others don't) to explain why some get rich and others remain poor. In the competition for favored positions and bigger shares of wealth, the strong, intelligent, and motivated naturally defeat the weak, less intelligent, and the lazy. So, people who get to the top deserve it, as do the people who remain at the bottom.

Marxism

Another reaction to the revolution in political thought was **Marxism**. The father of communism is generally acknowledged to be **Karl Marx**, who first wrote about his interpretation of history and vision for the future in *The Communist Manifesto* in 1848. He saw capitalism – or the free market – as an economic system that exploited workers and increased the gap between the rich and the poor. He believed that conditions in capitalist countries would eventually become so bad that workers would join together in a **Revolution of the Proletariat** (workers), and overcome the **bourgeoisie**, or owners of factories and other means of production. Marx envisioned a new world after the revolution, one in which social class would disappear because ownership of private property would be banned. According to Marx, communism encourages equality and cooperation, and without property to encourage greed and strife, governments would be unnecessary. His theories took root in Europe, but did not control European governments during the 19th century. It eventually took new forms in early 20th century Russia and China.

NATIONALISM

In older forms of political organizations, the glue of political unity came from the ruler, whether it is a king, emperor, sultan, or caliph. Political power generally was built on military might, and a ruler controlled the land that he conquered as long as he controlled it. Power was often passed down within one family that based the legitimacy of their rule on principles that held sway over their populations, often some kind of special contact with the spiritual world. The era 1750 to 1914 saw the creation of a new type of political organization – the **nation** – that survived even if the rulers failed. Whereas nations' political boundaries were still often decided by military victory, the political entity was much broader than control by one person or family. Nations were built on **nationalism** – the feeling of identity within a common group of people. Of course, these feelings were not new in the history of the world. However, the force of common identity became a basic building block for nations, political forms that still dominate world politics today. Nationalism could be based on common geographic locations, language, religion, or customs, but it is much more complex than that. The main idea is that people see themselves as "Americans" or "Italians" or "Japanese," despite the fact that significant cultural variations may exist within the nation.

Napoleon contributed a great deal to the development of strong nationalism in 19th century Europe. His conquests were done in the name of "France," even though the French monarchy had been deposed. The more he conquered, the more pride people had in being "French." He also stirred up feelings of nationalism within a people that he conquered: "Germans" that could not abide being taken over by the French. In Napoleon's day Germany did not exist as a country yet, but people still thought of themselves as being German. Instead Germans lived in a political entity known as "The Holy Roman Empire." However, the nationalism that Napoleon invoked became the basis for further revolutions, in which people around the world sought to determine their own sovereignty, a principle that Woodrow Wilson called **self-determination**.

RISE OF WESTERN DOMINANCE

A combination of economic and political transformations in Europe that began in the 1450 to 1750 era converged between 1750 and 1914 to allow the "West" (including the United States and Australia) to dominate the rest of the world. From China to the Muslim states to Africa, virtually all other parts of the world became the "have nots" to the West's "haves." With political and economic dominance came control in cultural and artistic areas as well.

NEW EUROPEAN NATIONS

A major political development inspired by growing nationalism was the consolidation of small states into two important new nations:

- **Italy** – Before the second half of the 19th century, Italy was a collection of city-states that were only loosely allied with one another. A unification movement was begun in the north by Camillo di Cavour, and in the south by Giuseppe Garibaldi. As states unified one by one, the two leaders joined, and Italy became a unified nation under King Vittore Emmanuele II. The movement was a successful attempt to escape the historical domination of the peninsula by Spain in the south and Austria in the north.

- **Germany** – The German Confederation was created by the Congress of Vienna in 1815, but it had been controlled by the Austrian and Prussian Empires. In 1848 major rebellions broke out within the confederation, inspired by liberals who envisioned a German nation ruled by parliamentary government. The revolutions failed, and many liberals fled the country, but they proved to be an excuse for the Prussian army to invade other parts of the Confederation. The Prussian military leader was **Otto von Bismarck**, who subjugated the rebels and declared the beginning of the German Empire. The government was a constitutional monarchy, with Kaiser Wilhelm I ruling, but for a number of years, Bismarck had control. He provoked three wars – with Denmark, Austria, and France – and appealed to German nationalism to create a strong new nation in the heart of Europe. He pronounced it the "2nd Reich" or ruling era (the 1st was the Holy Roman Empire and the 3rd was set up by Adolph Hitler in the 20th century).

These new nations altered the balance of power in Europe, causing established nations like Britain and France concern that their own power was in danger. Nationalism, then, was spurred on by a renewal of deep-rooted competition that European nations carried to the ends of the earth. They competed with one another through trade, industrial production, and colonization, setting up worldwide empires to bolster their attempts to outdo all the others.

EURASIAN EMPIRES

The Russian and Ottoman Empires – two land-based powers in Eurasia – suffered the disadvantages of being neighbors to the rising nations in Europe. Russia had its wins and losses during the era yet managed to retain its power, but the Ottomans were in steep decline during most of the period and on the brink of destruction by 1914.

THE RUSSIAN EMPIRE

The Russian Empire turned its attention to the west under the late 17th and early 18th century rule of Peter the Great. His moves to build Russia into a great western empire were reinforced by tsar **Catherine the Great** in the late 18th century. Although the tension between Slavic traditions and the new western orientation remained, Russia retained its growing reputation as a world power, especially after resisting Napoleon's invasion in 1812. However, Russia in the mid-19th century was a huge, diverse realm that was very difficult to rule from a central location, even with the power granted to an absolute tsar. Its economy remained agriculturally based, with most people as serfs bound to the land that they cultivated.

Russia got into trouble with powerful England and France when its formidable army attacked the Ottoman Empire to seize access to warm water ports around the Black Sea. Fearful of an upset in European balance of power, England and France supported the Ottomans in defeating Russian troops in the **Crimean War** (1853-1856). This defeat clearly showed Russian weakness, and it led Tsar Alexander II to attempt reform by emphasizing industrialization, creating elected district assemblies called *zemstvos*, and emancipating the serfs.

Russia's instability became apparent when Alexander II was assassinated by one of the many revolutionary groups that were growing rapidly within the country. Some of these revolutionary groups were Marxist, and their influence would eventually take over the country in 1917. However, Russia continued on under absolute rule until then, with an intense state-run industrialization program that did modernize Russia by the end of the 19th century.

THE OTTOMAN EMPIRE – "THE SICK MAN OF EUROPE"

The Ottoman Empire reached its peak during the 16th and 17th centuries when they won many of their encounters with European kingdoms, although their attack of Europe was stopped with their unsuccessful siege of Vienna. By the early 1800s the Ottoman Empire had many internal problems, including these:

- **Economic problems** – Military officers owned most of the land, a fact that created a great deal of resentment from others. Since military were exempt from taxes, the government had problems getting enough revenue to keep the army and government functioning. "Tax farming" – or relying on middlemen to collect taxes – became corrupt, and their demands created resentment from the taxpayers.

- **Problems with the Janissaries** – The Janissaries originally were Christian boys from the Balkans that had been recruited by the Ottomans to fight in their armies. By the early 1800s, the Janissaries were well established as military and political leaders. They often operated separately from the weakening sultan's court and gained a reputation for brutality and corruption.

- **Revolts in the Balkans and Greece** – At their heart, these revolts were evidence of nationalism – Balkan and Greek people who had loyalties to their ethnic identities, not the Ottoman Empire. Many people in these Christian areas resented Ottoman control, and they were inspired to revolt when Janissary governors treated them brutally. The Balkans appealed to Russia for help, which eventually led Russia to invade the Ottoman Empire, sparking the Crimean War. Greece gained its independence, supported in large part by western European nations. Most famously, the English poet Lord Byron, who fought and died in the Greek Revolution, saw the battle as one between western civilization (with roots in Ancient Greece) and the Islamic Ottomans.

When the Russian attack started the Crimean War, the Ottomans were aided by England and France. Even though Russia was defeated, an important result of the war was that the Ottomans found themselves increasingly dependent on western Europe. Even before the war, weak Ottoman rulers tried to restore their power by imposing western reforms, such as trials, rule of law, separation of church and state, and a Magna Carta type document. Young people were sent to France to learn modern military techniques and medicine. Education reforms featured textbooks written in French, and the army adopted French-style uniforms. The nickname that western nations bestowed on the Ottomans reflected their attitudes about the empire: "the sick man of Europe."

The decline of Ottoman power and prosperity had a strong impact on a group of urban well-educated young men who protested European domination of the empire's political, economic, and cultural life. Inspired by the European nationalist movements, they began to call themselves the **Young Turks**, and they pushed for a Turkish national state. A constitution was granted in 1876, but was later rescinded under a new sultan. However the Young Turk movement continued on through the era.

IMPERIALISM

Empire building is an old theme in world history. Societies have sought to dominate weaker neighbors as long ago as ancient Mesopotamia and Egypt, all the way through to the present. Motivations have been similar – to obtain natural resources, to subdue enemies, to accrue wealth, to win power and glory – but until the rise of the West, most empires have expanded to territories next to their borders. With the combination of sea power, centralized governments, and industrialized economies, European nations set out to build empires all over the world like none that had been seen before. They were driven by the need to provide raw materials for their industrial capacity, and the types of goods exchanged were determined by that need.

TYPES OF IMPERIALISM

Europeans began building their empires in the western hemisphere in the early 1500s, but by the 1800s, Spain and Portugal were no longer powerful countries, and the largest British colony had become the independent United States. Britain, France, Germany, Russia, and the Netherlands continued to colonize during this era, but they also devised other ways to spread their empires. In the late 19th century Japan and the United States joined the European nations as imperialist powers.

Types of imperialism in the 1800s included:

- **Colonial imperialism** – This form of imperialism is virtual complete takeover of an area, with domination in all areas: economic, political, and socio-cultural. The subjugated area existed to benefit the imperialist power, and had almost no independence of action. In this era, almost all of Africa and southern and Southeast Asia were colonized.

- **Economic imperialism** – This form of imperialism allowed the area to operate as its own nation, but the imperialist nation almost completely controlled its trade and other business. For example, it may impose regulations that forbid trade with other nations, or imperialist companies may own or have exclusive rights to its natural resources. During this era, China and most of Latin America were subjected to economic imperialism.

- **Political imperialism** – Although a country may have had its own government with natives in top political positions, it operated as the imperialist country told it to. The government was sometimes a relatively permanent "puppet government," as happened in late Qing China, and other times the control was temporary, as occurred in the Dominican Republic when the United States ran its government until it got out of debt.

- **Socio-cultural imperialism** – The dominating country deliberately tried to change customs, religions and languages in some of the countries. A good example was British India, where English was taught in schools, Indian soldiers dressed British-style, and western trading rules were set up. Generally, the imperialist countries assumed their cultures to be superior, and often times they saw themselves as bringing about improvements in the society.

IMPERIALISM IN AFRICA

Between 1450 and 1750 Europeans traded with Africa, but they set up very few colonies. By 1850, only a few colonies existed along African coastlines, such as Algeria (French), the Cape Colony (Great Britain,) and Angola (Portugal). Instead, free African states continued, and after the end of the slave trade in the early 1800s, a lively exchange took place between Europeans and African states, such as the Sokoto Caliphate in western Africa and Egypt and Ethiopia in northeast Africa. They traded manufactured goods for gold, ivory, palm oil (a substance used in soap, candles, and lubricants). Under the leadership of **Muhammad Ali**, and his grandson **Ismail**, Egypt grew to be the strongest Muslim state of the 19th century, producing cotton for export and employing western technology and business methods. They benefited from the American Civil War, when cotton shipments from the southern U.S. were cut off, but the Egyptian cotton market collapsed after American shipments resumed after the Civil War was over.

In the latter half of the 19th century, dramatic changes occurred, as Europeans began to explore Africa's interior, and by 1914, virtually the entire continent was colonized by one or the other of the competing European countries. European imperialists built on the information provided by adventurers and missionaries, especially the famous **Dr. David Livingstone** and **Henry Stanley**. Livingstone, a Scottish missionary, went to Africa in the 1840s and spent three decades exploring the interior of Africa and setting up missionary outposts all the way from central Africa to the Cape Colony on the southern tip. When people in Britain lost contact with Livingstone, journalist Henry Stanley became a news sensation when he traveled to Africa and found Livingstone. The two sparked interest in Africa and others followed, including the imperialists.

Belgium was one of the first countries to sponsor expeditions to develop commercial activities, first establishing the Congo Free State under the direction of Belgium's King Leopold II, and eventually seizing it as the Belgian Congo. This event set off the **Scramble for Africa**, in which Britain, France, Germany, and Italy competed with Belgium for land in Africa. The **Berlin Conference of 1884-5**, in an effort to avoid war, allowed European diplomats to draw lines on maps and carve Africa into colonies. The result was a transformation of political and economic Africa, with virtually all parts of the continent colonized by 1900.

IMPERIALISM IN INDIA

With the Mughal Empire significantly weakened, the French established trading cities along the Indian coast during the 18th century, but the British East India Company had pushed them out by the early 1800s. The British were still following the model of government support for private companies that they had used in colonizing North America during the 18th century. The company forced the Mughals to recognize company rule first over Bengal, and when the old Mughal Empire was defeated in the 18th century by Iranian armies, the British pushed for economic control over more and more areas. Again India fell into the familiar pattern of decentralized independent states ruled by *nawabs*, native princes who had nominally supported the Mughal emperor, and the company made agreements with them that were economically advantageous to the British.

The British "Raj" – 1818-1857

India was under "company" rule for almost forty years, but it was not actually a British colony during that time because the British East India Company was still private, even though the British government supported it. However, the company administered governmental affairs and initiated social reform that reflected British values. At the same time, they depended on the *nawabs* to support them, and so they also had to abide by Indian customs and rules as well. The contradictory roles they played eventually erupted in the **Sepoy Rebellion** of 1857. The Sepoys were Indian Muslims and Hindus who served the British as soldiers in the army that defended the subcontinent. The rebellion took the British by surprise, but they found out that the Indian fury could be traced to a new training technique that the soldiers refused to follow. It required them to put a bullet shell in their mouths that had been greased in either pork or beef fat, with the pork fat being highly offensive to the Muslims and the beef to the Hindu. The British changed the practice, but it was too late because nationalism had reached India, too, and a movement for a country based on Indian identity was beginning. The leaders of the movement would have to wait about 90 years, though, to fulfill their dreams.

British Rule – 1857-1947

The Sepoy Rebellion showed the British government how serious the problems in India were, and they reacted by removing the British East India Company from control and declaring India a British colony. British officials poured into India to keep control of its valuable raw materials for industry and trade, particularly cotton and poppies for opium. They expanded production, built factories in India, and constructed huge railroad, irrigation, and telegraph systems.

Rising Indian Nationalism

With growing industrialization and British controlled trade, a middle class of Indian officials and managers began to rise during the late 1800s. By and large, the British did not allow Indians to own companies or to hold top government positions, but they did provide education for people to fill middle level and professional jobs. Some Indians went to England for higher education, where they absorbed western political values of liberty, equality, and justice, and they began to apply those values to their own situations. For example, the **Brahmo Samaj** movement, led by **Rammouhan Roy**, advocated unity for Indians by combining traditional and modern ways. The **Indian National Congress** was formed in 1885, with the goals of promoting political unity and appointing more Indians into higher positions in the British Civil Service. The Congress was controlled by Hindus, and in 1906 another nationalist group was established for Muslims called the **All-India Muslim League**. Despite tensions between them, by 1914 both groups were demanding Indian independence from the British.

Were the British merely exploiting Indians for profit, or were they trying to "do the right thing" for India? Certainly the profit motive was strong, especially apparent in the takeover in the early years by the British East India Company, a profit-driven company. However, many British people of the time insisted that a major goals for the government was to improve Indian lives through modernization of their country. Perhaps the most famous defense for British motives was *The White Man's Burden*, a poem by Rudyard Kipling that promotes the vision of a British world leadership idealistically improving the lives of people in the areas they dominated. Of course, the Indian National Congress and the All-India Muslim League did not agree.

IMPERIALISM IN CHINA

After the long and prosperous rules of Kangxi and Qianlong in the 17th and 18th centuries, problems of the Qing Dynasty began to mount during the early 19th century. It suffered from many old land-based ailments, such as long borders to defend and the challenge of keeping transportation and communication routes operating, but they also faced other serious issues. The Manchu, rulers of the Qing dynasty, were originally a northern group that conquered the Han Chinese under Ming rule. Han Chinese, as they did under Mongol rule, pushed for restoration of rule to the natives. The dynasty also began to experience significant revolts from minorities, and the government, under an increasingly corrupt line of rulers, was not able to deal with them properly. As the Chinese dynastic cycle was clearly going into decline, Europeans sensed the problems, and began to push for trading rights that China had been reluctant to grant in earlier times.

The Opium Wars (1839-1842)

In 1759 Emperor Qianlong had restricted European commercial presence to Guangzhou, a port in the southeastern part of China. There the trade was very much supervised by Chinese under the *cohong* system, with specially licensed Chinese firms operating under government set prices. Trade with Europeans was also restricted by the fact that Europeans had very little that the Chinese wanted to buy, even though the reverse was far from true. So the British East India Company, using Turkish and Persian expertise, grew opium in India and shipped it to China. As a result, trade boomed, especially once the Chinese developed addictions to the drug. The weak Qing government failed to act, even after some Chinese officials began to support the trade by accepting bribes. In 1838, with about 40,000 chests of opium coming into Guangzhou that year, the government finally tried to stop it.

The Opium Wars began after the Qing refused to listen to British protests of the trade ban. The British sent well-armed infantry and gunboats to attack first Chinese coastal villages, and eventually towns along the Grand Canal. The British used the Canal to reach inland areas, fought the ill-equipped villagers all the way to the Yellow River, when the Qing surrendered. Although the British did not take over the government, they forced the Qing to sign a treaty allowing the trade.

The Unequal Treaties

The **Treaty of Nanjing**, signed by the Chinese after the Opium Wars, was oriented toward trade. The Chinese agreed to allow the trade of opium and open other ports to exclusive trade with Britain. Beyond that, it gave the British control of Hong Kong (near Guangzhou), and it released Korea, Vietnam, and Burma from Chinese control. This was the first of many **unequal treaties** signed by Asians with European nations, and they eventually led to **"spheres of influence"**. China was divided up into trading spheres, giving each competing European nation exclusive trading rights in a particular areas. By the early 20th century, most of China was split into these areas, and the Qing government was virtually powerless.

The Taiping Rebellion – 1850-1864

The Qing Dynasty was significantly weakened by the Taiping Rebellion, a revolt led by **Hong Xiuquan**, a village schoolteacher who hated the Manchus as foreigners. He gathered support among poor and unhappy farmers, and under his charismatic leadership, his armies captured the city of Nanjing as their capital, and came very close to toppling the government in Beijing. Hong was an unusual leader, believing that he was the younger brother of Jesus, and advocating abolition of private property and equality for women. The Chinese government finally ended the civil war, with a great deal of help from the Europeans, but the cost to the country was about 20-30 million killed in this 14-year struggle.

Although it is difficult to see the Taiping Rebellion as nationalism, its leader's ideas were similar in many ways to the radical political movements in the west. Chinese nationalism was more apparent in the 1900 **Boxer Rebellion**, in which a group called the Boxers led an army against the Qing with the express purpose of recovering "China for the Chinese." The group fed on their efforts to rid the country of European interests, and even though the rebellion was unsuccessful, the Boxers laid the foundations for the 1911 Chinese Revolution that finally ended the Qing Dynasty.

NEW IMPERIALIST NATIONS

By the late 1800s, two non-European nations – the United States and Japan – were rising to power through industrialization and imperialism. Both were destined to become important world powers in the 20th century.

The United States

As industrialization enriched and empowered the United States in the late 19th century, the country also began to experiment with imperialism. It began with the purchase of Alaska from Russia, and followed with a coup of the native government in Hawaii, a plot sponsored by American planters and growers in the Hawaiian Islands. Both Alaska and Hawaii became territories, and although many questioned the wisdom of the Alaska purchase, the Hawaii takeover clearly had an economic motive.

After a quarrel over Cuban independence, the United States defeated Spain in the **Spanish American War** in 1898, a fairly easy task since Spain was long past the peak of her colonial power. The peace treaty gave the Philippines, Puerto Rico, and the Pacific island of Guam to the United States as protectorates, as well as considerable economic control of Cuba. To keep their new empire intact, President Theodore Roosevelt advocated the building of a powerful American navy, and the United States sponsored the building of the **Panama Canal** to allow the new **Great White Fleet** access to both east and west coasts of the country.

Japan

United States sea captain Matthew Perry may take some credit for the destruction of the Tokugawa Shogunate. By the mid 19th century the Japanese were most concerned about European incursions in China, and so they kept up their guard against Europeans trying to invade their islands from the south. They were most surprised when Perry arrived from the east with his demands for opening of Japan to trade with the United States through an "unequal treaty." That was all the daimyos needed to join together in an insurrection against the Tokugawa, who indeed signed such a treaty. To legitimize their cause, the daimyos fought in the name of the emperor, and when they won, they declared that the legitimate government had been "restored." The **Meiji Restoration** took advantage of the fact that their geography made them less strategically important than the Chinese, so that the Europeans and Americans tended to leave them alone. They were left to their own devices – to create a remarkable state that built the foundations for Japan as a world power.

The *Meiji* (meaning "enlightened rule") claimed to have ended centuries of shogun-dominated governments that made the emperor totally powerless. They mystified and revered the position of the emperor, who became a very important symbol for Japanese unity. However, the new state did not give the emperor any real power, either. Japanese nationalism was built on the mysticism of the emperor, anxiety over the foreign threat, and an amazing transformation of Japan's military, economy, and government. The country was ruled by **oligarchs**, a small group of leaders who together directed the state. They borrowed heavily from the west to industrialize their country and to build a centralized, strong military. They gradually but systematically dissolved the daimyo and samurai classes, and they placed a great deal of emphasis on building a strong education system.

The era from 1750-1914 was clearly one of growing European power and domination of the globe. Industrialization created unprecedented wealth, and new western political ideas spawned strong, centralized states that directed empires around the world. However, the new political ideas encouraged nationalism, which on the one hand strengthened the industrialized countries, but on the other hand caused the people that they dominated to resent their control. The potential for worldwide power and riches also intensified the conflict and competition that had long existed among European states. In 1914 these conflicts came to the surface and erupted into a Great War that ushered in the new, very different era of the 20th century.

UNIT FOUR QUESTIONS

1. Which of the following is the best description of trade patterns between Africa and Europe during the mid-19th century?

    (A) Slaves were the most important trading good that Europeans wanted from Africa.
    (B) Most parts of Africa were colonies of European nations that supplied raw materials for industrial production.
    (C) Europeans traded manufactured goods to independent African states for gold, ivory, and palm oil.
    (D) Almost no trade existed between Europe and Africa after the slave trade had ended.
    (E) Trade between Africa and Europe only took place in a few places along the coastlines in West Africa and the tip of the African continent.

2. What is the demographic transition?

    (A) the shift in populations concentrations from Eurasia to the Americas
    (B) the movement of populations from rural to urban areas
    (C) the shift from high birth rates to low in industrialized countries
    (D) the decrease in death rates in Europe and the increase in death rates in China
    (E) a rise in the proportion of females to males in any given population area

3. Between 1750 and 1914 the "cult of domesticity" defined the lives of

    (A) middle class women in industrialized countries
    (B) lower class women in industrial cities
    (C) elite women in China
    (D) Muslim families in the Ottoman Empire
    (E) Indian women and children during the British raj

"There are three major races that historically have developed on earth: the Mongoloid, the Caucasian, and the Negroid. After careful research, it has been determined that the average brain size of the Caucasian is significantly larger than that of the Negroid."

4. The statement above most directly reflects the 19th century philosophy of

    (A) Social Darwinism
    (B) Marxism
    (C) Nationalism
    (D) Scientific racism
    (E) Positivism

5. Which of the following is the best explanation for the Sepoy Rebellion of 1857?

   (A) The British were cruel and inconsiderate of the wishes of the nawabs.
   (B) Sepoys were agitated by a charismatic leader who played upon the people's fear of imperialism.
   (C) The British had very little control over the discipline of their troops.
   (D) The British did not understand important cultural traditions of Indians.
   (E) The revolt was organized by the Indian National Congress to gain independence for India.

6. The "unequal treaties" were made by European countries with

   (A) Amerindians in Latin America
   (B) their colonies that sought independence
   (C) China, Japan, and other Asian countries
   (D) African political leaders
   (E) other imperialist nations that they competed with for colonies

7. What type of government was instituted in Japan by the *Meiji Restoration*?

   (A) a democracy
   (B) a shogunate
   (C) a military dictatorship
   (D) an oligarchy
   (E) a constitutional monarchy

8. Which of the following is the most fundamental cause of the French Revolution of 1789?

   (A) fear of invasion by other European countries
   (B) the attempted escape of Louis XVI and Marie Antoinette to Austria
   (C) the fall of the Bastille
   (D) the perception that political power and social privileges were unfairly distributed
   (E) the incompetence of Louis XVI's ministers

9. The North and South American independence movements of the late eighteenth and early nineteenth centuries shared which of the following?

   (A) limitation of civil rights to a minority of the population
   (B) reliance on Christian teachings to define revolutionary demands
   (C) industrial economies that permitted both areas to break free of European control
   (D) the desire of a majority of revolutionary leaders to create a politically united hemisphere
   (E) political instability caused by constant warfare among the new states

10. Which of the following developments in the Western Hemisphere most directly resulted from the French Revolution?

    (A) the expansion of the slave trade in the Americas
    (B) the extension of the plantation economy in the Caribbean
    (C) the colonization of Brazil
    (D) the British conquest of Quebec
    (E) the successful slave rebellion in Haiti

11. During the French Revolution the Jacobins favored the establishment of a(n)

    (A) representative democracy, granting wide powers to elected officials
    (B) radical republic, emphasizing equality
    (C) limited monarchy
    (D) absolute monarchy
    (E) empire

12. The concept of the European balance of power, as it emerged by the end of the eighteenth and the beginning of the nineteenth centuries, had which of the following as its most fundamental aim?

    (A) the elimination of war as an instrument of international relations
    (B) the prevention of the preponderance of one power in Europe
    (C) an approximate balance between the land and the sea powers
    (D) isolation of conflict to certain contested land areas
    (E) the division of Europe into two groups of states, both approximately equal in potential military power

13. Which phase of the French Revolution is William Wordsworth describing in the quote below?

    "The Mother from the Cradle of her Babe,
    The Warrior from the Field, all perished, all,
    Friends, enemies, of all parties, ages, ranks,
    Head after head, and never heads enough
    For those that bade them fall."

    (A) during the crisis that forced Louis XVI to call together the Estates General
    (B) at the time of the storming of the Bastille
    (C) at the time when the first Constitution was accepted
    (D) during the Reign of Terror
    (E) at the time that the Directory was ruling

(Questions 14 refers to the following quote):

"The National Assembly, considering that it has summoned to establish the constitution of the kingdom, to effect the regeneration of public order, and to maintain the true principles of monarch; that nothing can prevent it from continuing its deliberations in whatever place it may be forced to establish itself; and, finally, that wheresoever its members are assembled, there is the National Assembly;

Decrees that all members of this assembly shall immediately take a solemn oath not to separate, and to reassemble wherever circumstances required, until the constitution of the kingdom is established and consolidated upon firm foundations; and that, the said oath taken, all members and each one of them individually shall ratify this steadfast resolution by signature."

14. This document records an oath of unity taken by members of the

   (A) French Third Estate in opposition to Louis XVI, thus marking the beginning of the French Revolution
   (B) First Continental Congress in their opposition to George III, thus marking the beginning of the American Revolutionary War
   (C) French legislative assembly in response to the defeat of Napoleon I, thus marking the restoration of the French monarchy
   (D) first legislature of Gran Colombia, in defiance of Ferdinand VI, King of Spain
   (E) first legislature of Brazil, in defiance of Pedro II, King of Portugal

15. Which of the following best describes the role of western European countries in the world between 1750 and 1914?

   (A) Western European nations rose from positions of little world power in 1750 to dominating positions by 1914.
   (B) Western European nations gained world power during the era, but they still were not as powerful as were the Ottomans and the Chinese by 1914.
   (C) Western European nations solidified power gained between 1450 and 1750, so that they dominated world politics between 1750 and 1914.
   (D) Western European nations gained a great deal of power, especially since no countries/empires in Eastern Europe increased their power during the era.
   (E) Though still powerful in 1914, western European nations did not have as much world power as they had in 1750.

16. All of the following were key factors that helped Britain take an early lead in industrialization EXCEPT:

   (A) natural resources
   (B) human resources
   (C) large amounts of land relative to population
   (D) new technology
   (E) capital and demand

17. Which of the following was a major result of the Battle of Waterloo in 1815?

   (A) The French regained their domination of Europe.
   (B) Napoleon's army was defeated, but they made a comeback later on.
   (C) The battle had no major results, since it was fought to a draw.
   (D) In contrast to the battle of Trafalgar, the English were humiliated in battle.
   (E) The battle was Napoleon's final defeat.

18. Which of the following is the best explanation for why Western people were able to conquer or control many non-Western people during the era of New Imperialism?

   (A) Europe's absolute rulers were able to command expeditions efficiently.
   (B) Europeans made use of superior technology that allowed conquest.
   (C) Europeans had a more advanced understanding of scientific principles.
   (D) Christianity supported more aggressive behavior than other major religions did.
   (E) Europeans had a more favorable geographic location for conquering other nations.

19. Nationalism is a(n)

   (A) desire of people for self-expression
   (B) desire of people for democratic government
   (C) policy of redistributing national wealth
   (D) inevitable result of revolutions
   (E) feeling that unites people of the same language, history, and tradition

20. In general, which of the following characteristics of an area/region was most likely to attract the attention of imperialist nations seeking new opportunities?

   (A) highly developed industries
   (B) great natural beauty
   (C) few inhabitants
   (D) remote locations
   (E) undeveloped resources

21. The 1869 completion of which of the following vastly increased the geopolitical importance of Egypt?

    (A) the Suez Canal
    (B) the Aswan Dam
    (C) the Giza Canal
    (D) the Luxor Bridge
    (E) the Alexandria Dockyards

22. Which of the following is a correct statement regarding the relationship between industrialization and imperialism?

    (A) Only industrialized nations with absolute rulers practiced imperialism.
    (B) Competition among industrialized nations was a major motivation for imperialism.
    (C) Imperialist nations turned to manufacturing in order to make use of products from countries they controlled.
    (D) Industrialized nations generally had to free some of their colonies in order to concentrate on manufacturing.
    (E) Imperialist countries almost always encouraged industrialization in the countries that they controlled.

23. Which of the following groups of nations competed for colonial empires in Africa in the last half of the nineteenth century?

    (A) Germany, Belgium, and the United States
    (B) France, Italy, and the Netherlands
    (C) Germany, Belgium, and Great Britain
    (D) Spain, Great Britain, and Japan
    (E) Japan, Portugal, and Germany

24. Which of the following was the most significant factor that influenced the Spanish and Portuguese colonies in the Americas to declare independence?

    (A) Creole elites lost confidence in the Crowns' ability to administer their distant colonies.
    (B) When Napoleon invaded Spain and Portugal, the resulting political confusion in Europe encouraged Creoles to declare independence.
    (C) The treaties signed with Amerindians had expired, but the colonists did not want to give up their homes.
    (D) Christian beliefs and colonialism were incompatible.
    (E) The Spanish and Portuguese kings encouraged independence since they could no longer afford to support their American colonies.

25. Which Spanish colony experienced a major popular rebellion before a Creole-led military force succeeded in gaining independence?

   (A) Puerto Rico
   (B) Gran Colombia
   (C) Argentina
   (D) Cuba
   (E) Mexico

26. All of the following led armies to success in achieving independence for their countries EXCEPT:

   (A) Agustin Iturbide
   (B) George Washington
   (C) Father Miguel Hidalgo
   (D) Jose de San Martin
   (E) Simon Bolivar

27. Which of the following is the best reason why political power in Latin America frequently fell to military leaders?

   (A) Military leaders were needed to put down frequent slave insurrections and revolts by native peoples.
   (B) Since Latin American countries were always at war with each other, they needed strong military governments to defend themselves.
   (C) The military leaders had more experience running governments than the civilian authorities did.
   (D) Church officials usually condoned and cooperated with military leaders, and they influenced the people to submit to military rule.
   (E) Military leaders were popular with the people, and civilian authorities could not contain the political aspirations of charismatic military leaders.

28. Slavery in the western hemisphere lasted longest in

   (A) Argentina
   (B) Haiti
   (C) United States
   (D) British Caribbean colonies
   (E) Brazil

29. In a social sense the American, French, and Latin American revolutions can all be regarded as wars that

   (A) protested against taxes
   (B) established religious freedom
   (C) implemented governments that would foster commercial expansion
   (D) protected the populace from growing foreign dominance
   (E) reflected the growing power and culture of the bourgeoisie

30. During the 18th century, the migration of English workers from the countryside to the cities dramatically increased as a direct result of

   (A) faster and better water transportation
   (B) better living conditions in London and other industrialized cities
   (C) the enclosure movement
   (D) job opportunities in cities caused by the emigration of British citizens to the Americas
   (E) improved ground transportation, including the building of railroads

31. What do most historians regard as the root (or key) invention of the Industrial Revolution?

   (A) railroad
   (B) steam engine
   (C) steamboat
   (D) spinning jenny
   (E) pottery mold

32. Which of the following is the best reason why industrialization was slower in western European nations on the continent than in Britain?

   (A) Other countries did not see the value of industrialization.
   (B) Britain refused to trade with them.
   (C) The British discouraged the spread of industrialization by underpricing goods until the competition collapsed.
   (D) Revolutions and the Napoleonic Wars slowed industrialization on the continent.
   (E) The continent has few navigable rivers, so transportation to markets was more difficult than in Britain.

33. In which of the following ways did Europeans develop world domination in the era before 1750-1914?

(A) technology that allowed control of most sea and ocean trade routes
(B) far superior armies to those of the empires of the Middle East and Asia
(C) development and use of repeating rifles and smokeless powder
(D) development of railroad systems across areas of the world that they controlled
(E) construction of canals in key areas to shorten trade distances around the world

(Questions 34 and 35 are based on the following excerpt):

"Take up the White Man's burden –
Send forth the best ye breed –
Go bind your sons to exile
To serve your captives' need;
To wait in heavy harness,
On fluttered folk and wild –
Your new-caught, sullen peoples,
Half-devil and half-child."

Rudyard Kipling

34. What does Kipling mean by the "White Man's burden"?

(A) the responsibility to civilize people in non-industrialized areas
(B) the disadvantages that industrialization brings to the lower classes of European nations
(C) the conflicts caused when trade routes were opened to Africa, Asia, and South America
(D) the health and financial risks that Europeans take when they travel to foreign lands
(E) the right to seize property and power from non-industrialized areas

35. What does the poem reflect about Kipling's attitudes toward imperialism?

(A) Imperialism is the responsibility of European nations, but should not be practiced by the United States.
(B) The evils of imperialism are disguised by false beliefs that white men are just trying to help the people that they conquer.
(C) Imperialists have the responsibility to civilize the people in conquered nations, despite the fact that they will encounter resistance and resentment.
(D) The risks and disadvantages of imperialism are outweighed by its economic benefits.
(E) Imperialism helps Europeanizations more than it helps conquered lands.

COMPARITIVE ESSAY

During the 19th century, Britain built an empire that spanned the globe. Analyze and compare the different approaches that the British took in gaining imperialist domination of India and China.

UNIT FIVE

1914-Present

The world in 1914 was clearly dominated by European nations. Despite the rise of such powers as the United States, Japan, and Russia, huge empires around the globe were still headed by Britain and France. After the unification of Germany, the struggle for power intensified primarily as a contest among European nations. However, beginning in 1914, dramatic events shattered European hegemony, so that only three decades later, the dynamics of world power were transformed. Always competitive and contentious, European countries turned on one another, bringing a global network of countries into their arguments in two great world wars, but the ultimate losers were the very countries that had held the reins of global power in 1914. By the early 21st century, Europeans were again scrambling to patch up their differences through regional organizations and treaties, but by that point, European global domination had long disappeared.

QUESTIONS OF PERIODIZATION

20th century history is probably the most difficult to evaluate, primarily because we are still so close to it. We don't have the advantage of perspective that we have for earlier eras. After all, we don't know very much yet about the chapters that follow the end of the century, and even though some very dramatic events have occurred in the early 21st century, their meaning for the future is far from clear. However, even with our limited perspective, the 20th century appears to have been a pivotal one, with major changes and new patterns being established.

Major characteristics that distinguish the time period 1914 – present include:

- **Redefinition and repositioning of the West** – During the 20th century, the term "West" came to have a new meaning. In the early part of the century, the West was centered in Europe. Although the United States and Australia were considered to be western nations, they were more or less off-spins from the European colonial powers. After World War II the western center moved to the United States, and by the end of the century, the phrase "western dominance" was a clear reference to U.S. power. Even so, power centers in other parts of the world challenged the West: Japan in the 1930s and 40s, and the Soviet Union during the Cold War era. The United States emerged as the dominant world power after the Soviet Union collapsed in 1991, but significant checks on that power appear to be emerging in the early 21st century. Birth control has meant that the West currently has a smaller percentage of the world's population than ever before, a fact that adds to the question of whether or not the West will continue to dominate the world.

- **Increase in international contacts** – International trade and communication burgeoned during the 20th century, creating the phenomenon of **globalization**. Technological advancements were central to the swift, gigantic changes. In the beginning of the century, people marveled at the ability of ships and railroads to reach long-distance destinations in a few weeks, but by the end of the century, airplane point-to-point connections were measured in hours. Likewise, wired telephones were new in 1914, but by 2000 they were being replaced by cell phones and e-mail communication. Furthermore, automobiles, commercial airlines, and personal computers meant that more and more people were sharing the connections, although by century's end, many of the earth's people were still left out of the new communications network. Technological connections allowed the spread of culture and science to occur much more quickly than ever before. The century also saw the development of international organizations, starting with the League of Nations in 1918, and continuing with the United Nations, the World Bank, and the World Trade Organization. Migrations from Africa, Asia, and the Caribbean headed toward the leading industrial centers from the 1920s, leading many people to question whether or not regional identities were being lost.

- **The democratic transition** – Very few countries had the same type of government in 2000 that they had in 1914. Monarchies all over the world were replaced by democratic governments or authoritarian regimes, and by the late 20th century, many authoritarian regimes were being replaced by democracies. Western democratic governments were often used as models, not only for newly independent countries, but for former powerhouses, such as the Soviet Union.

- **Changes in belief systems** – For most of world history, organized religions in all parts of the globe have been important influences on almost every other area of life, including government, family life, and culture. Many scholars see a 20th century trend away from religion toward a new reliance on non-religious philosophies such as liberalism, nationalism, and communism. Furthermore, by century's end, people in western nations, as well as some in the East, appeared to be relying less on religious explanations for social and natural phenomena than on new and rapidly developing scientific explanations. However, religion cannot be discounted as a major force in the 20th century, especially in light of the resurgence of fundamentalist Islam in many parts of the world.

- **Questioning of systems of inequality** – Although people had challenged social inequalities for many years before 1914, widespread reforms characterize the 20th century. Industrialized countries had abolished slavery in the 19th century, but major civil rights movements for racial and ethnic minorities shook the social systems around the globe in such countries as the United States, South Africa, and India. Women's rights movements also have their roots in the 19th century, but only in the 20th century did women in industrialized countries win the right to vote. Likewise, people in lands conquered by imperialist powers in earlier eras challenged international inequities, although they were far from successful in their goals for equality by the end of the 20th century.

We will analyze these important characteristics of the period by examining these topics:

- **War and diplomacy** – The first half of the 20th century was marked by two world wars accompanied by genocide, and the second half saw a change in the nature of warfare with the Cold War between the United States and the Soviet Union. On the diplomatic front, international organizations proliferated to address the changing balance of power in the world.

- **New patterns of nationalism** – Nationalism continued to shape interactions among nations as large empires broke into smaller ethnic based countries. Widespread decolonization after World War II both reflected and promoted nationalism in former colonies.

- **Impact of major global economic developments** – The Great Depression affected some countries more than others, but it had a profound economic impact on both industrialized and non-industrialized areas as well as on world trade. New technologies promoted economic development in Pacific Rim countries and contributed to the emerging importance of multinational corporations.

- **Political revolutions and innovations** – Revolutions shook Russia, China, and many Latin American countries. Political leaders experimented with different versions of communism, socialism, and capitalism, with some turning to authoritarian methods and others to democracy, and monarchy declined in many parts of the globe.

- **Social reform and revolution** – Reform led to changes in gender roles, family structures, the rise of feminism, peasant protest, and international Marxism.

- **Globalization of science, technology, and culture** – Increasing international contacts encouraged the global spread of science and consumer culture, sparking varying local and regional reactions. Patterns of resistance to globalization raised questions of fragmentation, or the tendency for regions to turn toward local beliefs and values and resist influence from other areas.

- **Demographic and environmental changes** – Despite migrations of people from Africa, Asia, and the Caribbean to industrialized countries, population distributions changed, with North America and Europe having declining proportions of the world population. The environment was altered by continued urbanization and deforestation, and significant green/environmental movements emerged to resist these changes.

WAR AND DIPLOMACY

Wars are old occurrences during world history, but 20th century wars were unique in that they increasingly encompassed more and more of the globe. World War I began as a European conflict that spread into other regions, but World War II and the Cold War intensified international conflict to reach almost all parts of the globe. A series of international organizations formed in reaction to the wars, and provided a diplomatic alternative to world crises.

WORLD WAR I

World War I is an important marker event in modern history because it ushers in a new era in which the global framework changed dramatically. It also marks the collapse of European hegemony that had been solidly in place during the 1750-1914 era.

CAUSES

The onset of war in 1914 resulted from years of tensions among European nations:

- **Nationalism** – During the 19th century the identities of many European peoples intensified greatly. This nationalism set the stage for World War I in two ways:

  1. **National rivalries** – The unification of Germany threatened to topple the balance of power that had existed in Europe since the defeat of Napoleon Bonaparte in 1815. The competition took many forms: industrialization, a naval race, arms build-ups, and colonial disputes over territories. In 1870, Britain controlled about 1/3 of the world's industrial output, and Germany only about 13%. By 1914 Britain had dropped to 14%, putting it roughly comparable to Germany. (The U.S. was taking a huge percentage by 1914). Britain's great *dreadnought* ships were challenged as Germany began to build its own super battleships and develop an impressive submarine fleet. France and Russia joined the arms buildup as all countries beefed up armies, equipment, and weapons. When one increased their military, the others would try to match and outdo the others. Colonial disputes broke out all over the globe: Britain and Russia over Persia and Afghanistan; Britain and France over Siam and the Nile River Valley; Britain and Germany in East and Southwest Africa; Germany and France over Morocco and West Africa.

  2. **Nationalist aspirations** – Inherent in nationalism is **self-determination**, the right to form states based on ethnicity, language, and/or political ideals. This part of nationalism is apparent in the unification of Germany and Italy, and in the separation of Belgium from the Netherlands. However, in eastern Europe, Austria-Hungary and the Ottoman Empire resisted nationalist demands. Both empires confronted the nationalist aspirations of Slavic people – Poles, Czechs, Slovaks, Serbs, Croats, and Slovenes. Most threatening of all were the Serbs, who were encouraged by Russia's support and promotion of **Pan-Slavism**, a movement to unite all Slavic people.

- **Entangling alliances** – As countries and empires built their arms, they looked to one another for support and protection. Two hostile camps emerged, bound by treaties that stated conditions under which nations would go to war with one another in order to improve their chances for self-preservation. The two major alliances were the **Triple Entente** (Russia, England, and France) vs. the **Triple Alliance** (Germany, Austria-Hungary, and Italy). The allies generally had a common hatred for one or more or the countries on the other side.

SPARK FOR THE WAR

In June 1914 all of Europe was an armed camp, and rivalries were very intense. The war was precipitated by **Gavrilo Princip**, a member of a Serbian nationalist group known as the Black Hand. When he assassinated **Franz Ferdinand**, the heir to the Austrian throne, he set in motion a series of events in which one country after the other declared war on another. Austria-Hungary declared war on Serbia, who had an alliance with Russia. Russia declared war on Austria-Hungary, requiring Germany to declare war on Russia. And so the domino effect continued so that by August a local conflict had become a general European war.

NATURE OF THE WAR

World War I is often defined by the optimism that countries had going into the war in contrast to the horror, shock, and slaughter that traumatized them by the time the war ended in 1918. The balance of power struck in 1815 had been strong enough to delay conflict so that no one alive in 1914 could remember the devastation of war, and almost every nation glorified the excitement of war. The two sides settled into the **Allied Powers**-England, France, Russia, and Italy (who switched sides at the last minute) – and the **Central Powers** – Germany, Austria-Hungary, and the Ottoman Empire. The war was fought on two fronts:

- **Western Front** – The Western Front followed a line between France and Germany through Belgium. The French and British fought on one side against the Germans, eventually joined by Americans in 1917. The war bogged down quickly, with both sides digging trenches, and fighting from them until the war ended in 1918. The stalemate occurred partly because new technology – machine guns and poison gas – made any offensive attack so lethal that the army had to retreat to trenches. Attacks were followed by counter-attacks that resulted in huge casualties. It literally got to the point where each side simply hoped that the other would run out of young men first. Indeed that happened when the United States entered the war, and Germany could not match the combined forces on the Western Front.

- **Eastern Front** – The Eastern Front was on the opposite side of Germany from the Western Front. There Germany and Austria-Hungary fought Russia along a much more fluid battle line. The Central Powers overran Serbia, Albania, and Romania. The Russians took the offensive in Prussia, but by the summer of 1915 combined German and Austrian forces drove the Russian armies back eastward across Poland, and eventually back into Russia's borders. Russia's armies were poorly led and badly equipped, with the tsar sending men into battle without guns, food, or shoes. Mass desertions and loss of confidence in the tsar led to chaos in Russia, where a communist-inspired group called the **Bolsheviks** eventually took over the government and assassinated the tsar.

Russia withdrew from the war in 1917, releasing German soldiers to transfer to the Western Front, but U.S. soldiers supplemented French and British soldiers there so that the stalemate was finally broken, with the armistice occurring in November 1918. The net effect of the war was the slaughter of a huge portion of a generation of young men, primarily from Russia, Germany, Austria-Hungary, England, and France. Arguably, Europe never fully recovered from the loss.

THE VERSAILLES TREATY

The "Great War" is a marker event in world history because it is the first in a series of events that led to declining European power and ascending power for the United States and Japan. However, the Versailles Treaty at the end of the war is almost as important an event as the war itself because it changed the nature of international relations and set the stage for World War II.

Although 27 nations gathered at Versailles Palace in France in 1919 to shape a treaty, men from three nations dominated the proceedings: David Lloyd George from Britain, Georges Clemenceau from France, and Woodrow Wilson from the United States. Russia, who had pulled out of the war in 1917, was not represented. Woodrow Wilson came to the meetings with his plan, called the **Fourteen Points**, which was grounded in two important principles:

- **Self determination** – Wilson's document asserted the need to redraw the map of Europe and the old Ottoman Empire along the lines of self determination, allowing groups based on nationalism to determine their own governments.

- **The need for an international peace organization** – The Congress of Vienna had created the Concert of Europe in 1815, an organization of European nations bound to keep the balance of power in the region. Wilson's vision was broader, in that he advocated a worldwide organization charged with keeping the peace and avoiding another war like the one that had just occurred.

Britain and France came to Versailles with different motivations. After all, their countries had suffered a great deal more from the war than the United States had. For example, whereas Britain lost almost a million young men and France lost almost 1,400,000, the United States lost only about 115,000. A great deal of the war was fought on French soil, and so France suffered devastation of cities and countryside, and even French people who were not soldiers experienced the war first hand. As a result, George and Clemenceau were less idealistic than Wilson. Revenge and control of Germany – who was a more immediate threat to them than to the United States – were more important to them.

The treaty that resulted was a compromise among the three countries. The many provisions include these important ones:

- Germany lost land along all borders, including Alsace-Lorraine and the Polish Corridor.
- German military forces were severely restricted and a demilitarized zone was created along lands bordering France and Belgium.
- Germany had to pay very high reparations for war to specific Allied Powers.
- An international organization called the League of Nations was created.
- Germany's overseas possessions were placed under the control of the League, remaining as mandates until they were ready for independence.
- The map of Eastern Europe was redrawn along ethnic lines, recreating the country of Poland, and creating Czechoslovakia, Yugoslavia, Austria, and Hungary. Austria-Hungary as a political empire was destroyed.
- Although the Ottoman Empire was dismantled as well, the resulting pieces were designated as mandates, not independent countries.

The treaty was a fiasco that satisfied almost no one and infuriated many. The Turks and Arabs of the former Ottoman Empire, as well as people of Germany's colonies, couldn't understand why eastern European countries were created as independent countries and they weren't. What's more the British occupied many areas of the Middle East, and did not leave once the treaty was signed. The League of Nations excluded Germany and Russia from membership, and the United States Senate failed to ratify the treaty and never joined the League. As a result, the international peace organization had very limited authority from the beginning. However, the most immediate reaction came from Germany, who saw the treaty as unfairly blaming them for the war and punishing them so severely that they could not recover. Their discontent provided fertile grounds for the rise of a demagogue that of course happened in due time.

THE ROOTS OF WORLD WAR II

World War II is often described as Chapter 2 of the War that started in 1914. Only 20 years of peace lie in between the end of World War I and the beginning of World War II, and in many ways the hostilities never ceased.

THE RISE OF JAPAN

The Meiji Restoration of the late 19th century had greatly strengthened Japan in almost every way: militarily, politically, and economically. As the political oligarchy imitated western imperialist success and as China's strength faded, Japan's influence along the Pacific Rim grew. Japanese success against Russia in the Russo-Japanese War in the early 20th century surprised many western nations and proved that Japan was becoming a world power. When World War I broke out, Japan entered on the side of the Allied Powers, and almost immediately began to claim German territories around them. In 1915 Japan made **Twenty-one Demands** of China that allowed Japan a great deal of control over Chinese trade and production, even though China did not accept all of the demands.

Japan broke the post-war peace in 1931 by invading traditionally Chinese Manchuria, clearly reflecting their intention to expand their empire at the expense of China. This invasion angered the international community, and many nations reacted by enacting economic sanctions, but Japan was undeterred. From there, China itself was threatened, even after the League of Nations condemned Japanese actions. In 1937, they began a full-scale invasion of China, and rapidly began to control more and more of the mainland.

EXPANSIONISM IN EUROPE

Even as the Versailles Conference was going on, new stirrings of nationalism served as precursors of what was to come. Italy's representative to Versailles, Prime Minister Orlando, was called home early because his government had suffered a coup led by **Benito Mussolini**. Mussolini appealed to Italian nationalism in his quest to rebuild the glories of Ancient Rome through his military leadership. However, most menacing of all was the Nazi movement in Germany, led by an Austrian named **Adolf Hitler**.

Post-war Struggles in Germany

After World War I ended, Germany established a republican form of government under the leadership of General Hindenberg, a hero from the war. However, the government had countless obstacles in reestablishing order and stability. War debts were crushing, vital resources in the west had been claimed by France, and inflation became rampant as the country tried to rebuild itself after the devastation of the war. When the Great Depression spread throughout Europe in 1929-30, weakened Germany was the most vulnerable to its punch.

In their desperation, Germans were open to new political solutions, including those advocated by communism. On the other end of the political spectrum, Adolf Hitler, an Austrian artist who had fought in World War I, attracted attention as the leader of the German Socialist Workers Party. In a series of clever political moves, he established his party in the Reichstag, and eventually convinced Hindenberg to support him as chancellor. After Hindenberg died, he and his "Nazi" party came to dominate German politics with promises to restore German prosperity. That they did, but by blatantly breaking the provisions of the Versailles Treaty. He rebuilt the army, seized the resource-rich Rhineland from France, and played upon the loss of German pride suffered by the humiliations of the Versailles Treaty. His Nazi state was authoritarian and militaristic, and like Japan and Italy, also incredibly expansionistic.

German Expansion

Under Hitler, Germany began claiming territory around but outside its borders established by the Versailles Treaty. The claims were backed by military force, and at first they were only the lands that Germany believed had been unfairly taken from them by the Versailles Treaty. But eventually Hitler's forces attacked the **Sudetenland**, a part of Czechoslovakia with many German people, but also home to Czechs and other Slavs. Finally, with this action, Hitler experienced some reaction from the old Allied Powers.

The Munich Agreement and the Start of the War

England and France answered Czechoslovakia's pleas for help by calling a meeting with Hitler in Munich in 1938. Under the leadership of Britain's Prime Minister **Neville Chamberlain**, the Allies reached an agreement with Hitler, infamously known as **appeasement**, or giving Hitler the land he had already seized in exchange for his promise to not take any more. Chamberlain promised the British people upon his return home that he had achieved "peace in our time," but the war began the very next year when Hitler broke his promise by attacking Poland. England and France were still war-weary from World War I, but they reluctantly declared war on Germany. Chamberlain was replaced as Prime Minister by **Winston Churchill**, who had long warned Britain about the danger posed by Adolf Hitler.

THE NATURE OF THE WAR

The nations of the world aligned themselves with the **Allied Powers** (originally led by Britain and France, later joined by Russia and the United States) and the **Axis Powers** (led by Germany, Italy, and Japan.) Even though the causes of World War II were rooted in unsettled business from World I, the nature of the war was far different from any previous conflict in world history. Some distinct characteristics of World War II are:

- **Worldwide participation** – The war was truly fought in all corners of the globe. Only eleven countries did not become directly involved in th war: Afghanistan, Greenland, Iceland, Ireland, Mongolia, Portugal, Spain, Sweden, Switzerland, Tibet, and Yemen.

- **Fighting in "theatres" or "arenas"** – Whereas in most previous wars, including World War I, "fronts" where opposite sides clashed were identifiable, changing war technology and military techniques meant that the war was fought in two large arenas: Europe (including North Africa) and the Pacific Ocean. Fronts could sometimes be identified within arenas, but by and large the concept had become obsolete.

- **Technology** – Major war technologies contributed to changes in the nature of warfare. Although airplanes and tanks had been used to some extent in World War I, they came to dominate World War II. For example, in the Pacific, airplanes attacked from giant aircraft carriers that allowed the United States navy to "hop" from one set of island to the next, finally zeroing in on Japan. In Europe airplanes on both sides bombed their opponents with high explosives and incendiaries that killed millions of people and devastated the infrastructure, particularly in large urban areas. Other technologies, such as radar and more accurate and powerful weaponry, helped submarines and warships to target the enemy. The most unique and deadly technology – the atom bomb – was introduced at the end of the war.

- **Widespread killing of civilians** – Whereas civilian casualties were not unique to World War II, the war is characterized by deliberate targeting of non-military people. Because the bombings sought to destroy the industrial infrastructure, they focused on urban areas where many people lived. In some cases the bombs were intended to torment populations so that the enemy would surrender. The German Nazis deliberately killed Jews and many other groups of people that they considered to be inferior to them, and of course, the atom bomb killed all those in its path, regardless of their military or civilian status.

All of these characteristics combine to make World War II a **total war**, one that involved almost all citizens in all countries and mobilized deadly weapons created by the organizational capacity that accompanied industrialized economies. Overall, at least 35 million people died in World War II.

THE HOLOCAUST

Genocide (ethnic based mass killings) characterized World War II. For example, the Japanese tortured and killed as many as 300,000 Chinese citizens in Nanking after the city had fallen. The bombings of Hiroshima killed 78,000 Japanese, and Nagasaki killed tens of thousands more. The largest slaughter resulted from Hitler's decision to eliminate Jews in Germany and eastern Europe resulted in millions of deaths in concentration camps that specialized in efficient methods of extermination. The **Holocaust** was an unprecedented modern genocide that also targeted gypsies, political dissidents, and other special groups. The "final solution" to the "Jewish problem" included death by gassing, electrocution, phenol injections, flamethrowers, and machine guns. Others died in concentration camps from starvation and medical experiments.

THE COURSE OF THE WAR

The war officially began in Europe with Hitler's invasion of Poland in 1939. He used a war technique called ***blitzkrieg*** (lightning war) to quickly conquer Poland, Denmark, Norway, Holland, Belgium and France. *Blitzkrieg* involved bombing civilian targets and rapidly moving troops, tanks, and mechanized carriers. By 1940 only Britain resisted German attack. Germany could not execute his techniques on the island nation, so the Battle of Britain was fought primarily in the air between the Royal Air Force and the German

Luftwaffe. Germany stretched its armies when it decided to attack Russia to the east, despite an earlier non-aggression treaty signed between the two countries. The attack sparked Russia's entry on the Allied side in 1941, and the Germans suffered their first defeat of the war in Stalingrad in 1942.

The course of the war changed dramatically when Japan attacked Pearl Harbor in Hawaii in 1941, causing the United States to enter the war. The United States fought in both arenas – Europe and the Pacific – and played a much larger role in World War II than it did in World War I.

- **The European Arena** – The European war strategy, devised primarily by American and British generals, began in northern Africa where combined Allied forces defeated the German forces that occupied the area. From there, Allies attacked, defeated, and occupied Italy, depriving Germany of a major ally. In 1944, Allied forces – including Canadians – crossed the English Channel in the famous "D-Day" assault on Normandy that led to the liberation of France. From there, Allies attacked across Belgium and into western Germany, where they eventually joined Russian forces marching across eastern Germany. The meeting of the armies east and west represented the defeat of Germany.

- **The Pacific Arena** – By 1941 the Japanese occupied large parts of eastern Asia and were preparing to seize Australia, a major Allied Power in the area. British troops were fighting the Japanese in Southeast Asia when the Americans joined the war. With a navy seriously crippled by the Pearl Harbor attack, the United States first had to rebuild and reposition its ships, planes, and equipment, and then had to stop Japanese expansion eastward toward the American West Coast. Japan and the United States fought a great sea-air naval war that resulted in the blocking of Japanese attacks of Midway Island and the Aleutian Islands and in the successful defense of Australia. The "island hopping" campaign brought the United States very close to Japan, but the war ended with Japanese surrender after the United States dropped atom bombs on Hiroshima and Nagasaki in August 1945.

POST-WORLD WAR II INTERNATIONAL ORGANIZATIONS

Instead of being settled by one sweeping peace treaty, World War II ended with many negotiations and meetings. An important result of Allied discussions was the formation of the United Nations, only one of many international organizations that formed in the decades that followed World War II.

- **The United Nations** – The United Nations was chartered during an international meeting in San Francisco in September 1945. About 50 nations signed the charter, a number that swelled to over 180 by the end of the century. From the beginning, the United Nations had more members than the League of Nations had, and the United States not only joined it but also headquartered the new organization in New York City. The Soviet Union and China were given permanent seats on the Security Council (along with the United States, Britain, and France), so that internationalism expanded beyond the West. Like the League, the United Nations' main purpose was to negotiate disputes among nations, but it also has addressed other world issues, such as trade, women's conditions, child labor, hunger, and environmental protection.

- **North Atlantic Treaty Organization** – NATO was formed in 1949 as a defensive alliance among the U.S., Canada, and western European nations. In response, the Soviet Union formed the **Warsaw Pact**, including eastern European nations. The formation of these two international organizations was a reflection of changing politics and a new type of warfare called the **Cold War** that was to last until 1991.

THE COLD WAR

The Cold War describes the decades-long period after World War II that centered around tensions between the two most powerful countries that emerged from the war: the United States and the Soviet Union. The era marks the replacement of European hegemony with two competing power centers. The globe during this time was divided into three parts: the United States and its allies, the Soviet Union and its allies, and a **"Third World"** of unaligned, generally less developed countries that both "superpowers" competed to influence.

THE ROOTS OF THE COLD WAR

The World War II alliance between the Soviet Union on the one hand, and the United States and Britain on the other, was based primarily on a mutual enemy: Germany. The lack of trust between the two "sides" was apparent even before the war was officially over at two peace conferences:

- **The Yalta Conference** – Early in 1945 the three countries split Germany into four pieces, including liberated France as an occupying power. However, Britain and the United States believed that Germany should be reunited as a viable country, and the Soviets wanted to destroy German industrial might. The powers also quarreled over eastern European nations, with Britain and the United States insisting that they be democratic, and the Soviet Union wanting them to be communist. Compromise was reached, but the agreement was soon to be broken.

- **The Potsdam Conference** – Since the Soviet Union already occupied eastern Poland and eastern Germany, it was agreed that they could maintain control, with the Poles getting part of eastern Germany as compensation. With great difficulty, peace was negotiated with Italy, but the U.S. and the Soviet Union signed separate treaties with Japan. Tensions were high all during this conference held in July 1945.

The United States and the Soviet Union reacted by seizing control of lands that they occupied in Asia, with the northern half of Korea controlled by the Soviets, and the southern half by the United States. The U.S. maintained its occupation of Japan, China regained most of its former territory, and the old colonial powers maintained control in Southeast Asia. In Europe, the Soviet Union pushed its boundaries westward, and the nations of eastern Europe (with the exceptions of Greece and Yugoslavia) fell under Soviet domination. Since the countries of western Europe were seriously weakened by the war, they depended on the United States to help them maintain their democracies. The United States sent aid to them with the **Marshall Plan**, a program of loans to help them rebuild their infrastructures. The Soviets saw this as a vehicle for American economic domination, and in the words of Winston Churchill, an **"Iron Curtain"** descended across Europe, dividing east from west.

THE ARMS RACE

The competition between the United States and the Soviet Union extended to almost all areas, including a race to develop space technology and attempts to gain support from Third World countries. However, the deadliest competition came as both countries built their nuclear arsenals. In 1949 the Soviet Union developed the atom bomb, and from that point until the 1980s, the U.S.S.R. and the U.S. introduced new and increasingly powerful weapons, as well as new kinds of missile systems to support them.

The Cold War was at its height during the 1950s and 1960s, with people around the globe fearing the worst – the outbreak of a third world war, but this time with nuclear weapons that would almost certainly destroy the world. During the 1970s, both countries saw the need to compromise, and a series of negotiations led to arms reductions. Tensions eased further during the late 1980s, partly because the Soviet Union was on the verge of economic collapse and could no longer afford to finance their efforts.

NEW PATTERNS OF NATIONALISM

Nationalism was as important a force during the 20th century as it had been in the previous era. People under the control of imperialist nations continued to strive for their own identities, and new, independent nations popped up in Africa, the Indian subcontinent, and southeast Asia. Nationalist movements also were a major cause of the late 20th century breakup of the Soviet Union, again changing the balance of world power in the post-Cold War era.

NATIONALISM IN AFRICA

By the early 20th century Europeans had colonized most of the African continent. Christian missionaries set up schools that educated a new native elite, who learned not only skills and literacy but western political ideas as well. They couldn't help but notice the contrast between the democratic ideals they were being taught in class and the reality of discrimination that they saw around them. This observation sparked nationalist movements in many places, including:

- **Senegal** – **Blaise Diagne** agitated for African participation in politics and fair treatment by the French army.
- **South Africa** – Western-educated natives founded the **African National Congress** in 1909 to defend the interests of Africans.
- **Ethiopia** – Italy took over Ethiopia in the years leading up to World War II, and Emperor **Haile Selassie** led Ethiopian troops into his capital city to reclaim his title. Ethiopians, as well as many other people in northern Africa responded to Allied promises of liberation and helped the Allies defeat the Germans that had occupied the area.

POST WORLD WAR II STRUGGLES IN ALGERIA

World War II was a humiliating experience for the French. Their armies had folded under Hitler's *blitzkrieg* within a few days, and they had to be liberated from German control by the other Allied powers. Both world wars devastated the infrastructure of France, and the weak parliamentary government seemed to have little control over the economy. Despite these hardships (or perhaps because of them), the French were determined to hold on to Algeria and Vietnam in Southeast Asia after World War II ended. French persistence set off major revolts in both areas. In 1954 war in Algeria broke out with great brutality by both sides. In reaction to the government's inability to fight the war, the French government was totally restructured, with strong man Charles de Gaulle taking the reins of the country as its new president. Algeria finally gained their independence in 1962, but lingering bitterness and retaliation led to a stream of French-sympathizers flooding into France from Algeria.

DECOLONIZATION IN SUB-SAHARAN AFRICA

None of the wars for independence in sub-Saharan Africa matched the Algerian struggle in scale. One by one native leaders negotiated treaties with their imperialist masters, so that by the late 1960s, the African continent was composed primarily of independent nations. A **Pan-African** movement was started by **Kwame Nkrumah**, who in 1957 became the prime minister of Ghana, and **Jomo Kenyatta**, a leader of Kenya, but the focus of nationalism was on independence for the individual colonies.

Independence led to many new problems for African nations. Border disputes occurred, since colonial boundaries often did not follow ethnic lines. The borders of some countries, such as Nigeria and Zaire, encompassed several different ethnic groups that struggled with one another for control of the country. Race conflict became particularly severe in the temperate southern part of the continent, where Europeans clashed with natives for political and economic power. South Africa was left with **apartheid**, an attempt by European minorities to keep natives in subservient, and very separate, roles in society. The **African National Congress**, formed in South Africa in 1912, led a bloody struggle against apartheid, which eventually led to success when **Nelson Mandela** became the first black president of South Africa in 1994.

NATIONALISM IN INDIA

Native elites had formed nationalist groups in India before World War I began, and the struggle against British control continued until India finally won its independence in 1947. The movement was fractured from the beginning, largely because the diversity of people on the Indian subcontinent made a united independence movement difficult. Tensions were particularly high between Hindus and Muslims. Muslims constituted only about a quarter of the entire Indian population, but they formed a majority in the northwest and in eastern Bengal.

During World War I Indians supported Britain enthusiastically, hoping that they would be rewarded for their loyalty. However, Britain stalled on independence, and political tensions mounted. For the next twenty years, Indians and British clashed often and violently, and the colony threatened to descend into chaos. The downward spiral was halted by **Mohandas K. Gandhi**, a man known to his followers as "Mahatma," the "great soul." Gandhi, educated as a lawyer in Britain, had some unusual political ideas. He denounced violence and popular uprisings and preached the virtues of *ahisma* (nonviolence) and *satyagraha* (the search for truth.) He demonstrated his identification with the poor by wearing simple homespun clothing and practicing fasting. He was also a brilliant political tactician, and he had a knack for attracting public attention. His most famous gesture was the **Walk to the Sea**, where he gathered salt as a symbol of Indian industry, an action forbidden by the British government. Such non-violent persistence landed him in jail repeatedly, but his leadership gave Indians the moral high-ground over the British, who eventually agreed to independence in 1947.

The independence agreement was complicated because **Jawaharlal Nehru**, leader of the Indian National Congress, and **Muhammad Ali Jinnah**, the leader of the Muslim League, clashed openly. Violent riots between Hindus and Muslims broke out in Bengal and Bihar, so that the British negotiated with the two organizations to partition India into two states. Most of the subcontinent remained under secular rule dominated by Hindus, but the new Muslim state of Pakistan was formed in the northwest and northeast. Independence celebrations were marred by violence between Muslims and Hindus. The partition led to massive movements of Indians from one area to the other, and Gandhi himself was assassinated by a Hindu who was upset because the partition meant that he had to leave his home. Religious conflict continued to plague the subcontinent for the rest of the 20th century.

NATIONALIST MOVEMENTS IN SOUTHEAST ASIA

In Indonesia, a nationalist leader named simply **Sukarno** cooperated with the Japanese during World War II with the hope of throwing off the colonial control of the Dutch. Despite the Japanese defeat in the war, independence was negotiated in 1949, and Sukarno became the dictator until he was removed by a military coup in 1965. The British granted independence to Burma (now Myanmar) in 1948, and the United States negotiated independence with the Philippines in 1946. As in Africa, the French provided the most resistance to decolonization in Southeast Asia.

Throughout the area, independence leaders were also drawn to communism, and French Indochina was no exception. The Communist leader **Ho Chi Minh** led his supporters against the French, capturing the colonial stronghold of Dien Bien Phu in 1954. Ho Chi Minh's government took over in the north, and a noncommunist nationalist government ruled in the south, which eventually came to be heavily supported by the United States. In the 1960s and early 1970s, the United States waged an unsuccessful war with North Vietnam that eventually ended in the reunification of the country under communist rule in 1975.

NATIONALISM IN LATIN AMERICA

Nationalism in Latin America took the form of internal conflict, since almost all the nations had achieved independence during the 19th century. However, most were still ruled by an authoritarian elite. During the 20th century, many nations experienced populist uprisings that challenged the elite and set in motion an unstable relationship between democracy and militarism. Some teetered back and forth between democratically elected leaders and military generals who established power through force. *Coups d'etat* became common, and political legitimacy and economic viability became serious issues.

- **Mexico** – At the beginning of the century, Mexico was ruled by Porfirio Diaz, a military general who enriched a small group of elites by allowing them to control agriculture and welcoming businessmen from the United States to control industry. The Revolution of 1910 began not with the exploited poor, but with elites that Diaz did not favor, almost all of them military generals. As early as 1911 the revolutionary fervor had spread to peasants, who were led by regional strongmen, such as **Emiliano Zapata** and **Pancho Villa**. Despite the creation of a democratic-based Constitution in 1917, the revolution raged on, with every President assassinated during his term of office until **Lazaro Cardenas** took over in 1934. Finally, the country stabilized under an umbrella political party (PRI), which tightly controlled Mexican politics until the 1990s, when some signs of democracy began to appear.

- **Argentina and Brazil** – These two countries have many differences in language, ethnicity, and geographical settings, but both were controlled by elites. Early in the century, Argentina's government represented the interest of landowners that raised cattle and sheep and grew wheat for export, and Brazil's elite was made up of coffee and cacao planters and rubber exporters. In both countries, the gap between the rich and poor was great, with the elite spending lavishly on palaces and personal goods. However, the Great Depression hit both countries hard, and stimulated coups against the governments. **Getulio Vargas** took over in Brazil in 1930, and instituted a highly authoritarian regime. Military revolts characterized Argentina, with **Juan Peron**, supported by Nazi interests, leading a major coup in 1943. Authoritarian rule in both countries continued on into the second half of the century.

- **The Cuban Revolution and its aftermath** – Revolutions against dictators were often inspired by communism, especially after the Cuban Revolution led by **Fidel Castro** in 1959. Military leaders of Brazil led a conservative reaction by staging a coup of the democratically elected government in 1964. There the "Brazilian Solution" was characterized by dictatorship, violent repression, and government promotion of industrialization. A similar pattern occurred in Chile in 1974 where the socialist president **Salvador Allende** was overthrown in a military coup led by **General Augusto Pinochet**. Socialist **Sandinistas** led a rebellion against the dictator of Nicaragua in 1979, where their communist affiliations led them to disfavor with the conservative United States government led by **Ronald Reagan**. The Reagan administration supported **Contras** (counterrevolutionaries) who unsuccessfully challenged the Sandinistas. By the 1990s, most Latin American nations had loosened the control by the military, and democratic elections appeared to be gaining ground. However, they continued to be economically and militarily dominated by the United States.

MAJOR GLOBAL ECONOMIC DEVELOPMENTS

World War I not only shattered the power of European nations, it also left their economies seriously weakened. However, after a period of post-war recession, economic prosperity returned by the mid-1920s, most markedly in the United States. Mass consumption rates rose for several years, fed by new technologies such as the radio, rayon, household appliances, and the automobile. However, the stock market crashes of 1929 put an end to the recovery in Europe as well as the boom in the United States.

THE GREAT DEPRESSION

The stock markets in the United States had boomed during the late 1920s, but the optimism of investors that drove the markets upward far outstripped the strength of the economy. When the bubble burst in October 1929, the New York Stock Exchange tumbled, losing half of its value within days. Millions of investors lost money, as did the banks and brokers who had lent them money. New York banks called in their loans to Germany and Austria who in turn could no longer pay war reparations to France and Great Britain. The series of events led to a domino effect of crashing markets in Europe and other industrialized countries, ushering in the deepest and most widespread depression in history. Companies laid off thousands of workers, farm prices fell, and unemployment rates soared. The catastrophe caused many to rethink the free-enterprise system, and increased the appeal of alternate political and economic philosophies, such as communism and fascism.

The Depression had a serious effect on the global economy, with global industrial production dropping about 36 percent between 1929 and 1932, and world trade sinking by 62 percent. France and Britain escaped the worst by making their colonies and dependents buy their products instead of products from other countries. However, Germany suffered greatly. Already crippled by the Versailles Treaty, the depression in Germany meant that half of its population lived in poverty by the early 1930s. Japan's economy also took a nosedive, partly because the country's economy was very dependent on exports from the distressed international market to pay for imported food and fuel. The Depression devastated other countries that depended on international trade, such as Brazil and Columbia for their coffee, Argentina for its wheat and beef, Malaya and the Dutch East Indies for their rubber, and Ceylon and Java for their tea. Countries less dependent on international markets managed to escape the worst of the economic malaise.

The Depression only ended with the advent of World War II, when production demands from the war stimulated the U.S. economy sufficiently to create jobs for workers and sell agricultural products on the world market.

TWENTIETH CENTURY TECHNOLOGY

The new inventions sparked by the Industrial Revolution in the 19th century continued to develop during the 20th century. New military technologies resulted from the two world wars, including tanks, poison gas, airplanes, jet engines, radar, submarines, and improved weaponry. The most dramatic and dangerous new type of weapon was nuclear, but nuclear energy also had the potential to be harnessed for power for peaceful endeavors. When applied to industry, many of the World War II technologies increased productivity, reduced labor requirements, and improved the flow of information. After both world wars, pent-up demand for consumer goods spawned new inventions for peacetime economies. Improvements in existing technologies kept economies healthy during the 1950s and 60s, especially as European countries began to recover from the war. Trucks, airplanes, and trains became bigger and faster, cutting transportation costs. Both the United States and the Soviet Union built highway systems and airports and constructed nuclear power plants.

THE COMPUTER AGE

One of the most important new technologies of the 20th century was the computer. At first they were large and very expensive, so that only large corporations, governments, and universities could afford them. However, desktop computers began replacing typewriters by the mid-1980s, and by century's end, computers were smaller, more powerful, and more affordable than ever before. The internet rapidly developed and expanded during the 1990s, and its ability to connect computers to one another and access information transformed communications by the early 21st century.

MULTINATIONAL CORPORATIONS

Computers helped make possible the proliferation of **multinational corporations**. As early as the 18th century, large companies had conducted business across national borders. However, with improved transportation and communications, these corporations became truly international in the late 20th century with their multinational ownership and management. International trade agreements and open markets reinforced the trend. Many of the companies were American (General Motors, Exxon, Microsoft) or Japanese (Honda, Sony), but by 2000 many other multinational corporations were headquartered in countries with smaller economies.

One result of the growth of transnational corporations was the increasing difficulty that national government had in regulating them. Often the companies simply repositioned their plants and labor force by moving their bases to countries with fewer regulations and cheaper labor. As a result, the worst cases of labor and environmental abuses tended to occur in poor nations.

THE PACIFIC RIM

Another important development of the late 20th century was the increasing economic strength of many countries and cities along the **"Pacific Rim"**, such as Japan, South Korea, Singapore, Taiwan, and Hong Kong.

Japan experienced a faster rate of economic growth in the 1970s and 1980s than did any other major developed economy, growing at about 10 percent a year. In contrast to the American model of free enterprise, giant Japanese business conglomerates known as *keiretsu* have close relationships with government. The government supports business interests in industry, commerce, construction, automobiles, semiconductors, and banking through tariff and import regulations. By 1990 Japan enjoyed a trade surplus with the rest of the world that caused many observers to believe that Japan would soon pass the United States as the world's strongest economy. However, by 2000 the Japanese economy was slowed by overvalued stocks and housing, speculation, and corruption.

South Korea, as one of the **Asian Tigers** (along with Taiwan, Hong Kong, and Singapore), followed the model of close cooperation between government and industry. Through a combination of inexpensive labor, strong technical education, and large capital reserves, South Korea experienced a **"compressed modernity"** that transformed the country into a major industrial and consumer economy that, despite a recession in 1997, continued into the early 21st century. The initial economic bursts of Singapore and Hong Kong were based on shipping and banking and commercial services, and Hong Kong eventually developed highly competitive textile and consumer electronic industries. Despite the conflict with mainland China, Taiwan's economy grew rapidly, beginning with small, specialized companies.

In China after Mao Zedong's death in 1976, **Deng Xiaoping** emerged as the new communist leader. He advocated a **socialist market economic**, a practical blend of socialism and capitalism, to solve China's economic woes. By century's end, China's economy had expanded rapidly, and by the early 21st century, China was granted membership in the World Trade Organization, and was rapidly become one of the most important trading nations in the world.

IDEOLOGIES AND REVOLUTIONS

Many of the conflicts of the 20th century, including World War II and the Cold War, represent important ideological clashes between industrialized democracies and industrialized totalitarian powers. Two important ideologies that greatly influenced the century were communism and fascism.

- **Communism** – Karl Marx's communist theory was revolutionized during the early 20ths century in Russia by **Vladimir Lenin**, a leader of the **Bolsheviks**, a group that eventually took over the country. Whereas Marx envisioned revolutions of the proletariat (workers) as occurring in capitalist countries where workers were most oppressed, Lenin advocated **democratic centralism**. He and a small group of leaders became a **"vanguard of the revolution"**, leading in the name of the people, but concentrating control in the hands of a few. Even though his version of communism emphasized equality and the destruction of class distinctions, the highly centralized control translated into totalitarian power. In China, **Mao Zedong's** communism stressed the importance of agriculture and the peasants, but he also exercised totalitarian power after his takeover of the country in 1949.

- **Fascism** – As communism became more popular in Europe, especially as capitalism faltered with the Great Depression, **fascism** developed as an alternative doctrine to countries in economic distress. Fascism, an authoritarian political movement that sought to subordinate individuals to the service of the state, first developed under **Benito Mussolini** in Italy. Mussolini advocated an extreme nationalism that claimed to regain the power and glory of the ancient Roman Empire. Fascism spread to other countries, including Germany, where **Adolf Hitler** fashioned it into **Nazism**. Struggling under the oppressive restrictions of the Versailles Treaty and the economic stresses of the Great Depression, Germany was particularly susceptible to Hitler's message of restoring glory and strength to the nation. The Nazis not only suppressed communism, but their highly centralized government destroyed trade unions, crushed the judiciary and the civil service, took control of all police forces, and removed enemies of the regime. Nationalism assumed the face of racism with the purging of Jews and other eastern European people.

Whereas fascism played an important role in World War II, communism sparked numerous revolutions, including those in Russia and China.

COMMUNISM IN RUSSIA

During World War I Russia had the largest army in the world, but its generals were incompetent and the soldiers were poorly equipped. The war inflicted incredible hardship on the Russian people, and by early 1917, soldiers were deserting en masse from the war front, citizens were demonstrating, and workers were striking. In the chaos that followed, the tsar abdicated, and a provisional government was put in place. When the autocratic government toppled, revolutionary groups that had been repressed for decades became active, and the communist-inspired **Bolsheviks** seized control of parliament. Under the leadership of **Vladimir Lenin**, Russia withdrew from the war and was named the **Union of Soviet Socialist Republics**. After a four-year civil war, Lenin established his control over the country, and the U.S.S.R. became the first communist regime of the 20th century.

STALINISM

When Lenin died in 1924, his position as General Secretary of the Communist Party was eventually claimed by **Joseph Stalin**. Stalin emphasized internal development, and set in place **Five-Year Plans** that set industrial goals designed to strengthen the power of the Soviet Union. Stalin did not focus on producing consumer goods. Instead his plans increased the output of electricity and heavy industry, such as iron, steel, coal, and machinery. Agriculture was **collectivized**, a process that abolished small private farms and forced farmers to work on large government-controlled farms that produced food to support industry.

Stalinism was characterized not only by industrialization and collectivization, but by brutal, centralized control of government that held little resemblance to Marxist doctrine. Despite his purges of untold millions of people, Stalin did lead the Soviet Union to industrialize faster than any country had ever done. By the late 1930s, the U.S.S.R. was the world's third largest industrial power, after the United States and Germany.

POST-STALIN ECONOMIC CRISES

Russia emerged from World War II as a superpower, largely as a result of Stalin's focus on industrial strength. However, economic development was uneven. The USSR produced a great army, developed a sophisticated missile program, and participated in a "race to space" with the United States. Much money was spent on maintaining control over satellite states, but the consumer economy failed to grow. By the mid-1980s, the country was on the verge of economic collapse, although the severity of its problems was largely unknown to outsiders. **Mikhail Gorbachev** attempted to revive the country through a 3-pronged program:

- **Perestroika** – Economic reforms attempted to infuse some capitalism into the system, reduce the size of the army, stimulate under-producing factories, and stabilize the monetary system.
- **Glasnost** – Loosely translated as "openness", glasnost attempted to loosen censorship restrictions and allow nationalist minorities to address their concerns to the government.

- **Democratization** – Gorbachev's plan allowed some choice of candidates for the national congress, a body that in turn selected a president.

The Gorbachev reforms backfired after a conservative coup attempt in 1991. Although the coup failed, and Gorbachev retained his position as president, the crisis resulted in unrest that quickly brought an end to the U.S.S.R. as the republics one by one declared their independence. By the year's end, Gorbachev had no job because he had no country, and Russia – the largest of the republics – emerged under the leadership of **Boris Yeltsin**. The 1990s saw a weakened Russia struggling to establish a democracy and regain some of its former power.

COMMUNISM IN CHINA

Communism emerged in the early 20th century shortly after the Bolshevik Revolution in Russia. The Communist leader, **Mao Zedong**, accepted a great deal of support from the U.S.S.R., but he did not gain control of China until 1949. Until then, the country was ruled by nationalist leader **Chiang Kai-shek**. Mao gained strength as a result of the **Long March** of 1934-5, as he and his followers evaded Chiang's army that pursued him for thousands of miles. With the Japanese occupation of China before and during World War II, the two men called a truce, but when the war ended, Mao's army emerged as the stronger one, with Chiang and his supporters finally being driven to the island of Taiwan. In 1949, Mao claimed main land China for communism, renaming the country the **People's Republic of China**.

CHINA UNDER MAO

At first, Mao accepted a great deal of aid from the Soviet Union, establishing Five-Year Plans modeled after those instituted by Stalin. However, **Maoism** always differed from the Soviet-style communism, partly because Mao believed in the importance of keeping an agricultural-based economy. He broke with the Soviet Union in the late 1950s and instituted his **Great Leap Forward** to compensate for the loss of Soviet aid. This program emphasized both agricultural and industrial development, but the economy nose-dived. Mao responded with the **Cultural Revolution** in 1966 – a much more profound reform in that it encompassed political and social change, as well as economic. Mao was still unhappy with China's progress toward true egalitarianism, and his main goal was to purify the party and the country through radical transformation.

A primary goal of the Cultural Revolution was to remove all vestiges of the old China and its hierarchical bureaucracy and emphasis on inequality. Scholars were sent into the fields to work, universities and libraries were destroyed. Emphasis was put on elementary education – all people should be able to read and write – but any education that created inequality was targeted for destruction.

CHINA UNDER DENG XIAOPING

When Mao died in 1976, the country was on the verge of collapse, traumatized by massive changes brought by the Cultural Revolution. His successor, **Deng Xiaoping**, encouraged a practical mix of socialism and capitalism called the **socialist market economy**, a tactic that brought better economic health to China. During the late 20th century, China became more and more capitalistic while still retaining centralized control by the government. Tensions between economic reform and the centralized communist political system erupted into popular disruptions, most famously at **Tiananmen Square** in Beijing in 1989. By the early 21st century, China remained the largest (and one of the only) communist-controlled country in the world, but had become increasingly prosperous with the government openly encouraging trade with capitalist countries.

SOCIAL REFORM AND SOCIAL REVOLUTION

The 20th century saw the spread of **international Marxism**, as first the Soviet Union, and eventually the People's Republic of China, sought to influence other countries to turn to communism. Their efforts were countered by the United States, that sought to spread capitalism and its form of democratic government. However, by mid-century, communist parties were entrenched in countries in many parts of the globe, especially in Latin America and Southeast Asia. As communism supported egalitarian revolts, democratic countries of the West instituted their own versions of social reform.

FEMINIST MOVEMENTS

Both World Wars had the effect of liberating western women from their old subservient roles of the 19th century. In both cases, when men left for war, women stepped into jobs that kept the economies going during wartime. One effect was the granting of suffrage to women after World War I, first in the United States, but eventually to most countries in western Europe. After World War II, women saw no comparable gain, partly because of the **Red Scare** that developed in the late 1940s and early 1950s in the United States. The fear of the international spread of communism led to increased suspicions about citizens' loyalty to their country, and so many responded by embracing a traditional way of life.

After the Red Scare faded, the feminist movement revived during the 1960s to claim other rights than suffrage for women. One area of change came with abortion and birth control rights, as feminists asserted that only with birth control measures would women be able to free themselves from the age-old tendency of "biology determining destiny." Birth control pills ensured this freedom, and some legal protections for abortion emerged during the 1970s. Another area of change was economic employment of women, which by century's end was 40-50% of the workforce in most industrialized countries. The U.S. Civil Rights Act of 1964 prohibited discrimination on the basis of both race and sex.

BLACK NATIONALISM

The women's movement was spurred by a surge of black nationalism during the 1950s. Blacks in Africa asserted themselves through independence movements that resulted in the widespread decolonization of the era. Blacks in the United States responded to the leadership of **Martin Luther King**, who relied openly on Indian leader Mohandas Gandhis's methods of passive nonresistance and boycotting to attain equality in the United States.

The Soviet Union often pointed to the discrimination that black Americans experienced as an indication of the evils of capitalism. One result was the **civil rights movement**, led by King, that led to vast legal changes in the United States for blacks. Segregation was ruled unconstitutional by the U.S. Supreme Court in 1954, and national legislation outlawed many other forms of discrimination in 1964 and 1965. During the 1980s an **anti-apartheid** movement in South Africa led to similar legislation there, and eventually to the 1994 election of the first black president, **Nelson Mandela**.

GLOBALIZATION OF SCIENCE, TECHNOLOGY, AND CULTURE

Since the classical period, world history has involved a tension between the differing natures of individual civilizations and the forces of interaction that cause civilizations to share common culture, science, and technology. By the late 20th century these two counter-trends were apparent in the interactions of nations worldwide: **globalization** and **fragmentation**. Globalization is an integration of social, technological, scientific, environmental, economic, and cultural activities of nations that has resulted from increasing international contacts. On the other hand, fragmentation is the tendency for people to base their loyalty on ethnicity, language, religion, or cultural identity. Although globalization and fragmentation appear to be opposite concepts, they both transcend political boundaries between individual countries. At the beginning of the 21st century it is possible to predict that new homogenizing forces will further reduce variations between individual cultures or that a new splintering among civilizations is taking place, with each region advocating its own self-interest.

FORCES FOR GLOBALIZATION

The cross-cutting forces of the past century or so have increasingly homogenized cultures. Most civilizations find it very difficult to isolate themselves from the rest of the world since they are tied together in so many ways. Some factors that promote globalization include:

- **Modern transportation and communication** – People are able to go from one area of the world to another much more easily than at any previous time in history. Likewise, communication is faster and more reliable than ever before. Satellites transmit images and voices instantaneously across great distances, and the internet allows people to communicate regularly and extensively often with one person not knowing exactly where the other's message actually is coming from.

- **Increasing international trade** – Trade among different geographical areas is just about as old as civilization itself, but many barriers to international trade were removed during the second half of the 20th century.

- **Spread of "popular culture"** – The popularity of western fads and fashions, from clothes to television to sports, leads to cultural contact between ordinary people in everyday life. Although this phenomenon may be seen as the "westernization" of world culture, in recent years culture from other lands has influenced the west as well.

- **Sharing of international science** – Today scholars in both science and social science come together at international conferences and confer by e-mail or telephone to discuss ideas and share information. Nationality is secondary to their mutual interests.

- **International business** – Like scientists, businessmen from around the globe meet together, especially since large corporations headquartered in one country often have branches is other areas of the world. As a result, business leaders learn from other organizational forms and labor policies.

FORCES FOR FRAGMENTATION

All through history, regions and civilizations have combined distinctive traditions, experiences, and beliefs that unify them at the same time that they set them apart from others. The late 20th and early 21st centuries are no exception. To date, no pattern of modernization has obliterated key boundaries between the major civilizations. Some factors that encourage fragmentation include:

- **The decline of European power** – A major factor that led to the mid-20th century decolonization in Africa and Asia was the desire for cultural and political independence from European nations that had dominated them during the preceding decades.

- **The breakup of multicultural empires** – During the 20th century, many multicultural empires broke apart, leaving their subject people to quarrel among themselves. When British India broke into two countries – India and Pakistan – old hostilities between Hindus and Muslims came to the surface. Likewise, when the Ottoman Empire broke up after World War I, Slavic and Muslim peoples fragmented so deeply that intercultural wars broke out in the Balkans many decades later.

- **The end of the cold war** – The end of the cold war gave many nations dependent on American or Soviet aid the opportunity to reassert themselves in new ways. For example, the Soviet breakup gave independence to many subject states that have fragmented into different countries. In the Middle East, leaders of the 1979 revolution in Iran committed themselves to ousting U.S. influence and reinvigorating Islamic traditions.

Do supranational regional organizations such as NATO, NAFTA, OPEC, and the European Union encourage globalization or fragmentation? The case may be argued either way. The fact that nations within each organization must cooperate with others may be seen as a stepping-stone to internationalism since trade and communications barriers have decreased within the regions. From this point of view, regional organizations represent a movement away from national organizations toward international ones. On the other hand, it may be argued that they are just larger units that represent conflicting regions, each with their own loyalties and points of view that separate them from the others.

DEMOGRAPHIC AND ENVIRONMENTAL CHANGES

Dramatic changes occurred in the 20th century in migration patterns, birthrates and death rates, and types of urbanization. Continued industrialization, expansion of agricultural production, and technological innovations also impacted the world's ecosystem, inspiring "green" movements to pop up in many areas.

MIGRATIONS

Two distinct types of migrations characterized the 20th century:

- **Rural to urban** – The industrialized nations saw significant migrations from the farm to the city during the 19th century, and that pattern continued well into the 20th century. However, developing nations experienced this shift in population even more profoundly, with migrations from rural areas to urban centers increasing threefold from 1925 to 1950. Cities such as Rio de Janeiro, Mexico City, and Johannesburg developed shantytown sprawls that impressed developed countries as signs of economic failure. However, most migrants to cities made economic gains until the scale of the migration grew to such proportions that many cities have not been able to keep up with the demand for services. Nearly every poor nation today still faces the challenge of rapidly growing cities.

- **Global migration** – Whereas most countries of the 20th century experienced internal migration from rural to urban areas, another major migration occurred among countries, with people leaving the developing world to emigrate to industrialized nations. For example, illegal immigration across the border from Mexico to the United States has increased significantly. In Europe, migrations from Islamic countries were encouraged beginning in the 1960s when an expanding European economy needed new sources of labor. However, as the size of the immigrant populations grew and the economies slowed, right-wing anti-immigration political movements sprang up in reaction, especially in Germany and France.

POPULATION INCREASES

Human reproductive and life expectancy patterns changed profoundly in the second half of the 20th century. By the late 1960s Europe and other industrial societies had made a **demographic transition** to lower fertility rates and reduced mortality. Lower birthrates occurred as more women went to work, couples married at later ages, and birth control methods became more effective. Death rates declined as well, as modern medicine and better health led to increased longevity. The number of births in the developed nations was just enough to replace the people that died, and populations began to stabilize. Many experts predicted that the same thing would occur in developing nations once their industrialization process was more advanced. However, as of the early 21st century, the demographic transition has not occurred in developing or less developed countries around the globe.

THE GROWTH OF DEVELOPING NATIONS

Whether the transition will occur in the future is open to debate. However, some political leaders of developing nations have encouraged high birth rates, thinking that a larger population would increase political power. In other areas, cultural patterns enforce values that support large families. Whatever the reasons, at current rates, most of the population increases of the 21st century will almost certainly take place in developing nations. Areas of rapid population increase include most nations of Africa and Latin America. In Asia, the populations of India and China have continued to grow despite government efforts to reduce family size. In China, efforts to enforce a limit of one child per family have led to female infanticide as rural families have sought to produce male heirs. In India, forced sterilization led to public protest and electoral defeat of the ruling political party. In both countries, population rates have slowed, but the population bases are already so large that a real slowdown is unlikely to occur in the foreseeable future.

CONTRASTING POPULATION PYRAMIDS

Population pyramids show the distribution of a country's population by age group and by gender. At the beginning of the 21st century, these pyramids for industrialized nations contrasted greatly with those of developing nations. The slow rates of growth in industrialized nations and the contrasting rapid growth in developing nations create strikingly different population compositions. In industrialized nations, the percentage of older people is increasing, and the percentage of younger people is decreasing. These differences create demands for social security and healthcare for senior citizens that challenge the ability of a shrinking labor pool to finance through taxes. In contrast, the populations of young people are exploding in developing countries, resulting in job shortages and unmet demands on the education systems. Poor nations, then, often find it impossible to create wealth since education and jobs are in such short supply.

"GREEN" MOVEMENTS

During the 1960s environmental activists began movements devoted to slowing the devastating consequences of population growth, industrialization, and the expansion of agriculture. These "green" movements raised public awareness of the world's shrinking rainforests and redwood trees, the elimination of animal species, and the pollution of water and air. Predictably, pressure on environments is greatest in developing countries, where population is increasing the most rapidly. By the early 21st century, environmental movements were most effective in industrialized nations, where they have formed interest groups and political parties to pressure governments to protect the environment. Some governments have rewarded energy-efficient factories, fuel-efficient cars, and alternative energy sources such as solar and wind power. However, these movements have had less success in developing nations, where deforestation and pollution continue to be major problems.

THE IMPORTANCE OF THE 20TH CENTURY

Although the 20th century is so recent that our analytical perspective is limited, in many ways the era appears to be a pivotal one, with major changes and new patterns being established. Since 1914 two world wars and a cold war have led to the decline of European power and the rise of the United States. Politically, more and more nations are experimenting with democratic governments, and authoritarian regimes appear to be on the decline. Social inequality has been challenged on many fronts, and gender, racial, and social class distinctions have been altered radically in at least some areas of the world. By the early 21st century, the forces of globalization clash with those that encourage fragmentation. Perhaps it is this dynamic that will shape our future. Will advances in global connections, trade, and communication lead to a more unified world, or will regional differences fragment the world in ways that will lead to division and conflict? Both patterns have occurred in world history, but never before has either encompassed virtually all people on earth. Despite the fact that these tendencies are deeply rooted in time, they promise that at least some developments of the 21st century will be new, different, and extremely challenging.

UNIT FIVE QUESTIONS

1. Which of the following is not usually considered to be a major cause of the Great War (World War I)?

   (A) nationalist aspirations
   (B) alliance systems
   (C) nationalist rivalries
   (D) the rise of German power
   (E) socialism

2. Which of the following countries was a member of the Triple Alliance?

   (A) Japan
   (B) Great Britain
   (C) Russia
   (D) Germany
   (E) Netherlands

3. All of the following were effects of the First World War in Russia EXCEPT:

   (A) The old societal structure was destroyed.
   (B) The land was distributed to the peasants.
   (C) The door to revolution and civil war was opened.
   (D) A radical new political system was introduced.
   (E) Land was gained on their western border, as settled in the Versailles Treaty.

4. Which of the following countries never joined the League of Nations?

   (A) Japan
   (B) Belgium
   (C) France
   (D) Great Britain
   (E) The United States

5. Which of the following countries was NOT carved out of the Versailles Treaty?

   (A) Czechoslovakia
   (B) Poland
   (C) Yugoslavia
   (D) Greece
   (E) Lithuania

6. According to the Versailles Treaty, mandates were

   (A) orders to redraw the borders of eastern European countries according to ethnic identities
   (B) former colonies/lands of the Central Powers placed under the control of the League of Nations
   (C) requirements that Germany repay war debts
   (D) orders for all the Central Powers to disarm and to reduce the size of their armies and navies
   (E) declarations that blamed Germany for starting the war

7. Which of the following is an accurate statement describing combat on the Western and Eastern Fronts during World War I?

   (A) Fighting on the Eastern Front degenerated into stalemate, whereas conditions on the Western Front were much more fluid.
   (B) Fighting on the Western Front degenerated into stalemate, whereas conditions on the Eastern Front were much more fluid.
   (C) Conditions on both fronts were roughly the same.
   (D) The level of technology on the Eastern Front was significantly higher than on the Western Front.
   (E) There were no aircraft used on either front.

8. What best describes the relationship between Woodrow Wilson and his fellow Allied Powers, Georges Clemenceau and David Lloyd George, at the Paris Peace Conference?

   (A) Out of gratitude, Clemenceau and Lloyd George agreed to almost all of Wilson's proposals.
   (B) Wilson opposed most of the so-called Fourteen Points supported by Clemenceau and Lloyd George.
   (C) Wilson's thirst for revenge clashed with the lofty idealism of Clemenceau and Lloyd George.
   (D) Clemenceau's and Lloyd George's thirst for revenge clashed with the lofty idealism of Wilson.
   (E) Clemenceau and Lloyd George vetoed Wilson's plan for a League of Nations, but readily agreed to decolonize the French and British empires.

9. After the Versailles Conference, Arab leaders

(A) were frustrated by the limited autonomy granted them as mandate states
(B) were content with their new-found independence
(C) were overjoyed by the Balfour Declaration
(D) were grateful to the Turkish government for standing up on behalf of the Middle East at the conference
(E) were angry that Middle Eastern affairs had not been discussed at all during the conference

10. The leader of the Red Army in the Russian civil war that lasted from 1918 to 1921 was

(A) V.I. Lenin
(B) Karl Marx
(C) Leon Trotsky
(D) Alexander Kerensky
(E) Joseph Stalin

11. Which of the following is the best explanation of the importance of the Long March in Chinese history?

(A) It effectively marked the end of the Qing Empire, the last dynasty in China.
(B) It brought the Nationalists under Chiang Kai-shek to power.
(C) It established the reputation of Mao Zedong and paved the way for the creation of a communist state in China.
(D) It reflected the Chinese resolve to resist Japanese invasion by establishing a fighting base outside the Japanese Occupation area.
(E) It affirmed the continuing importance of the Mandate of Heaven in determining who rules China.

12. Which of the following political belief systems rose most directly from the misery caused by the Great Depression?

(A) Maoism
(B) Leninism
(C) Fascism
(D) Marxism
(E) Liberalism

(Questions 13 and 14 are based on the following quote):

[The Five-Year Plan] has undermined and smashed the kulaks as a class, thus liberating the poor peasants and a good half of the middle peasants from bondage to the kulaks...It has thus eliminated the possibility of the differentiation of the peasantry into exploiters – kulaks – and exploited – poor peasants. It has raised the poor peasants and the lower stratum of the middle peasants to a position of security..."

Report issued in January 1933

13. The author of the report is

   (A) Vladimir Lenin
   (B) Joseph Stalin
   (C) Mao Zedong
   (D) Chiang Kai-shek
   (E) Sun Yat-sen

14. The kulaks that the report mentions had revolted against the regime's practice of

   (A) collectivization of agriculture
   (B) industrialization
   (C) purging dissidents
   (D) excessive taxation of the middle class
   (E) confiscating lands for the private use of government elites

15. Which of the following countries experienced a dramatic increase in world power between World War I and World War II?

   (A) Japan
   (B) China
   (C) Britain
   (D) France
   (E) Russia

16. Which of the following changes occurred for women in the years following World War I?

    (A) Women working outside the home became commonplace in most parts of the globe.
    (B) Women became more active in politics and held many important leadership roles in industrialized countries.
    (C) Women gained the right to vote in a number of industrialized countries.
    (D) Women in the middle classes began to work outside the home, but working class women were expected to remain at home.
    (E) Women gained important rights in some countries, but those that lived under communism experienced setbacks in terms of gaining equal rights to men.

17. This policy was enacted by Britain and France toward Hitler in 1938. It was inspired by fear of war, fear of communism, and the expectation that agreements would be honored. The policy was known as

    (A) containment
    (B) détente
    (C) appeasement
    (D) preemption
    (E) balance of power

18. Which of the following does NOT accurately compare military tactics and practices of World War I and World War II?

    (A) Airplanes were much more important during World War II than they were in World War I.
    (B) Trench warfare was much more characteristic of World War I than of World War II.
    (C) World War I was fought on "fronts;" World War II was fought in "theatres" or "arenas."
    (D) Machine gun technology was used in World War II but not in World War I.
    (E) Tanks were used more effectively during World War II than they were in World War I.

19. By December 7, 1941 the Japanese occupied all of the following areas of Asia and the Pacific EXCEPT:

    (A) Australia
    (B) Korea
    (C) Taiwan
    (D) Manchuria
    (E) Large areas of mainland China, including Beijing, Shanghai, and Nanjing

20. "Leap-frogging" or "island hopping" during the World War II era describes

(A) the Japanese technique of capturing control of islands off the coast of Asia during the years just prior to the war
(B) the retreat of Japanese forces as they were overwhelmed by Allied attacks in the Pacific
(C) the U.S. technique of capturing strategic islands in the Pacific to put themselves in a position to invade Japan
(D) the necessity during World War II for airplanes to have to make frequent stops for fueling as they traveled across the Pacific and Atlantic Oceans
(E) the use of bases in the Dutch East Indies by Allied forces as a way to drive the Japanese out of mainland China

(Questions 21 and 22 are based on the following photograph):

AP/Wide World Photos

21. The man in the photo is

(A) Vladimir Lenin
(B) Cecil Rhodes
(C) Mohatma Gandhi
(D) Nelson Mandela
(E) Mutafa Kemal

22. The spinning wheel represents

   (A) Indian national consciousness
   (B) imperialist demands on African colonies
   (C) gender equality
   (D) ceaseless, fruitless work
   (E) Pan-Africanism

23. Which of the following was an important consequence of World War II for American women?

   (A) large-scale entry of women into the labor force
   (B) large-scale entry of women into the armed forces
   (C) better access to consumer goods that allowed them to take better care of their families
   (D) uprooting of many women from their homes, especially on the West Coast
   (E) a delay in the women's rights movement by confirming traditional values that kept women at home

(Questions 24 and 25 are based on the following quote):

"All the great civilizations of the past died out because contamination of their blood caused them to become decadent…In other words, in order to protect a certain culture, the type of human who created the culture must be preserved…If we were to divide mankind into three categories – the founders of culture, the bearers of culture, and the destroyers of culture, only the Aryans can be considered to be in the first category."

24. The quote is from

   (A) *The Communist Manifesto*
   (B) *Mein Kampf*
   (C) *What is to be Done?*
   (D) *The Diaries of the Nanking Massacre*
   (E) *Wealth of Nations*

25. The quote is meant to justify the belief in

   (A) democratic centralism
   (B) the pillaging of cities during times of war
   (C) imperialism
   (D) the existence of a master race
   (E) wars of national liberation

26. What dramatic political change occurred in Africa in the years that followed World War II?

   (A) African kingdoms were colonized by European nations.
   (B) A Pan African movement combined nations under a strong continental government.
   (C) Many African colonies gained independence from imperial powers.
   (D) Most African nations formed strong alliances with the Soviet Union.
   (E) Strong democratic governments were established in many nations.

27. Which of the following countries experienced a rapid growth in industrial output during the late 20th century?

   (A) China
   (B) England
   (C) Sweden
   (D) Peru
   (E) Haiti

(Questions 28 and 29 are based on the following chart):

POPULATION FOR MAJOR AREAS OF THE WORLD, 1900-2050

Major Area	1900	1950	1998	2050
Asia	947	1402	3585	5268
Africa	133	221	749	1766
Europe	408	547	729	628
Latin America	74	167	504	809
North America	82	172	305	392
Oceania	6	13	30	46
World (total)	1650	2521	5901	8909

28. What area of the world will experience the largest percentage increase in population growth between 1998 and 2050?

   (A) Asia
   (B) Africa
   (C) Europe
   (D) Latin America
   (E) North America

29. Which of the following predictions for future population distributions is supported by the data in the chart?

(A) North American populations will surpass European populations by 2050.
(B) Between 1998 and 2050, Asian populations will increase at higher percentage rates than they have in the past.
(C) Latin American population growth will level off by 2050.
(D) The low population levels in Oceania will almost certainly keep it from having much political and economic power in the world.
(E) Europe's share of world population has declined significantly since 1900, and the trend will continue in the future.

30. All of the following are major characteristics that distinguish the time period 1914-present from earlier eras EXCEPT:

(A) redefinition and repositioning of the west
(B) decrease in international contacts
(C) the democratic transition
(D) new reliance on non-religious philosophies
(E) questioning of systems of inequality

31. Which of the following revolutions/reforms did not take place during the 20th century?

(A) revolution for Mexican independence from Spain
(B) Bolshevik Revolution
(C) Chinese Cultural Revolution
(D) Revolution against apartheid in South Africa
(E) Indian nationalist revolution

32. Which of the following types of migrations most characterized the 20th century?

(A) from North America to South America
(B) from non-industrialized countries to industrialized countries
(C) from industrialized countries to non-industrialized countries
(D) from urban to rural areas
(E) from Southeast Asia to Korea and Japan

33. The Warsaw Pact formed directly as the result of the formation of

(A) the United Nations
(B) NATO
(C) the Yalta Conference
(D) the African National Conference
(E) the People's Republic of China

34. Migrations from which former colony created a large Muslim minority in France during the late 20th century?

(A) Egypt
(B) Syria
(C) Pakistan
(D) Indonesia
(E) Algeria

35. Which of the following is an important political consequence of the formation of multinational corporations in the late 20th century?

(A) Asian governments, such as those in China and Japan, have become more powerful than those in the West.
(B) The United Nations now strictly regulates business practices of multinational corporations.
(C) National governments have experienced increasing difficulty in regulating multinational corporations.
(D) Many more equal trade agreements have been made between multinational corporations and the governments of non-industrialized countries.
(E) Worst cases of labor and environmental abuses have tended to occur in capitalist countries where governments ignore the problems.

DOCUMENT BASED QUESTION

Directions: The following question is based on the accompanying Documents 1-7. The documents have been edited for the purpose of this exercise.

This question is designed to test your ability to work with and understand historical documents. Write an essay that

- Has a relevant thesis and supports that thesis with evidence from the documents.
- Uses all or all but one of the documents.
- Analyzes the documents by grouping them in as many appropriate ways as possible, and does not simply summarize the documents individually.
- Takes into account both the sources of the documents and the authors' points of view.

You may refer to relevant historical information not mentioned in the documents.

Using the documents, analyze the forces of cultural convergence and diversity in the world during the modern time period (1914-Present). Is cultural convergence or diversity the best model for understanding increased intercultural contact in the modern time period? **What additional kinds of document(s)** would help assess the historical significance of convergence and diversity in this period?

Document 1

October 9, Macau. Here we are, halfway around the world, in the Portuguese colony of Macau – a little nub jutting from the coast of China. Few people here speak English, and life on the streets seems a world apart from the urban rhythms of New York, Chicago, or Los Angeles. Then I turn the corner and stand face to face with (who else?) Ronald McDonald! After eating who-knows-what for so long, forgive me for giving in to the lure of the Big Man. But the most amazing thing is that the food – the burger, the fries, and the drink – looks, smells, and tastes exactly the same as it does back home 10,000 miles away!

George Ritzer, American Sociologist
The McDonaldization of Society, 1993

Document 2

[A man sits in a coffee house in some Middle Eastern city] drinking a cup of coffee or tea, perhaps smoking a cigarette, reading a newspaper, playing a board game, and listening with half an ear to whatever is coming out of the radio or television installed in the corner…In modern times the dominating factor in the consciousness of most Middle Easterners has been the impact of Europe, later of the West more generally, and the transformation – some would say dislocation – which it has brought.

Bernard Lewis
British Writer
The Middle East, 1995

Document 3

Our...goal is to prevent regimes that sponsor terror from threatening America or our friends and allies with weapons of mass destruction. Some of these regimes have been pretty quiet since September the 11th. But we know their true nature. North Korea is a regime arming with missiles and weapons of mass destruction, while starving its citizens.

Iran aggressively pursues these weapons and exports terror, while an unelected few repress the Iranian people's hope for freedom.

Iraq continues to flaunt its hostility toward America and to support terror. The Iraqi regime has plotted to develop anthrax, and nerve gas, and nuclear weapons for over a decade...This is a regime that agreed to international inspections – then kicked out the inspectors. This is a regime that has something to hide from the civilized world.

States like these, and their terrorist allies, constitute an axis of evil, arming to threaten the peace of the world. By seeking weapons of mass destruction, these regimes pose a grave and growing danger. They could provide these arms to terrorists, giving them the means to match their hatred. They could attack our allies or attempt to blackmail the United States. In any of these cases, the price of indifference would be catastrophic.

George W. Bush
President of the United States
State of the Union Address, January 29, 2002

Document 4

How should countries go about their relations with one another in this complicated and diverse world? It is a question that is on the minds of many people.

We are of the view that for a smooth conduct of state-to-state relations and for lasting peace and common prosperity, all countries should act in compliance with the following principles:

First, politically, they should respect each other, seek common ground while putting aside differences and endeavour to expand areas of agreement. Our world is a diverse place like a rainbow of many colours. Civilizations, social systems, development models, as different as they may be, should nonetheless respect one another, learning from each other's strong points to make up for one's own weakness amid competition and comparison and achieving common development by seeking common ground while shelving differences.

Second, economically, they should complement and benefit one another, deepen their cooperation and achieve common development. With economic globalisation developing in such depth, no country can expect to achieve economic development without going for effective economic and technological cooperation with other countries and actively participating in international division of labour.

Third, culturally, they should step up exchanges and enhance understanding and mutual emulation. Diversity in the world is a basic characteristic of human society, and also the key condition for a lively and dynamic world as we see today. The proud history, culture and traditions that make each country different from others are all parts of human civilisation. Every nation, every culture, must have some strong points of its own, and all should respect one another, draw on each other's strength to make up for its own weakness and strive to achieve common progress.

Hu Jintao
President of China
Speech to the Australian Parliament, October 24, 2003

Document 5

The first transatlantic telegraph cable was laid in 1866. By the turn of the century, the entire world was connected by telegraph, and communication times fell from months to minutes. The cost of a three-minute telephone call from New York to London in current prices dropped from about $250 in 1930 to a few cents today. In more recent years, the number of voice paths across the Atlantic has skyrocketed from 100,000 in 1986 to more than 2 million today. The number of internet hosts has risen from 5000 in 1986 to more than 30 million now.

Martin Wolf
Economics Commentator, *The Financial Times*
2001

Document 6

Just beyond the horizon of current events lie two possible political figures – both bleak, neither democratic. The first is a retribalization of large swaths of humankind by war and bloodshed: a threatened [nationalization of states] in which culture is pitted against culture, people against people, tribe against tribe – a Jihad in the name of a hundred narrowly conceived faiths against every kind of interdependence, every kind of artificial social cooperation and civic mutuality. The second is being borne in on us by the onrush of economic and ecological forces that demand integration and uniformity and that mesmerize the world with fast music, fast computers, fast food – with MTV, Macintosh, and McDonald's, pressing nations into one homogeneous global network: one McWorld tied together by technology, ecology, communications, and commerce. The planet is falling precipitously apart and coming reluctantly together at the very same moment.

Benjamin Barber
"Jihad vs. McWorld"
1992

Document 7

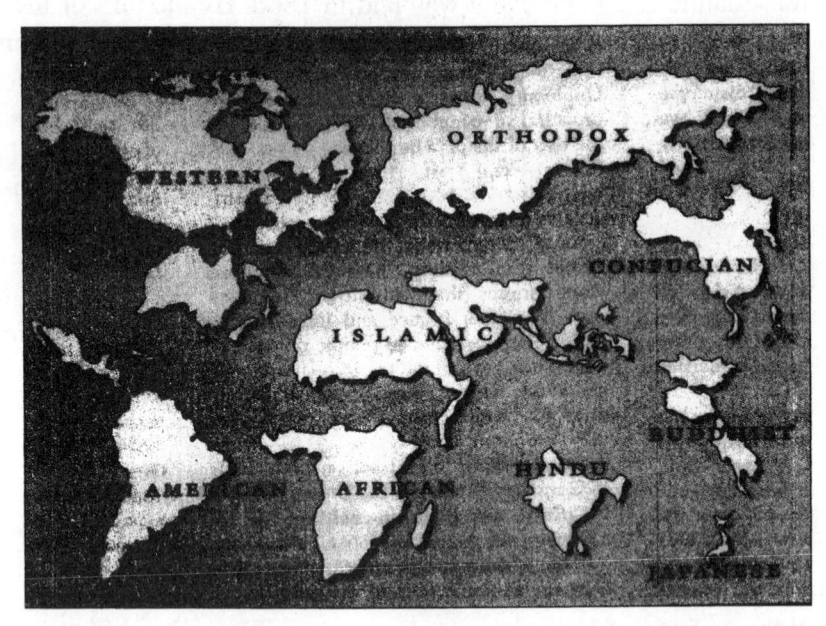

© 1996 The Economist Newspaper Ltd. All rights reserved. Reprinted with permission, Further reproduction prohibited. www.economist.com

PART III

Sample Examinations

Sample Examination I

This section should be completed in 55 minutes.

Directions: Each of the questions or incomplete statements is followed by five suggested answers or completions. Select the one that best answers the question or completes the statement.

1. All of the following are geographical characteristics that isolated the development of early Chinese civilization EXCEPT:

    (A) The Gobi Desert was north of Ancient China.
    (B) The deserts of the Xinjiang lay to the west of Ancient China.
    (C) The great east/west rivers of Ancient China were not navigable.
    (D) The Himalayas lay to the southwest, blocking China from other early civilizations.
    (E) The vast Pacific Ocean lay to the east of Ancient China.

2. Which of the following is NOT true of the major Amerindian civilizations in Central and South America prior to the arrival of Europeans?

    (A) Their economies were based primarily on trade.
    (B) They constructed monumental buildings.
    (C) They had major urban centers.
    (D) They had differentiation of labor.
    (E) They had social classes.

3. "Pax Mongolica" is a reference to the

    (A) disruption caused by Muslim invasions all across Eurasia
    (B) disease that spread along the trade routes protected by Mongols
    (C) land controlled by the Great Khan
    (D) peace brought about by Mongol rule across Eurasia
    (E) tax farming practices of the Mongols

4. Which of the following did Mohandas Gandhi, Martin Luther King, and Nelson Mandela have in common?

(A) They practiced non-violence to relieve oppression of the groups they represented.
(B) They led equality movements in the United States during the 20th century.
(C) They led independence movements during the 20th century.
(D) They were religious leaders before they were political leaders.
(E) None ever held formal political leadership positions in their respective countries.

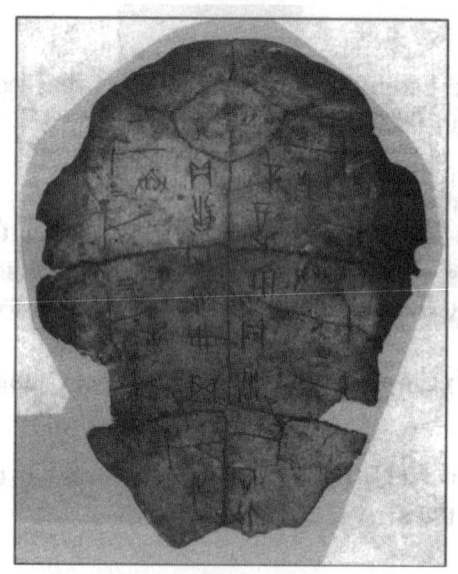

Bulliet, Richard. The Earth and its Peoples, Second Edition. Copyright © 2001 by Houghton Mifflin Company. Used with permission.

5. The tortoise shell pictured above was used in Ancient China for what purpose?

(A) to teach children Confucian sayings
(B) to designate social class
(C) to communicate with the ancestors
(D) to record agricultural production
(E) to map directions to various places in China

6. During which era in world history was a sharp divide created between "have" and "have not" countries by industrialization?

(A) 200 B.C.E. to 600 C.E.
(B) 600 C.E. to 1450 C.E.
(C) 1450 to 1750 C.E.
(D) 1750-1914 C.E.
(E) 1914-Present C.E.

7. "Brahmans, Kshatriyas, Vishniyas, Shudras" are examples of different

   (A) types of Buddhist monks
   (B) Indian gods
   (C) areas conquered by the Romans
   (D) early Indian castes
   (E) aspects of a single Indian god as represented by the arms

8. Which of the following best describes both the Abbasid Caliphate and Europe during the late 1st millennium?

   (A) Both were united under strong central governments.
   (B) Both had many characteristics of advanced levels of civilization.
   (C) Both were united by strong religious organization.
   (D) Neither had strong religious or political organizations.
   (E) In both areas, Jews generally were considered to be inferior to polytheistic people.

9. Which of the following was a characteristic of the time period 1750-1914 that distinguished it from others as a distinct period in world history?

   (A) European dominance globally of long-distance trade
   (B) the democratic transition
   (C) the eastern hemisphere's first contact with the western hemisphere
   (D) Islam's emergence as the largest religion in the world
   (E) slavery as the dominant labor system for most western societies

10. All of the following were significant differences between North American and Latin American colonies EXCEPT:

    (A) North American colonies depended more heavily on slave labor than did Latin American colonies.
    (B) Many North American colonies were established by joint stock companies; Latin American colonies were established by Spanish and Portuguese governments.
    (C) Gold and silver were more important to the overall economy of Latin America.
    (D) Latin American colonies employed the mita and encomienda labor systems; North American colonies did not.
    (E) The government structures of Latin American colonies were less likely to incorporate ideas of self-government into their political systems.

11. During the time period from 600 to 1200 C.E., in which part of the world did women have the right to own property and to divorce their husbands?

(A) western Europe
(B) Tang/Song China
(C) Muslim lands of Southwest Asia
(D) India
(E) Western Africa

(Questions 12 and 13 refer to the following engraving)"

General Research Division
The New York Public Library
Astor Lenox and Tilden Foundations

12. The woman in the engraving is

(A) sacrificing herself to the gods in order to bring good fortune to her people
(B) following societal expectations that a widow jump into her husband's funeral pyre
(C) acknowledging European dominance of her country by following rules set by an imperialist country
(D) demonstrating her ability to survive a death by fire
(E) taking part in a ceremony meant to pay honor to European visitors

Sample Examination I

13. In what part of the world did Europeans encounter the scene depicted in the engraving?

    (A) the Ottoman Empire
    (B) the Swahili states in eastern Africa
    (C) India
    (D) Southeast Asia
    (E) South America

14. They wandered from place to place throughout medieval Europe representing the church. Some of them emphasized the spread of knowledge and learning, and others were noted for their kindness and love of people and animals.

    What were they?

    (A) bishops
    (B) cardinals
    (C) abbots
    (D) friars
    (E) legates

15. Which of the following correctly contrasts Tang and Song China?

    (A) Buddhism was politically influential during the early Tang, whereas most political elites during Song times were neo-Confucian.
    (B) Song China was militarily superior to Tang, and Song rulers controlled much more land space in Asia than Tang did.
    (C) Women during Song times had more equal status to men than Tang women did.
    (D) Song cities had more extensive and regular contact with foreigners than Tang cities had.
    (E) Song China occupied lands to the north, whereas Tang China dominated southern Asia from India to Annam (Vietnam).

16. Which part of the world showed a significant decline in its proportion of world population during the 20th century?

    (A) South America
    (B) East Asia
    (C) The Indian subcontinent
    (D) Europe
    (E) Oceania

17. Which of the following was NOT a characteristic of the Neolithic (Agricultural) Revolution?

    (A) Agriculture began in one place (the Middle East) and gradually spread to other areas of the world.
    (B) The first farmers most likely used both fire and specialized tools to raise their crops.
    (C) In all likelihood, women played a major role in the transition from food gathering to food cultivation.
    (D) Emmer wheat and barley were among the first plants to be cultivated.
    (E) In most cases the Agricultural Revolution included both the domestication of animals and the cultivation of food crops.

18. Which of the following was NOT an invention of the Industrial Revolution of the late 18th and 19th century?

    (A) cotton gin
    (B) railroad engine
    (C) spinning mule
    (D) flying shuttle
    (E) moveable type

19. According to the belief in the Mandate of Heaven, dynasties fall primarily because the rulers

    (A) have less power than their warlords
    (B) do not fulfill their obligations to be good and benevolent
    (C) become too soft and charitable
    (D) are no longer able to effectively communicate with the ancestors
    (E) forget that they are gods on earth to be worshipped and revered as divinities

(Questions 20 and 21 refer to the following chart):

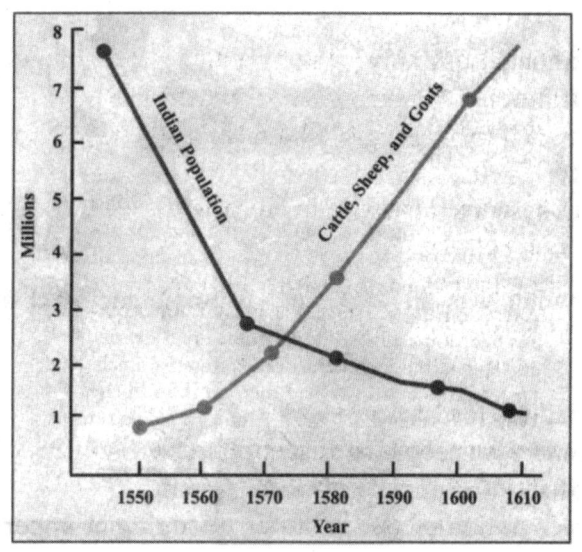

WORLD CIVILIZATIONS, 3rd ed. by Peter N. Stearns, Michael Adas, Stuart B. Schwartz and Marc Jason Gilbert. Copyright © 2001 by Addison-Wesley Educational Publishers Inc. Reprinted by Permission of Pearson Education, Inc.

20. Which of the following is the best explanation for the trends shown in the chart above?

   (A) The Indian population migrated north, and the Spanish began a special breeding program for cattle, sheep, and goats.
   (B) Overgrazing of animals led to the death of many Indians.
   (C) The Spanish brought both livestock and knowledge of birth control methods with them from Europe.
   (D) The Indian population died of disease, and cattle, sheep, and goats were first introduced to the New World from Europe.
   (E) Fewer Indians were needed for subsistence farming because livestock meant that food was more plentiful.

21. The patterns shown in the chart reflect a phenomenon in world history known as the

   (A) Middle Passage
   (B) Land bridge Crossing
   (C) Great Trek
   (D) Social Contract
   (E) Columbian Exchange

22. Which of the following was formed as a conservative reaction to late 18th and early 19th century revolutions in Europe?

   (A) the French National Assembly
   (B) the Concert of Europe
   (C) NATO
   (D) Triple Alliance
   (E) the continental system

23. Which of the following was an important principle included in Woodrow Wilson's Fourteen Points?

   (A) German reparations for war damages
   (B) self determination for people in Eastern Europe
   (C) the creation of an international mandate system
   (D) nation-state recognition of all territories belonging to imperialist countries
   (E) reconstruction of war-torn France and Britain

24. All of the following are similarities of the socio-economic foundations of the Roman and Han Empires EXCEPT:

   (A) Both empires were economically based in agriculture.
   (B) Both empires built great roads that improved commerce and troop movement.
   (C) Both empires allowed almost no social mobility, so that individuals had little opportunity to enhance their socio-economic standing.
   (D) Both empires had major cosmopolitan cities linked together by commerce and communication.
   (E) Conflicts over who owned the land and how the land was to be used caused turmoil in both empires.

25. "Certain women, who were called acllas, or 'the Chosen,' were destined for lifelong virginity...[They were] known for their beauty as well as their chastity."

   The phrase above describes a practice of the

   (A) Aztecs
   (B) Anasazi
   (C) Inca
   (D) Toltecs
   (E) Maya

Sample Examination I

26. The Vedic Age of Indian civilization gave rise to all of the following important traditions EXCEPT:

    (A) a caste system
    (B) literary epics
    (C) Sanskrit as a writing system
    (D) strong central governments
    (E) Buddhism

27. Before 600 C.E. the Bedouin social structure on the Arabian peninsula was characterized most fundamentally by

    (A) loyalty to kinship groups and clashes with rival clans
    (B) their tributary status to the Sasanid Empire
    (C) urbanization supported by strong connections to Indian Ocean trade routes
    (D) strong religious ties to Zoroastrianism
    (E) an extremely large gap between the rich and poor

28. The manorial system in medieval Europe was characterized by all of the following EXCEPT:

    (A) relative self-sufficiency
    (B) a well-defined relationship between agricultural workers and landlords
    (C) a barter economy
    (D) structures built to protect inhabitants from outside attacks
    (E) regular tributes paid to dominating civilizations to the east

29. The status of women in Zhou China is best described as

    (A) higher than that of women in Ancient Egypt and Mesopotamia
    (B) subordinate to the status of men, as defined within the confines of a highly patriarchal family structure
    (C) equal yet different to the status of men, as evidenced by the enduring influence of yin and yang
    (D) subordinate to the status of men, although Zhou China was a matrilineal society
    (E) very low in the early part of the dynasty, but much improved by the time the dynasty ended in the 3rd century B.C.E.

30. Which of the following achievements is mismatched with the civilization?

    (A) Japan: strong steel swords
    (B) Yuan: cannons
    (C) Mongols: conquest of Russia
    (D) Islamic Eurasia: astronomy and engineering
    (E) Koreans: horse stirrups

31. Which of the following experienced a rapid growth of industrial output in the late 19th century?

   (A) Japan
   (B) China
   (C) India
   (D) Mexico
   (E) Spain

32. Which technology was first used during World War II?

   (A) airplanes
   (B) tanks
   (C) the atom bomb
   (D) machine guns
   (E) submarines

33. Though the Ming dynasty is not known for its technological advancement, they did excel in

   (A) metallurgy
   (B) tools for agriculture
   (C) porcelain production
   (D) firearm production
   (E) bridge building

34. The most powerful political figures in this government were senators. The senate elected consuls to serve for one year, and other assemblies, such as tribunals, were also allowed. This government existed in

   (A) Ancient Greece
   (B) Ancient Rome
   (C) Han China
   (D) Mauryan India
   (E) Gupta India

Sample Examination I 219

35. Which of the following is the most important factor that fostered the spread of Islam in the century after the death of Muhammad in 632?

    (A) the lack of political unity in India
    (B) the decline of the military power of the Seljuk Turks
    (C) political and religious divisions within the Byzantine and Sasanid Empires
    (D) the failure of the Christian knights from Europe to defeat the Muslims during the Crusades
    (E) the political solidarity among the Muslim leaders that followed Muhammad

© Library of Congress

36. For which 20th century war was the poster above designed?

    (A) World War I
    (B) World War II
    (C) Korean War
    (D) Vietnam War
    (E) Boxer Rebellion

37. The political and social structure of the Mongols in the years preceding their conquests was based primarily on

    (A) education; only highly educated people could be elites
    (B) kinship ties; powerful clans dominated weaker families
    (C) trading skills; merchants had the highest status
    (D) religious ties; Muslims and Christians were given low status
    (E) Confucian scholarship

38. Which of the following ancient civilizations had a city-state form of government?

   (A) Sumeria
   (B) Egypt
   (C) Persia
   (D) China
   (E) Rome

39. What was the main purpose of the Marshall Plan?

   (A) to form an all-European Union
   (B) to protect eastern Europe from attack by the Soviet Union
   (C) to form an international peace organization
   (D) to help to rebuild war-torn countries of western Europe
   (E) to arrange for independence for African colonies

40. Sumerians, Akkadians, Babylonians were all civilizations that were centered in ancient

   (A) Mesopotamia
   (B) Indus Valley
   (C) Egypt
   (D) China
   (E) India

41. Which of the following was a rebellion that defied occupation by an imperialist power in the 19th century?

   (A) Crimean War
   (B) Meiji Restoration
   (C) Boer War
   (D) Russian Revolution
   (E) Sepoy Rebellion

42. Which of the following was NOT a factor that caused the Western Roman, Han, and Gupta Empires to fall between 200 and 600 C.E. EXCEPT?

   (A) All suffered devastating attacks from the Huns.
   (B) All experienced significant deterioration in the power of their belief systems to affect their citizens' lives.
   (C) All had problems protecting and maintaining their borders.
   (D) All experienced a deterioration of political institutions.
   (E) Plagues and epidemics followed the trade routes, reducing populations in many areas.

43. All of the following characterize the era between 600 and 1450 EXCEPT:

(A) Many belief systems crossed cultural groups and political boundaries.
(B) Hegemony was established by China.
(C) Cross cultural exchange broadened to include Africa and Europe.
(D) The Mongol conquests/migrations affected almost all areas of Eurasia.
(E) Continuing contacts were establishes among three areas of the world: Eurasia, the Americas, and Oceania.

Louvre, Paris, France/Bridgeman Art Library

44. The tablet above is an example of

(A) Egyptian hieroglyphics
(B) Inca Quechan
(C) early Chinese writing
(D) Korean hangul
(E) Mesopotamia cuneiform

45. All of the following were inventions/contributions attributed to the Chinese EXCEPT:

(A) gothic architecture
(B) chain-driven mechanical clock
(C) gunpowder
(D) the mariner's compass
(E) moveable type printing

46. All of the following are characteristics of western Europe in the 1500s EXCEPT:

    (A) the growth of trade
    (B) the increasing strength of the Roman Catholic Church
    (C) the decline of the feudal system
    (D) an increasingly urban population
    (E) the development of improved weaponry

47. Which of the following civilizations had the longest life span?

    (A) Ancient Greece
    (B) Ancient Rome
    (C) Han China
    (D) Mauryan India
    (E) Gupta India

48. The Berlin Conference of 1884-5 was called to avoid war as a result of

    (A) competition between the United States and western European nations
    (B) conflict over national borders among European nations
    (C) imperialist competition for land in Africa
    (D) quarreling over spheres of influence in China
    (E) widespread rebellions in areas of the world controlled by imperialist nations

49. The Twenty-One Demands issued in 1915 allowed Japan a great deal of control over

    (A) Russia
    (B) Korea
    (C) The Philippines
    (D) Southeast Asia
    (E) China

50. Which of the following societies had the least contact with foreign nations during the period from 1450-1750?

    (A) Japan
    (B) India
    (C) Ottoman Empire
    (D) Latin America
    (E) China

51. Which of the following countries was least affected by the Great Depression of the 1930s?

(A) Germany
(B) The United States
(C) Argentina
(D) Britain
(E) Japan

52. Which of the following statements accurately compares the Mughal and Ottoman Empires?

(A) The Indian government was more highly centralized.
(B) The Mughal rulers were Hindu, and the Ottoman sultans were Muslim.
(C) Indian culture was much less diverse than Ottoman culture was.
(D) India was Shi'ite Muslim; the Ottoman were Sunnis
(E) Most Indian people were non-Muslim, as compared to a mostly Muslim citizenry in the Ottoman Empire.

53. Westernization of Russia during the 17th and 18th centuries came about largely through the

(A) efforts of Peter the Great and his successors
(B) invasion of Russia by Sweden
(C) desire of European countries to seek new markets to the east
(D) establishment of the Eastern Orthodox Church as the official religion
(E) invasion of Slavic areas by the Mongols

54. This 20th century philosophy emphasized equality and the destruction of class distinctions, although political power was held centrally by a few people. It also stressed the importance of agriculture and the peasants. What is it?

(A) Leninism
(B) Stalinism
(C) Maoism
(D) Fascism
(E) Liberalism

55. Which of the Jesuit compromises with Chinese culture most upset the Catholic Pope?

   (A) their adoption of Chinese dress and mannerisms
   (B) the memorization of Confucian texts and use of this ideology to explain Christianity
   (C) their use of the Chinese language during Mass
   (D) their acceptance of ancestor worship as compatible with Christianity
   (E) their acceptance of the 8-fold path as compatible with Christianity

56. Which of the following European nations unified as a nation during the late 19th century?

   (A) France
   (B) The Netherlands
   (C) Spain
   (D) Germany
   (E) Britain

(Questions 57 and 58 are based on the following quotes):

"On the first day of January, as a sign of rejoicing, wishes for the new year and century will be exchanged...

We have...given orders, made dispositions, and founded institutions indispensable for increasing our trade with foreigners....

Learn how to draw plans and charts and how to use the compass and other naval indicators....

Western dress shall be worn by all the boyars, members of our councils and of our court...

All court attendants....provincial service men, government officials of all ranks, military men......must shave their beards and moustaches..."

57. The quotes are from decrees issued by

   (A) Peter the Great
   (B) Suleiman the Magnificent
   (C) Kangxi
   (D) Babur
   (E) Wanli

58. The decrees set in motion which of the following conflicts within the ruler's country?

    (A) asceticism vs. more practical religious requirements
    (B) isolationism vs. active trading with other nations
    (C) absolutism vs. rule by law
    (D) military vs. civilian rule
    (E) Slavic vs. western values and customs

59. Which of the following is the best reason why constitutional experiments were more successful in North America than in South America during the 19th century?

    (A) North American experiments were based on the parliament of the mother country. Mother countries in South America were authoritarian.
    (B) South American governments generally ruled more independently from their mother countries.
    (C) Military leaders were much stronger in North America.
    (D) South American revolutions occurred much earlier in history.
    (E) Colonial governments in North America were led by the educated elite; South American governments were usually controlled by peasants.

(Questions 60 and 61 are based on the following plaque):

*Plaque/Edo peoples/Nigeria/Mid 16th-17th century/copper alloy/
H x W x D: 47 x 34.2 x 8.2 cm (18 1/2 x 13 7/16 x 3 1/4 in.) Gift of Joseph H. Hirshhorn to the Smithsonian Institution in 1979. Photograph by Franko Khoury. National Museum of African Art, 85-19-18, Smithsonian Institution.*

60. The plaque was made by craftsmen in

    (A) Benin
    (B) South Africa
    (C) Swahili
    (D) Zimbabwe
    (E) Egypt

61. The soldiers in the top background came "from the sea" and were from

    (A) Britain
    (B) Southeast Asia
    (C) Portugal
    (D) Brazil
    (E) Korea

62. During the 18th century, the migration of English workers from the countryside to the cities dramatically increased as a direct result of

    (A) Faster and better water transportation
    (B) better living conditions in London and other industrialized cities
    (C) the enclosure movement
    (D) job opportunities in cities caused by the emigration of British citizens to the Americas
    (E) improved ground transportation, including the building of railroads

63. During which of the following centuries did the largest number of governments experiment with democracy?

    (A) 16th century
    (B) 17th century
    (C) 18th century
    (D) 19th century
    (E) 20th century

64. Which country(ies) made use of joint stock companies in order to participate in the Great Circuit trade?

    I. England
    II. The Netherlands
    III. Spain
    IV. Portugal

    (A) I only
    (B) I and II only
    (C) I, II, and III only
    (D) II and III only
    (E) I, II, III, and IV

65. Under this political rule, Japan developed a "cult of the emperor," but was ruled by a few very powerful men who emphasized modernization of military, political, and economic systems. They also promoted trade with western nations. The political rule was known as

   (A) the Fujiwara reign
   (B) the Tokugawa Shogunate
   (C) the Meiji Restoration
   (D) the Strengthening Movement
   (E) the Minimoto Era

66. The nickname "Banana Republic" was granted to many South American countries because they

   (A) exported only agricultural products
   (B) imported most of their food from other countries
   (C) had no natural mineral resources
   (D) depended heavily on one product for economic health
   (E) tried to be self-sufficient, with few or non imports and exports

(Questions 67 and 68 are based on the following excerpt):

WE THE PEOPLES...DETERMINED

- to save succeeding generations from the scourge of war, which twice in our lifetime has brought untold sorrow to mankind, and
- to reaffirm faith in fundamental human rights, in the dignity and worth of the human person, in the equal rights of men and women and of nations large and small, and
- to establish conditions under which justice and respect for the obligations arising from treaties and other sources of international law can be maintained, and
- to promote social progress and better standards of life in larger freedom,

AND FOR THESE ENDS

- to practice tolerance and live together in peace with one another as good neighbours, and
- to unite our strength to maintain international peace and security, and
- to ensure, by the acceptance of principles and the institution of methods, that armed force shall not be used, save in the common interest, and
- to employ international machinery for the promotion of the economic and social advancement of all peoples,

67. The excerpt is from the

    (A) Versailles Treaty
    (B) Charter of the United Nations
    (C) Congress of Vienna Agreement
    (D) Munich Agreement
    (E) Marshall Plan

68. The people that wrote the excerpt formed as a group

    (A) after the Napoleonic Wars
    (B) in the years immediately following World War I
    (C) immediately before World War II broke out
    (D) immediately after World War II ended
    (E) in the late 20th century

69. Which of the following statements most accurately describes changes in China from the time period 1450-1750 to the era between 1750 and 1914?

    (A) China's political and economic power was significantly stronger during the later era.
    (B) During the later era, China's political system became less centralized with power shifting to regional leaders, but Chinese merchants became much more prosperous.
    (C) During the later era, the highly centralized Chinese government focused successfully on keeping foreign influence to a minimum.
    (D) Between 1450 and 1750 China participated broadly in world trade circuits; between 1750 and 1914 China traded primarily with other East Asian countries.
    (E) Chinese political and economic power was very strong between 1450 and 1750, but was seriously disrupted by western imperialist countries between 1750 and 1914.

70. Which of the following revolutions happened first?

    (A) French Revolution
    (B) Haitian Revolution
    (C) Russian Revolution
    (D) Chinese Communist Revolution
    (E) American Revolution

DOCUMENT BASED QUESTION

(suggested writing time – 40 minutes)

Directions: The following question is based on the accompanying Documents 1-7. This question is designed to test your ability to work with and understand historical documents. Write an essay that:

- Has a relevant thesis and supports that thesis with evidence from the documents.
- Uses all or all but one of the documents.
- Analyzes the documents by grouping them in as many appropriate ways as possible. Does not simply summarize the documents individually.
- Takes into account both the sources of the documents and the authors' points of view.

You may refer to relevant historical information not mentioned in the documents.

During the time period between 1100 and 1500 C.E., great cities existed in many parts of the world. Are these cities best understood by analyzing their commonalities or by analyzing their differences? Historians support both views.

Based on the following documents, discuss the commonalities and differences among cities around the world between 1100 and 1500. What kinds of additional documentation would help you better evaluate the importance of commonalities vs. differences?

Document 1

Source: Charter of Henry I for London (1130-1133)

Henry, by the grace of God, king of the English, to the archbishop of Canterbury, and to the bishops and abbots, and earls and barons and justices and sheriffs, and to all his liegemen, both French and English, of the whole of England, greeting.

…the citizens shall appoint as sheriff from themselves whomsoever they may choose, and shall appoint from among themselves as justice whomsoever they choose to look after the pleas of my crown and the pleadings which arise in connexion with them. …and a man of London shall not be fined at mercy except according to his "were," [ability to pay] that is to say, up to one hundred shillings: This applies to an offence which can be punished by a fine.

…And let all debtors to the citizens of London discharge their debts, or prove in London that they do not owe them; and if they refuse either to pay, or to come and make such proof, then the citizens to whom the debts are due may take pledges within the city either from the borough or from the village or from the county in which the debtor lives. And the citizens shall have their hunting chases, as well and fully as had their predecessors, to wit, in Chiltern and Middlesex and Surrey.

Document 2

Source: "A Description of Foreign Peoples," Zhau Rugua, mid-13th century

The capital of the country [Arabia], called Maluoba, is an important center for the trade of foreign people…The streets are more than fifty feet broad; in the middle is a roadway twenty feet broad and four feet high for use of camels, horses, and oxen carrying goods about. On either side, for the convenience of pedestrians' business, there are sidewalks paved with green and bluish black flagstones of surpassing beauty….

Very rich persons use a measure instead of scales in business transactions of gold or silver. The markets are noisy and bustling, and are filled with a great store of gold and silver damasks, brocades, and similar wares. The artisans have the true artistic spirt. The king, the officials, and all the people serve Heaven.

They also have a Buddha by the name of Mahiawu [Muhammad]. Every seven days they cut their hair and clip their fingernails. At the New Year for a whole month they fast and chant prayers. Daily they pray to Heaven five times.

Document 3

Source: *The Travels of Marco Polo*, 1324

The new royal city is a perfect square, each of its sides being 6 miles long. The city wall has 12 gates, 3 on each side of the square. The whole city was laid out by line. The streets are so straight that if you stand at one gate, you can see the gate on the other side of the city.

....there were in the city twelve guilds of the different crafts, and that each guild had twelve thousand houses in the occupation of its workmen. Each of these houses contains at least twelve men, whilst some contain twenty and some forty....

The throngs of inhabitants and the number of houses in Khanbalik are greater than the mind can grasp. The suburbs have even more people than the city itself. Within each suburb, there are many hotels at which merchants can stay.

Everything that is most rare and valuable in the world finds its way to this city. This is particularly true for rich goods from India, such as precious gems, pearls, and spices. From other parts of Cathay [China] itself, at least 1,000 carriages and packhorses loaded with raw silk enter the city each day.

Since the Great Kaan occupied the city he has ordained that each of the twelve thousand bridges should be provided with a guard of ten men, in case of any disturbance, or of any being so rash as to plot treason or insurrection against him.

...In the center of the city is a great bell, which is rung every night. After the third stroke, no one dares to be found on the streets, except for some emergency. In such necessary cases, the person is required to carry a light. Groups of 30 or 40 guards patrol the streets all night, looking for people who are out of their houses after the great bell has rung.

Document 4

Source: *History of Florence from 1380 to 1405*, Gregorio Dati

When springtime comes and the whole world rejoices, every Florentine begins to think about organizing a magnificent celebration on the feast day of St. John the Baptist [June 24]... For two months in advance, everyone is planning marriage feasts or other celebrations in honor of the day. There are preparations for the horse races, the costumes of the retinues, the flags, and the trumpets; there are the pennants and the wax candles and other things which the subject territories offer to the Commune. Messengers are sent to obtain provisions for the banquets, and horses come from everywhere to run in the races. The whole city is engaged...

Early on the morning of the day before the holiday, each guild has a display outside of its shops of its fine ware, its ornaments, and jewels. There are cloths of gold and silk sufficient to adorn ten kingdoms...Then, at the third hour, there is a solemn procession of clerics, priests, monks, and friars, and there are so many [religious] orders, and so many relics of saints, that the procession seems endless.

Document 5

Source: Hernan Cortes' diary, 1519

…From up there [the top of the city's central pyramid] we saw the three causeways that led into Mexico – the causeway of Iztapalapan, by which we had come four days earlier, the causeway of Tiapcopan, by which we were later to flee, on the night of our great defeat…and that of Tepeyacac. We saw the aqueduct that comes from Chapultepec to supply the town with sweet water, and at intervals along the three causeways the bridgeswhich let the water flow from one part of the lake to another. We saw a multitude of boats upon the great lake, some coming with provisions, and some going off loaded with merchandise…and in these towns we saw temples and oratories shaped like towers and bastions, all shining white, a wonderful thing to behold. And we saw the terraced houses, and along the causeways other towers and chapels that looked like fortresses. So, having gazed at all this and reflected upon it, we turned our eyes to the great marketplace and the host of people down there who were buying and selling: the hum and the murmur of their voices could have been heard for more than a league. And among us were soldiers who had been in many parts of the world, at Constantinople, all over Italy and at Rome: and they all said they had never seen a market so well ordered, so large, and so crowded with people.

Document 6

© *Sandro Santioli*

An Ancient Map of Florence, Italy

Document 7

Source: "Of the Kingdom of Tombuto [Timbuktu]", Leo Africanus [visitor from Morocco, early 16th century]

The houses here are built in the shape of bells, the walls are stakes or hurdles plastered over with clay and the houses covered with reeds. Yet there is a most stately temple to be seen, the walls whereof are made of stone and lime; and a royal palace also built by a most excellent artist from Granada. Here are many shops of artificers, and merchants, and especially of such as weave linen and cotton cloth. And hither do the Barbary merchants bring cloth of Europe. All the women of this region except maidservants go with their faces covered, and sell food. The inhabitants, and especially strangers that reside there, are exceeding rich, inasmuch, that the king that now has married both his daughters unto rich merchants. Here are many wells, containing most sweet water; and so often as the river Niger overfloweth, they convey the water thereof by certain sluices into the town. Corn, cattle, milk, and butter this region yieldeth in great abundance, but salt is very scarce here; for it is brought hither by land from Tegaza, which is five hundred miles distant....

Here are great store of doctors, judges, priests, and other learned men, that are bountifully maintained at the king's cost and charges. And hither are brought diverse manuscripts or written books out of Barbary, which are sold for more money than any other merchandise....

The inhabitants are people of a gentle and cheerful disposition, and spend a great part of the night in singing and dancing through all the streets of the city....

CHANGE OVER TIME ESSAY

(suggested planning and writing time – 40 minutes)

Choose ONE of the areas listed below and analyze how political structures/sources of political power changed from the era beginning in 1450 to the era ending in 1914. Be sure to describe the area's political structures/sources of power around 1450 as your starting point, and describe both changes AND continuities within a global historical context.

East Asia   Sub-Saharan Africa

Western Europe   The Middle East

South Asia

COMPARATIVE ESSAY

(suggested planning and writing time – 40 minutes)

Between 1450 and 1750 rulers of the so-called "Gunpowder Empires" faced many problems in building and/or maintaining the strength of their empires. Choose TWO of the empires below and compare the problems that each faced, as well as the solutions that their respective rulers tried in order to solve the problems. Include within your essay your estimation of which of the two empires was more successful and why.

Ottoman Empire
Saffavid Empire
Mughal Empire
Russian Empire
Ming Empire
Qing Empire
Tokugawa Shogunate

No testing material on this page.

Sample Examination II

This section should be completed in 55 minutes.

Directions: Each of the questions or incomplete statements is followed by five suggested answers or completions. Select the one that best answers the question or completes the statement.

1. All of the following were pastoral nomads that invaded and/or settled in lands around the Mediterranean in ancient times EXCEPT:

    (A) Celts
    (B) Bantus
    (C) Hittites
    (D) Hyksos
    (E) Israelites

2. Which of the following correctly compares belief systems in Ancient Egypt and Mesopotamia?

    (A) Egyptians believed in an afterlife; the Mesopotamians did not.
    (B) Egyptians were polytheistic; most Mesopotamians were monotheistic.
    (C) Egyptian beliefs tended to be more optimistic and positive than Mesopotamian beliefs.
    (D) Mesopotamians had more female deities than the Egyptians.
    (E) Egyptian gods tended to be more anthropomorphic (human-like) than the Mesopotamian gods.

Bridgeman-Giraudon/Art Resource, NY

3. The statue above represents Shiva, a figure that is important in the religion of

   (A) Hinduism
   (B) Buddhism
   (C) Islam
   (D) Daoism
   (E) Christianity

4. Which of the following is a correct statement about the fall of classical civilizations between 200 and 600 C.E.?

   (A) The fall of the Gupta Empire probably had the most impact of all.
   (B) The fall of the Han Dynasty brought about the end of the influence of major belief systems that shaped earlier Chinese Dynasties.
   (C) The fall of the Gupta Empire meant that Indian trade connections on the Indian Ocean were broken.
   (D) The spread of Christianity almost certainly delayed the fall of the Western Roman Empire.
   (E) After its fall, the Western Roman Empire never united politically again in history.

Tomb of Qin shi Huang Di, Xianyang, China/Bridgeman Art Library

5. The famous clay soldiers pictured above guard the tomb of the "first" Chinese emperor, Shi Huangdi, whose rule is most closely associated with the doctrine of

    (A) Confucianism
    (B) Daoism
    (C) Shintoism
    (D) Legalism
    (E) Buddhism

6. The Punic Wars are an example of

    (A) hostilities that existed between Ancient Rome and Ancient Greece
    (B) infighting among Indian princes during the time of Ashoka
    (C) the tendency for trading people on the Mediterranean Sea to frequently quarrel and fight
    (D) conflict in SubSaharan Africa caused by the Bantu migration
    (E) the constant state of warfare that existed between Athens and Persia

7. The philosopher Confucius formulated a code of conduct whose chief purpose was to

    (A) improve society and government
    (B) prepare man's soul for the hereafter
    (C) enable the Zhou rulers to maintain power
    (D) encourage the Chinese to conquer all of Asia
    (E) encourage people to find "The Way"

8. The Viking attacks of Europe during the 8th and 9th centuries C.E. encouraged the development of the political and economic system known as

(A) capitalism
(B) feudalism
(C) nomadism
(D) Pan-Slavism
(E) absolutism

9. "When Gabriel took him up to each of the heavens and asked permission to enter he had to say whom he had brought and whether he had received a mission and they would say 'God grant him life, brother and friend!' until they reached the seventh heaven and his Lord. There the duty of fifty prayers a day was laid upon him."

The quote describes

(A) an apostle's conversion to Christianity
(B) events leading up to the building of the first Jewish temple
(C) Muhammad's Night Journey and ascent to heaven
(D) the death and resurrection of Jesus
(E) the hajj to Mecca

10. An important consequence of Japan's successful resistance of two attacks by Yuan China was that

(A) Japan took over the Korean peninsular as a buffer zone against further attacks
(B) Japan continued to maintain its relative autonomy in the region
(C) China turned its attention to the south, successfully invading India
(D) China turned to Korea to help execute a third attacks
(E) Japan came to dominate China by the 15th century

11. Ports of call in the Indian Ocean maritime system in the period 600-1450 C.E. were located in all of the following places EXCEPT:

(A) the South China Sea
(B) Chang'an
(C) Southeast Asia
(D) India
(E) East Africa

Sample Examination II

12. Which of the following Amerindian civilizations is well known for its use of "floating" gardens?

    (A) the Hopewell
    (B) the Maya
    (C) the Inca
    (D) the Anasazi
    (E) the Aztecs

13. Under the political, military, and economic structure of Japanese feudalism, the samurai were

    (A) military support personnel
    (B) bureaucrats
    (C) warriors
    (D) farmers
    (E) regional lords

(Questions 14 and 15 are based on the following diagram):

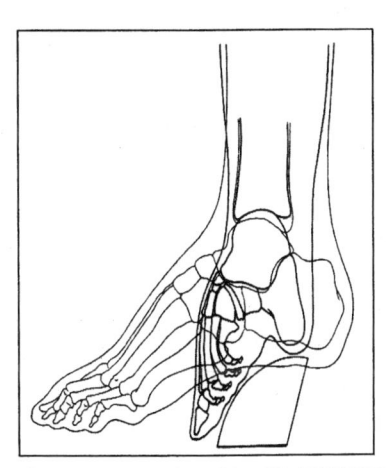

Fairbank, John K., Reischauer, and Albert Craig, EAST ASIA: TRADITION AND TRANSFORMATION, Revised Edition. Copyright © 1989 by Houghton Mifflin Company. Used with permission.

14. The diagram shows a deformity caused by

    (A) high fashion shoes in Indonesia
    (B) intensive peasant labor in Ancient Champa
    (C) poor nutrition in Yuan China
    (D) footbinding in Song China
    (E) the bubonic plague in Japan

15. Which of the following principles is best illustrated by the deformity?

    (A) effects of trade along the Silk Road
    (B) women as property of men
    (C) the inability to harness the forces of nature
    (D) effects of a growing gap between the rich and the poor
    (E) the power of religion to determine social practices

16. What response did the Spanish and Portuguese governments have when the encomienda system failed in their American colonies?

    (A) They encouraged the importation and use of African slaves.
    (B) They improved the diets and medical care of the natives that worked successfully within the system.
    (C) They replaced incompetent plantation owners with peninsulares.
    (D) They turned to the mita system instead.
    (E) They replaced the plantation system with numerous small farms and encouraged immigrants from Europe to populate them.

17. Which of the following is the best description of the overall demographic effects of the Atlantic slave trade on Africa?

    (A) The slave trade dramatically depopulated the African continent.
    (B) The slave trade had almost no demographic impact on Africa.
    (C) The slave trade impacted southern Africa far more than it affected northern Africa.
    (D) Whereas the slave trade acutely affected certain areas, it probably had little effect on the overall population.
    (E) Coastal areas of western Africa were severely affected, but virtually no slaves were taken from the African interior.

18. The power of which of the following European kings/queens was significantly checked by a parliament during the era between 1450 and 1750 C.E.?

    (A) Elizabeth I
    (B) Louis XIV
    (C) Ferdinand and Isabella
    (D) Philip II
    (E) Charles V

19. Which of the following is a correct observation of the Ottoman Empire during the 16th century?

    (A) It made good use of its strategic location between Europe and Asia to build its power and influence.
    (B) Its landlocked status was an obstacle that was almost impossible for them to overcome.
    (C) It had control over most of Western Europe.
    (D) It was not as strong as it would be by the 19th century.
    (E) It had many natural resources, but none of its sultans were strong military or political leaders.

20. European Enlightenment philosophers of the 18th century generally viewed the Qing emperors as

    (A) foolish children
    (B) cruel tyrants
    (C) model philosopher-kings
    (D) religious demagogues
    (E) weak and ineffectual.

21. Peter the Great of Russia welcomed all of the following Western influences EXCEPT:

    (A) shipbuilding technology
    (B) western style clothing
    (C) Jesuit missionaries
    (D) western architecture
    (E) western military technology

22. What motivation lay behind Matteo Ricci's attempts to entertain the Chinese with Western gadgets and inventions?

    (A) He wanted to secure Chinese trade for the European countries that he represented.
    (B) He exchanged them for Chinese gadgets and inventions that he wanted to introduce in Europe.
    (C) He used them to gain the emperor's ear to discuss political philosophy.
    (D) He wanted to show the Pope how advanced Chinese society was.
    (E) He used them to accomplish his underlying goal – converting the Chinese to Christianity.

23. Which of the following has generally not been true of nomadic groups in world history?

   (A) Nomadic societies are patriarchal.
   (B) Nomadic societies have some social hierarchy.
   (C) Themes of nomadic art tend to be centered on their animals.
   (D) Nomadic societies have had few positive influences on settled peoples.
   (E) Nomadic societies have often engaged in peaceful trade.

24. During which era did industrialization first create "have" and "have not" nations in the world?

   (A) Foundations (before 600 C.E.)
   (B) 600-1450 C.E.
   (C) 1450-1750 C.E.
   (D) 1750-1914 C.E.
   (E) 1914-Present

25. Enclosure of land in Britain by wealthy landowners during the 18th century had the important effect of

   (A) discouraging experimentation with new techniques of farming
   (B) stimulating the need for more agricultural workers
   (C) forcing small farmers to the cities to look for work
   (D) depleting the soil of nutrients necessary for successful farming
   (E) creating instability within the British government

26. Which industry first took the lead in Britain as the Industrial Revolution began?

   (A) textiles
   (B) opium
   (C) glass
   (D) armaments
   (E) farm equipment

27. Which of the following is the best example of a "Banana Republic" that emerged during the era from 1750 to 1914?

   (A) France
   (B) China
   (C) The Ottoman Empire
   (D) Brazil
   (E) Russia

28. An influential spokesperson for the abolitionist movement in the late 18th century was

   (A) Olaudah Equiano
   (B) Jethro Tull
   (C) John Locke
   (D) Susan B. Anthony
   (E) Emiliano Zapata

29. Which of the following countries directly experienced the demographic transition from high to low birth rates by the end of the 19th century?

   (A) Argentina
   (B) Mexico
   (C) Russia
   (D) Ethiopia
   (E) The United States

"When in the course of human events, it becomes necessary for one people to dissolve the political bands which have connected them with another, and to assume, among the powers of the earth, the separate and equal station to which the laws of nature and of nature's God entitle them..."

The Declaration of Independence
The United States, 1776

30. The quote above most directly reflects the philosophy of

   (A) balance of power
   (B) the social contract
   (C) collective security
   (D) natural selection
   (E) self-determination

31. Which of the following general demographic patterns characterized the 20th century?

   (A) The proportion of world population in North America increased.
   (B) The proportion of world population in Europe increased.
   (C) The proportion of world population in Africa increased.
   (D) The proportion of world population in Asia decreased.
   (E) The proportion of world population in the Middle East decreased.

32. "Britain's great *dreadnought* ships were challenged as Germany began to build its own super battleships and develop an impressive submarine fleet...colonial disputes broke out all over the globe..."

The quote above best describes the buildup to

(A) the Crimean War
(B) World War I
(C) World War II
(D) The Korean War
(E) The Persian Gulf Wars

33. Which of the following was a major provision of the Versailles Treaty of 1919?

(A) Germany gained land along most of its borders, although it lost overseas possessions.
(B) Poland, Czechoslovakia, Yugoslavia, Austria, and Hungary were all combined into one big empire.
(C) The concept of self-determination was applied, but only to nations in western Europe.
(D) The demilitarized zone between France and Germany was removed.
(E) The Ottoman Empire was dismantled into mandates, not independent countries.

34. Which of the following Allied Powers during World War II was defeated by Germany in 1940?

(A) the United States
(B) Britain
(C) Australia
(D) France
(E) China

35. The United Nations was formed in 1945 with the main purpose of

(A) protecting the environment
(B) creating an international bill of rights
(C) seeing that Germany was punished for beginning the war
(D) creating a balance of power among nations of the world
(E) negotiating disputes among nations

36. The "Iron Curtain" divided

   (A) Eastern Europe from Western Europe
   (B) the U.S.S.R. from China
   (C) Africa from Southwest Asia
   (D) the United States from Mexico
   (E) the U.S.S.R. from Eastern Europe

37. All of the following became independent nations in the years following World War II EXCEPT:

   (A) India
   (B) Algeria
   (C) Mexico
   (D) Vietnam
   (E) Nigeria

38. Which of the following is the best example of change in social structure that resulted from industrialization?

   (A) narrowing of the gender gap
   (B) better working conditions for ordinary citizens
   (C) strengthening of family ties
   (D) more emphasis on land ownership for status distinctions
   (E) growing gap between the rich and the poor

(Questions 39 and 40 are based on the following map):

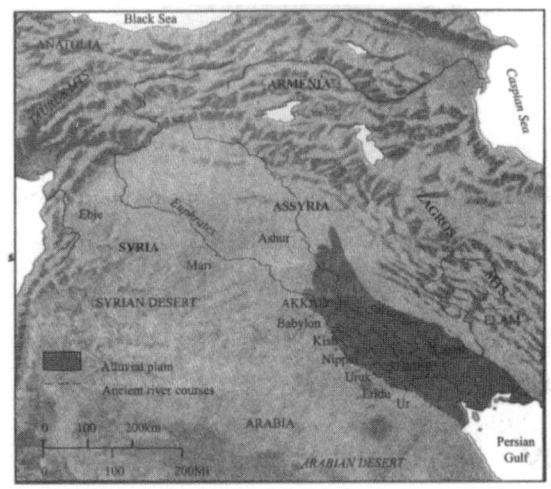

Bulliet, Richard. The Earth and its Peoples, Second Edition. Copyright © 2001 by Houghton Mifflin Company. Used with permission.

39. The map shows ancient

 (A) Egypt
 (B) India
 (C) China
 (D) Mexico
 (E) Mesopotamia

40. Which of the following was a famous ruler of the area shown in the map?

 (A) King Tut
 (B) Hammurabi
 (C) Xerxes
 (D) Shi Huangdi
 (E) Montezuma

41. Which of the following is the best explanation for why Egyptian Pharaohs of the Old Kingdom exercised unusual authority over their subjects?

 (A) They served as military commanders of a highly successful army.
 (B) They were respected for developing a lucrative trade with Mesopotamia, Crete, and Palestine.
 (C) They were recognized as supreme rulers by the royal family and nobility.
 (D) They inherited their position in the dynastic order through their mother's family.
 (E) They were worshipped as gods who ruled the society through an extensive theocracy.

42. The jaguar man and/or jaguar god were prevalent in which of the following civilizations?

 I. Olmec
 II. Hittite
 III. Assyrian
 IV. Chavin

 (A) I only
 (B) I and II only
 (C) I, II, and III only
 (D) I and IV only
 (E) I, II, III, and IV

43. Buddha believed that a state of grace or nirvana could be reached by

 (A) changing one's karma
 (B) following the moral duties of one's caste
 (C) being reincarnated as a Brahman
 (D) following the eight-fold path
 (E) renouncing asceticism

(Questions 44 and 45 refer to the photo below):

© Kim Karpeles

44. The primary function of the structure was to

 (A) transport troops across the river
 (B) impress rival empires
 (C) divert the river for irrigation of crops
 (D) carry water from one area to another
 (E) serve as a backdrop for important religious ceremonies

45. This structure that still exists in modern day was built by the

 (A) Ancient Greeks
 (B) Carthaginians
 (C) Song Chinese
 (D) Mauryans
 (E) Romans

46. All of the following were significant technological advancements of the Chinese during the Song Dynasty EXCEPT:

    (A) gunpowder
    (B) the camel saddle
    (C) improvements in shipbuilding
    (D) moveable type
    (E) metallurgy:

47. Which of the following is (was) religious law, often applied by religious courts?

    (A) the Code of Justinian
    (B) the Twelve Tables
    (C) Magna Carta
    (D) Shari'a
    (E) Five Pillars of Faith

48. All of the following were characteristic of the Aztec and Inca Civilizations prior to the arrival of the Europeans EXCEPT:

    (A) Their economies were based primarily on trade.
    (B) They constructed monumental buildings.
    (C) They had major urban centers.
    (D) They had conquered nearby peoples and established large empires.
    (E) They had job specialization and distinct social classes.

49. All of the following groups invaded Europe between 400 and 1000 C.E. EXCEPT:

    (A) Huns
    (B) Vikings
    (C) Magyars
    (D) Mongols
    (E) Vandals

50. All of the following are reasons why China's discovery voyages ceased after Zheng He's death EXCEPT:

    (A) The sponsoring emperor also died.
    (B) Confucian court officials resisted cross-cultural contacts and trade.
    (C) Court officials did not believe that Chinese sailors were sufficiently skilled to voyage any further than they did.
    (D) War broke out in the Western provinces, so the government needed to spend money there.
    (E) Court officials criticized Zheng He's voyages for not being profitable.

51. What two events directly led to the successful Spanish claim of most of Latin America during the early 16th century?

    (A) the successful voyages of Christopher Columbus and Ferdinand Magellan
    (B) the Spanish defeats of Portugal at Lepanto and the invention of the caravel
    (C) the 100 Years War and the 30 Years War, both of which weakened England and France
    (D) the union of Castile and Aragon and the defeat of the Muslim Almorids
    (E) the defeat of the Aztec by Cortes and the Inca by Pizarro

52. The Columbian Exchange developed as a result of the establishment of which new trade route during the 16th century?

    (A) the Indian Ocean trade
    (B) the South China Sea trade
    (C) the Great Circuit
    (D) Sub-Saharan trade
    (E) The Silk Road

53. The most important result of the Siege of Vienna in 1529 was the

    (A) halt of the Ottoman invasion of Europe
    (B) spread of Islam to Eastern Europe
    (C) growth in the political and military power of Russia
    (D) decline of the Hapsburg family as a major power in Europe
    (E) strengthening of the political power of English and French monarchs

54. In which of the following European kingdoms did the idea of limited monarchy first develop?

    (A) the Holy Roman Empire
    (B) France
    (C) Spain
    (D) Portugal
    (E) England

55. Suleiman the Magnificent was one of the most famous rulers of the

    (A) Safavid Empire
    (B) Mughal Empire
    (C) Ottoman Empire
    (D) Mongol Empire
    (E) Abbasid Caliphate

56. Songhay and Kongo were powerful kingdoms that developed in

   (A) northern Africa
   (B) subSaharan Africa
   (C) the Indian subcontinent
   (D) Southeast Asia
   (E) Oceania

(Questions 57 and 58 refer to the following quote):

"Women were seen as stable and pure, the vision of what kept men devoted to the tasks of running the economy. Women as standard-setters, then became the important force in shaping children to value respectability, lead moral lives, and be responsible for their own behaviors."

57. The above description of the role and responsibility of women in 19th century industrialized societies is known as the

   (A) cult of domesticity
   (B) social contract
   (C) demographic transition
   (D) feminine revolution
   (E) balance of power

58. The quote describes expectations that defined gender roles of those in

   (A) all social classes
   (B) the upper class
   (C) the middle class
   (D) the working class
   (E) the lower class

59. Which of the following was a social problem in France that directly led to the Revolution in 1789?

   (A) The nobles held much more power than the king did.
   (B) Working class people in the cities were much better off economically than the rural peasants were.
   (C) The clergy were both poor and powerless.
   (D) A huge influx of immigrants from northern Africa created overcrowding in the cities.
   (E) The economic prosperity of the bourgeoisie grew, but it was not accompanied by increasing political power.

60. Which of the following leaders of revolution in the Americas was a member of the colonial elite?

   (A) Emiliano Zapata
   (B) Simon de Bolivar
   (C) Pancho Villa
   (D) Miguel Hidalgo
   (E) Toussaint L'Ouverture

61. "a revolution, the beheading of a king, a terrorizing egalitarian government, and finally a demagogue who attacked all of Europe."

   The quote above describes

   (A) England during the 17th century
   (B) France during the late 18th and early 19th centuries
   (C) China during the 20th century
   (D) Germany during the late 19th century
   (E) Russia during the 19th century

62. The 19th century philosophy that explained inequality between the rich and the poor in terms of natural selection was called

   (A) radicalism
   (B) Social Darwinism
   (C) self-determination
   (D) the white man's burden
   (E) cohong

63. What was the main reason that the United States sponsored the building of the Panama Canal in the early 20th century?

   (A) to facilitate trade with China
   (B) to help the economies of struggling Latin American countries
   (C) to allow the U.S. navy access to both east and west coasts of the country
   (D) to shorten the voyage between California and Europe
   (E) to add an important leg to the Great Circuit trade routes

64. What was the name of the U.S. program set up to help Western European nations rebuild their economies after World War II?

    (A) the New Freedom
    (B) containment
    (C) the Square Deal
    (D) the Marshall Plan
    (E) self-determination

65. Which of the following was the last to gain its independence as a country?

    (A) Haiti
    (B) Argentina
    (C) Ethiopia
    (D) India
    (E) Algeria

66. Juan Peron and Augusto Pinochet are both examples of 20th century

    (A) socialist presidents in South America
    (B) PRI-sponsored presidents of Mexico
    (C) rulers that relied on the ballot box rather than military force
    (D) martyrs assassinated by Latin American political elites
    (E) military dictators in South America

67. During which era of the 20th century was the free-enterprise economic system most seriously challenged by alternative political and economic philosophies?

    (A) pre-World War I
    (B) 1930s
    (C) post-World War II
    (D) 1970s
    (E) 1990s

68. Advocacy of the socialist market economy is most associated with

    (A) Deng Xiaoping
    (B) Mao Zedong
    (C) Ho Chi Minh
    (D) Sukarno
    (E) Joseph Stalin

69. Which of the following accurately describes a fundamental difference between fascism and communism?

   (A) Communism is based on democratic centralism; fascism is not.
   (B) Communist leaders are more totalitarian than fascist leaders.
   (C) Fascism is based on corporatism; communism is not.
   (D) Communism emphasizes nationalism; fascism does not.
   (E) Communist leaders are popularly elected; fascist leaders are not.

70. The anti-apartheid movement in South Africa was most directly strengthened by the growing

   (A) number of white Europeans settling in South Africa
   (B) number of converts to Islam in South Africa
   (C) appeal of black nationalism to the oppressed majority
   (D) centralization of the Zulu state
   (E) isolationism of South Africa from world trade and contact

DOCUMENT BASED QUESTION

(suggested writing time – 40 minutes)

Directions: The following question is based on the accompanying Documents 1-8. This question is designed to test your ability to work with and understand historical documents. Write an essay that:

- Has a relevant thesis and supports that thesis with evidence from the documents.
- Uses all or all but one of the documents.
- Analyzes the documents by grouping them in as many appropriate ways as possible. Does not simply summarize the documents individually.
- Takes into account both the sources of the documents and the authors' points of view.

You may refer to relevant historical information not mentioned in the documents.

Which is the best explanation for the evolution of large, powerful empires during the classical era (1000 BCE - 600 CE): independent invention or cultural diffusion? Historians support both views. Based on the following documents, discuss independent invention and cultural diffusion as shapers of the classical civilizations. What additional types of documents would help assess the development of the empires?

Document 1

The Master [Confucius] said, "Filial piety is the root of virtue and the source of civilization. Sit down again and I will explain it to you. Since we receive our body, hair, and skin from our parents, we do not dare let it be injured in any way. This is the beginning of filial piety. We establish ourselves and practice the Way, thereby perpetuating our name for future generations and bringing glory to our parents. This is the fulfillment of filial piety. Thus filial piety begins with serving our parents, continues with serving the ruler, and is completed by establishing one's character."

Classic of Filial Piety
Early Han Period

Document 2

Seng Du said, "Serving the king, as demanded by Confucianism, is to assist in the ruling of one's country. That cannot be compared with pursuing the Buddhist path for all peoples. Serving one's parents means to establish a family of one's own; but that cannot be compared with following the Buddhist path for the sake of all beings in the three realms. The dictum 'Never to harm your body or hair' is the narrow advice of those committed to the world. I am ashamed that my present virtue has not extended itself to cover even that filial duty. However, small baskets of earth add up to a mountain: all beginnings are small. Thus I put on my monk's gown, drink the pure water, and laud the wisdom of the Buddhas. Although the dress of princes, the food of the eight rarities, the sound of music and the color of glories are all fine, I would not trade my lot for them. If our minds are in tune to one another, we will meet in nirvana. However, people's hearts are different, just as their faces are. Your distaste for the hermit's way is like my indifference to the world."

Zhu Seng Du
Chinese Buddhist Scholar

Document 3

[The true appearance of the deity is described]

It was a multiform, wondrous vision,
with countless mouths and eyes
and celestial ornaments,
everywhere was boundless divinity
containing all astonishing things,
wearing divine garlands and garments,
anointed with divine perfume.
if the light of a thousand suns
were to rise in the sky at once,
it would be like the light
of that great spirit.
Arjuna saw all the universe
in its many ways and parts,
standing as one in the body of the god of gods.

The Bhagavad-Gita

Document 4

"For a long time in the past, for many hundreds of years have increased the sacrificial slaughter of animals, violence toward creatures unfilial conduct toward kinsmen, improper conduct toward Brahmins and ascetics. Now with the practice of morality of King [Ashoka], the sound of war drums has become the call to morality….You [government officials] are appointed to rule over thousands of human beings in the expectation that you will win the affection of all men. All men are my children. Just as I desire that my children will fare well and be happy in this world and the next, I desire the same for all men….King [Ashoka] …desires that there should be the growth of the essential spirit of morality or holiness among all sects….there should not be glorification of one's own sect and denunciation of the sect of others for little or no reason. For all the sects are worthy of reverence for one reason or another.

Inscribed Edict from Ashoka
3rd Century BCE

Document 5

During the nine years of his command this is in substance what he [Julius Caesar] did. All that part of Gallia which is bounded by the Pyrenees, the Alps and the Cévennes, and by the Rhine and Rhone rivers, a circuit of some 3,200 miles [Roman measure, about 3,106 English miles], with the exception of some allied states which had rendered him good service, he reduced to the form of a province; and imposed upon it a yearly tribute of 40,000,000 sesterces. He was the first Roman to build a bridge and attack the Germans beyond the Rhine; and he inflicted heavy losses upon them. He invaded the Britons too, a people unknown before, vanquished them, and exacted moneys and hostages. Amid all these successes he met with adverse fortune but three times in all: in Britannia, where his fleet narrowly escaped destruction in a violent storm; in Gallia, when one of his legions was routed at Gergovia; and on the borders of Germania, when his lieutenants Titurius and Aurunculeius were ambushed and slain…

Having ended the wars, he celebrated five triumphs, four in a single month, but at intervals of a few days, after vanquishing Scipio; and another on defeating Pompeius' sons. The first and most splendid was the Gallic triumph, the next the Alexandrian, then the Pontic, after that the African, and finally the Hispanic, each differing from the rest in its equipment and display of spoils…. he mounted the Capitol by torchlight, with forty elephants bearing lamps on his right and his left. In his Pontic triumph he displayed among the show-pieces of the procession an inscription of but three words, "I came, I saw, I conquered," ['Veni, vidi, vici'] not indicating the events of the war, as the others did, but the speed with which it was finished.

The Lives of the Caesars, The Deified Julius
Suetonius, written c. 110 CE

Document 6

Bristol City Museum and Art Gallery, UK/Bridgeman Art Library

The Acropolis in Athens

Document 7

© *Gerald Oskoboiny*

The Roman Forum

Document 8

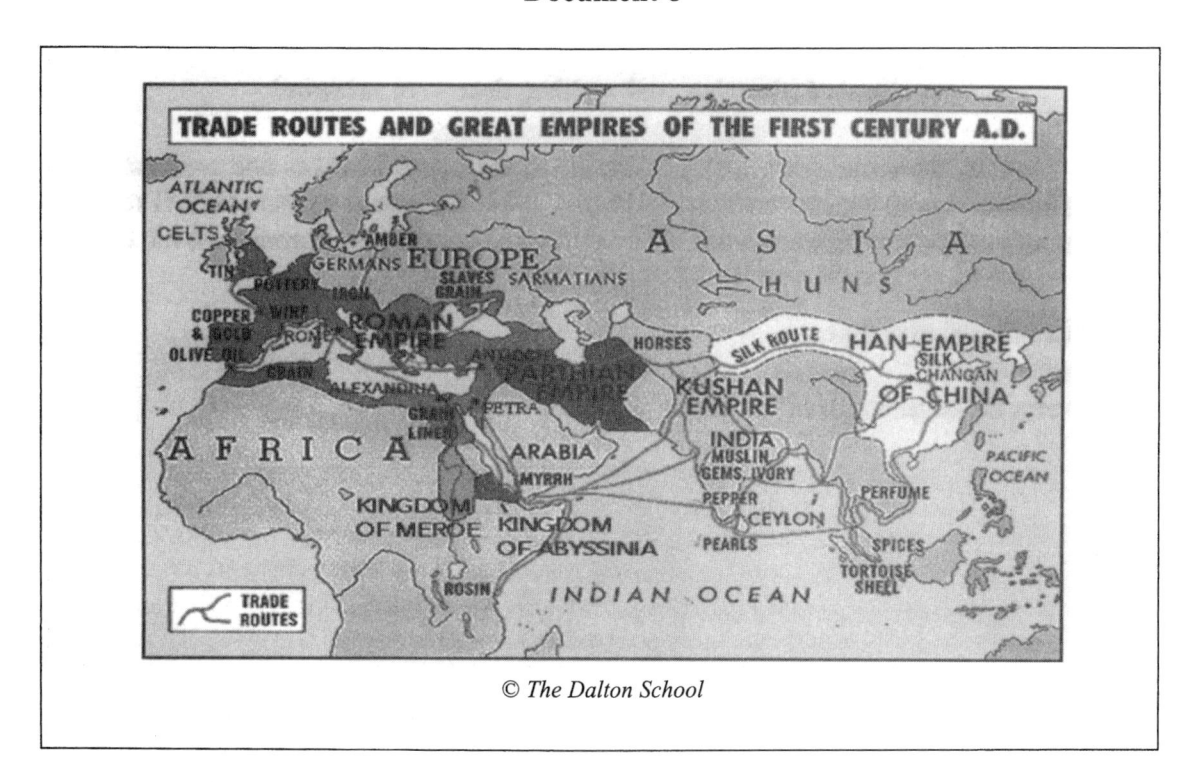

TRADE ROUTES AND GREAT EMPIRES OF THE FIRST CENTURY A.D.

© *The Dalton School*

CHANGE OVER TIME ESSAY

(suggested planning and writing time – 40 minutes)

Choose TWO of the areas listed below and analyze important changes and continuities in Chinese history during the eras between 1450 and 1914. Be sure to explain BOTH regional and international factors that produced the changes and continuities throughout the eras.

- Cross cultural exchanges
- Belief systems
- Systems of social organization/gender structure

COMPARATIVE ESSAY

(suggested planning and writing time – 40 minutes)

A series of revolutions brought major changes in world history during the period between 1750 and 1914. Discuss the major similarities and differences between TWO of the revolutions listed below in terms of causes, nature of the conflict, and consequences.

The American Revolution
The French Revolution
Revolution in Haiti
Revolution in Venezuela
Mexican Revolution (1821)

No testing material on this page.

Sample Examination III

This section should be completed in 55 minutes.

Directions: Each of the questions or incomplete statements is followed by five suggested answers or completions. Select the one that best answers the question or completes the statement.

1. All of the following were common consequences of the fall of the Western Roman, Han, and Gupta Empires (200 -600 C.E.) EXCEPT:

    (A) Long distance trade on the Silk Road was disrupted but survived.
    (B) The spread of Christianity was limited to areas around the eastern Mediterranean until about 1000 C.E.
    (C) The importance of religion increased as political authority decreased.
    (D) Political disunity in the Middle East forged the way for the appearance of a new religion – Islam – in the 7th century.
    (E) Long distance trade on the Indian Ocean increased as conflict and decline of political authority affected overland trade.

2. According to most anthropological studies, in what part of the world did the first human beings appear?

    (A) the Middle East
    (B) Europe
    (C) China
    (D) Australia
    (E) eastern and southern Africa

3. All of the following are common characteristics of classical civilizations EXCEPT:

    (A) They all had patriarchal family structures.
    (B) In all civilizations, the emperor's position was passed down from father to son.
    (C) All had agricultural-based economies.
    (D) They all participated in long-distance trade.
    (E) They all were "root" civilizations that directly influenced many civilizations that came later.

4. The Chinese philosopher Laozi taught that people could achieve peace of mind by

   (A) accepting, with humility, one's lot in life
   (B) relying on the government for protection
   (C) pursuing wealth and giving it to the poor
   (D) turning to one's family and friends for solace in an unfriendly world
   (E) reforming the evils of the world

"Ruler/subject, father/son, elder brother/younger brother, husband/wife, friend/friend"

5. The above relationships are basic to

   (A) polytheism
   (B) legalism
   (C) Daoism
   (D) Confucianism
   (E) Zoroasterism

Bristol City Museum and Art Gallery, UK/Bridgeman Art Library

6. The building above was built as a

   (A) tribute to the Roman god Juno
   (B) place of honor to the city's special deity
   (C) palace for the civilization's emperor
   (D) symbol of victory over Persia's King Darius
   (E) trade center on the western end of the Silk Road

7. Which of the following is the best description of the geographical extent of the Gupta Empire?

   (A) It covered northern India from the Himalaya Mountains to the Deccan Plateau.
   (B) It encompassed the old Srivijaya Empire as well as land that extended to the Tibetan Plateau.
   (C) It covered virtually the entire Indian subcontinent.
   (D) It extended from Carthage in the west to Ghana in the east.
   (E) It included the Xinjiang and the Ganges River Valley.

British Museum, London, UK/Bridgeman Art Library

8. The civilization that produced the above painting was characterized by

   (A) a lush natural environment with plenty of rainfall
   (B) a profound interest in the afterlife
   (C) decentralized government
   (D) a short but intense period of existence
   (E) self-sufficiency, little contact with other civilizations

9. All of the following accurately describe Charlemagne's accomplishments EXCEPT:

   (A) He protected the pope from invaders.
   (B) He built the largest empire in Europe between 500 and 1000 C.E.
   (C) He established a center for learning.
   (D) His empire remained intact for hundreds of years following his death.
   (E) He inspired support from a large army that won most of its battles.

10. Which of the following BEST describes what happened to Chinese women's status during the Song dynasty (961-1279 C.E.)?

   (A) The status of women fell significantly from the relatively high levels that existed in previous dynasties.
   (B) Women had been subordinate to men in previous dynasties, but their status fell to new lows during the Song Dynasty.
   (C) Although still relatively low, women's status improved significantly during the Song era.
   (D) No significant change occurred; women's status remained low throughout the eras.
   (E) No significant change occurred; women's status in China remained high in comparison to other contemporary societies.

11. Christian monasteries performed all of the following functions EXCEPT:

   (A) They were the primary centers of literacy and learning.
   (B) They sometimes planted Christianity in new lands.
   (C) They preserved ancient Latin manuscripts.
   (D) They usually made a great deal of money for the Pope.
   (E) They sometimes served as places of refuge for those that needed protection.

(Questions 12 and 13 refer to the following artifact):

Courtesy the Library, American Museum of Natural History

12. The animal represented by the artifact was important to which of the following civilizations?

    (A) Aztec Empire
    (B) Kingdom of Songhay
    (C) Ming China
    (D) Mughal Empire
    (E) Inca Empire

13. The animal was particularly valuable to the people that made use of it because it was

    (A) surefooted for travel in a mountainous terrain
    (B) durable and reliable for use in cross-desert trade
    (C) able to carry much larger amounts of trade products than horses or camels
    (D) good for herding small animals, such as goats and sheep
    (E) able to travel much more rapidly than humans and other animals

14. All of the following describe Mongol reactions to those that they conquered EXCEPT:

    (A) Despite their many conquests, they acquired few of the customs and beliefs of lands they occupied.
    (B) Their most important goal was almost always to collect sizeable tribute from defeated peoples.
    (C) They provided protection for trade routes that crossed the lands that they acquired.
    (D) They practiced "tax farming."
    (E) They sometimes formed alliances with native leaders in order to subjugate others.

(Questions 15 and 16 refer to the following painting):

The Chester Beatty Library

15. Although the painting above refers to religious figures, its design includes no attempt to capture their images. The best reason for this emphasis on geometric designs rather than images is that

    (A) religious doctrine forbids artistic representations that might encourage the worship of images as idols
    (B) artists of the time period were much more skilled at drawing geometric designs than human figures
    (C) paintings were used as monetary exchange, so they had to include numeric calculations
    (D) human forms were considered to be shameful; only spiritual values should be captured in art
    (E) the geometric figures are actually language symbols, and the painting tells a story

16. The painting reflects the religious doctrines of

    (A) Hinduism
    (B) Daoism
    (C) Islam
    (D) Buddhism
    (E) Judaism

17. Under the "Sun King," Louis XIV, the king's power was strengthened by

   (A) establishing a tribute system for all conquered lands
   (B) proclaiming the Edict of Nantes
   (C) extending the reach of the central bureaucracy throughout France
   (D) defeating the supporters of parliamentary government in a civil war
   (E) sponsoring pirate expeditions that robbed Spanish galleons laden with gold and silver from the Americas

"It began in Europe, ran south to Africa, and then turned west to South America, Central America, the Caribbean, and North America. Finally, it swept back from various points in the Americas to Europe."

18. The quote above best describes the trade connections known as the

   (A) Great Circuit
   (B) Middle Passage
   (C) Triangular Trade
   (D) The Route of the Manila Galleons
   (E) The African Diaspora

19. Which of the following is the best comparison of European and Islamic contacts with Africa during the 16th and 17th centuries?

   (A) The Islamic countries traded a larger amount of goods with the Africans.
   (B) A greater number of slaves were traded across the Sahara to Islamic countries than were traded across the Atlantic to European colonies.
   (C) Islamic cultural and religious influences were far greater than European influences on the African continent.
   (D) Muslims believed that slavery was ethically wrong, so they left the slave trading to the Europeans.
   (E) Both Islamic and European countries were primarily interested in trading, not settling or controlling the mainland.

20. Which of the following statements most clearly supports the argument that the institution of slavery caused racism to rise as a belief system?

   (A) All people are ethnocentric and assume that their race is superior to all others.
   (B) Europeans did not believe that it was immoral to enslave people in Africa because their cultures were so clearly inferior to those in Europe.
   (C) The harsh treatment of slaves on the trans-Atlantic crossing proves that traders did not think of them as human.
   (D) Africans enslaved only other cultural groups in Africa; Europeans did the same thing by only enslaving non-Europeans
   (E) The Atlantic trade routes were set up for profit. Slave labor was needed in the Americas to reap profits for European nations.

21. Which of the following empires was primarily land-based but also maintained a great navy in the era 1450-1750?

    (A) Britain
    (B) Ottoman Empire
    (C) Mughal Empire
    (D) Spain
    (E) Ming China

22. Which of the following is an accurate description of the Qing (Manchu) Dynasty during the 17th and 18th centuries?

    (A) Two great emperors ruled over a "golden age" in Chinese history.
    (B) The empire had almost no contact with Europeans or other foreigners.
    (C) Confucianism weakened significantly as a major philosophical influence.
    (D) The Manchu intermarried with the Han Chinese and lost their separate identity as as a people.
    (E) The size of the empire was much smaller than it had been during the earlier Song Dynasty.

23. Which of the following is the BEST explanation for why Russian Tsar Peter is granted the title "the Great"?

    (A) He defeated the Swedes and the Ottomans – two major powers of the day.
    (B) He extended Russian territory to the Pacific Ocean.
    (C) He westernized Russia because he recognized the important shift in world power away from land-based empires toward seafaring European nations.
    (D) He ruled with absolute power, willing to sacrifice the lives of relatives and friends for the good of Russia.
    (E) He understood the importance of preserving Slavic values and customs and built the country on the strength of those traditions.

24. What general attitude did Europeans have toward Chinese merchandise during the 18th century?

    (A) Europeans greatly respected and demanded Chinese silk, tea, porcelain, wallpaper, and other decorative items.
    (B) They considered European merchandise to be superior.
    (C) They valued Chinese merchandise, but considered it to be more appropriate for the homes of middle class people than for those of the rich.
    (D) They valued items from southern China, but believed any designs influenced by the Manchu to be inferior.
    (E) Europeans ignored Chinese merchandise because so few Chinese products made their way back to Europe.

25. During the 19th centuries, many European colonies became independent in

(A) Southwest Asia
(B) Sub-Saharan Africa
(C) Southeast Asia
(D) Latin America
(E) North Africa

26. Of the following groups, which benefited most directly from the Industrial Revolution?

(A) the middle class
(B) the factory workers
(C) the landed nobility
(D) women
(E) monarchs

27. Which of the following characteristics distinguished the era 1750 to 1914 from all previous eras?

(A) the rising hegemony of China
(B) the establishment of democracy as a new type of political organization
(C) the beginning of the first sustained contact and trade between the eastern and western hemispheres
(D) the first appearance of "Gunpowder Empires"
(E) Islamic control of most long-distance trade circuits

28. During the era 1750 to 1914 labor systems around the world experienced a major change as

(A) coercive labor systems expanded rapidly
(B) percentages of the total work force employed in factories declined
(C) agricultural workers became more independent, more likely to be self-employed
(D) coercive labor systems declined in use
(E) percentages of workers employed in long-distance trade declined

29. The flying shuttle, the spinning jenny, the water frame, and the spinning mule were all important elements that transformed

(A) Britain after 1750
(B) China during the Song Dynasty
(C) Japan after 1870
(D) Northern African kingdoms after 1500
(E) Russia after 1650

30. Environmental changes in 19th century Europe include all of the following EXCEPT:

(A) Coal mining increased substantially.
(B) Towns grew rapidly, and major cities formed.
(C) "Industrial belts" formed, especially in Britain.
(D) Iron was used extensively as a natural resource.
(E) Deforestation increased.

31. "Green movements" of the 20th century had their greatest successes in

(A) developing countries in South America
(B) less developed countries in Sub-Saharan Africa
(C) industrialized nations of Europe and North America
(D) densely populated countries such as India and China
(E) less densely populated countries such as Australia and Russia

32. During the 20th century population migrations from rural to urban areas were most intense in

(A) industrialized countries in North America
(B) industrialized countries in Europe
(C) developing nations in Latin America and South Africa
(D) less developed nations in Southwest Asia
(E) industrializing nations in East Asia

33. Which of the following most clearly reinforced the late 20th century trend toward fragmentation?

(A) increasing international trade
(B) invention and use of the internet
(C) spread of Western "pop culture"
(D) the end of the cold war
(E) sharing of international science

34. In industrialized countries feminist movements of the early 20th century tended to focus most on

(A) promoting widespread acceptance of birth control methods
(B) gaining the vote for women
(C) gaining abortion rights for women
(D) equal employment opportunities for women
(E) child care issues

35. The Great Leap Forward, the Cultural Revolution, and the creation of the socialist market economy all characterize 20th century

    (A) China
    (B) Japan
    (C) Russia
    (D) Mexico
    (E) France

36. Which of the following concepts was a central argument that promoted the Revolution of 1917 in Russia?

    (A) socialist market economy
    (B) *keiretsu*
    (C) compressed modernity
    (D) democratic centralism
    (E) *détente*

37. A major influence on the early development of Western Europe (5th and 6th centuries) was

    (A) the movement of the Mongols
    (B) Attila the Hun's advance against Rome
    (C) the spread of Islam into Spain by the Moors
    (D) the pressure put on Germanic peoples by the movement of the Huns
    (E) the emergence of a unified Frankish kingdom

38. "The New York Stock Exchange tumbled, markets crashed in Europe and other industrialized countries, companies laid off thousands of workers, Germany could not pay war reparations, and countries dependent on international trade suffered a terrible economic malaise."

    The passage describes the state of the world economy during the

    (A) late 1800s
    (B) late 1920s and 1930s
    (C) post World War II era
    (D) 1980s
    (E) early 21st century

39. The *Upanishads*, the *Ramayana*, and the *Bhagavad Gita* are considered to be significant pieces of Indian literature because they

(A) provide guidelines for Hindu living and behavior
(B) identify basic Buddhist principles
(C) show the constant class struggle in early southern Asian societies
(D) reflect the similarities between the Hindu and Muslim religions
(E) teach economic and political skills that have allowed Indian civilization to survive many invasions

40. Which of the following best describes the reaction of Hindu leaders to Buddhism in India in the years following Buddha's death?

(A) Hindu leaders welcome the new religion because it reinforced belief in a universal spirit.
(B) Hindu leaders allowed Buddhism among the lower classes because it kept them out of trouble.
(C) Hindu leaders in the Ganges River area allowed it to flourish, but Southern leaders suppressed it.
(D) Hindu leaders suppressed the religion because it threatened existing beliefs and social structures.
(E) Hindu leaders were largely indifferent to Buddhism.

41. Hinduism and Buddhism both agree that life on earth

(A) is destined to perpetual, inescapable reincarnations
(B) is preparation for immediate entrance to heaven
(C) must conform to caste rules
(D) has as its ultimate goal the achievement of nirvana
(E) is one of sorrow

Martha Cooper/Peter Arnold, Inc.

42. The above ruins of Tikal in modern Guatemala reflect the central role of

   (A) religion in the lives of the Maya
   (B) trade in the lives of the Aztecs
   (C) beasts of burden in the lives of the Toltecs
   (D) the Inca ruler in controlling his subjects
   (E) Spanish colonization and exploitation

43. Which of the following empires combined political and religious authority almost completely?

   (A) Holy Roman Empire
   (B) The Mongol Empire
   (C) The Abbasid Caliphate
   (D) The Gupta Empire
   (E) Roman Empire

44. Which of the following is a characteristic shared by most Amerindian civilizations in Central and South America prior to the arrival of Europeans?

   (A) All had hieroglyphic writing systems.
   (B) All gave priests high social status.
   (C) All had centralized governments.
   (D) None used mortar for their public buildings.
   (E) None used beasts of burden to carry out work.

Erich Lessing/Art Resource, NY

45. This suit of jade sewn together with gold threads to serve as burial dress tells us that the Han Chinese

    (A) were very much influenced by Confucianism
    (B) believed in a Supreme Being
    (C) traded with other empires
    (D) believed that the emperor had a Mandate of Heaven
    (E) had distinct social classes

"Generally, an adult male had to spend 1/7 of his time working for the ruler, a few months at a time. When his obligation to the state was complete, he would return home until his service time came up again. The Spanish adopted this system, but when so many natives died, the Spanish had to increase the time natives committed to projects that it became impractical."

46. The passage above describes the mita labor system originally used in the western hemisphere by the

    (A) Aztecs in MesoAmerica
    (B) Anasazi in North America
    (C) Inca in South America
    (D) Maya in Central America
    (E) Moundbuilders in North America

Cathedral of Notre Dame, Amiens, France/Peter Willi/Bridgeman Art Library

47. The architecture above represents a grand achievement of

    (A) Renaissance Italy
    (B) Medieval Europe
    (C) the Byzantine Empire
    (D) Romans in Europe
    (E) Europeans in the Age of Enlightenment

48. An important consequence of the journeys and writings of Marco Polo and Ibn Battutu was

    (A) increased knowledge of other parts of the world among people in the eastern hemisphere
    (B) the successful resistance of Mongol control by African and European kingdoms
    (C) intensification of trade between eastern and western hemispheres
    (D) increased hostility between Europeans and Africans
    (E) the spread of Christianity and Islam to Eastern Asia

(Questions 49 and 50 refer to the following map):

Bulliet, Richard. The Earth and its Peoples, Second Edition. Copyright © 2001 by Houghton Mifflin Company. Used with Permission

49. The above map portion reflects a 14th century Mediterranean geographer's view of

    (A) South Africa
    (B) Southwest Asia
    (C) Northern Africa
    (D) India
    (E) Europe

50. The man with the crown and scepter in the middle of the map is holding an example of which major resource of the area during the 14th century?

    (A) a ball of silk
    (B) gold
    (C) a large diamond
    (D) iron
    (E) fruit

51. Why do most historians consider the voyages of Bartolomeu Diaz and Vasco da Gama to be more important Marker Events in world history than those of Zheng He?

(A) Diaz and da Gama's voyages were much longer than those of Zheng He.
(B) The Portuguese sailing technology was more advanced than that of the Chinese.
(C) Diaz and da Gama's voyages began the first sustained interactions between western and eastern hemispheres.
(D) Zheng He did not bring wealth back to China; Diaz and da Gama were responsible for making Portugal rich.
(E) Zheng He's ships disappeared in storms in the Indian Ocean; Diaz and da Gama made it back home to Portugal.

52. Which of the following is an important consequence of the Columbian Exchange?

(A) increasing population levels in the western hemisphere during the 16th century
(B) introduction of cattle and sheep to Africa for the first time
(C) better nutrition for many people around the world
(D) widespread death from disease in Europe and Africa
(E) decrease of long distance trade across the Pacific Ocean

53. The best reason why the Magna Carta is an important document in world history is that it was an important step toward

(A) limiting the rights of English nobles
(B) promoting centralization of power in the hands of the king
(C) establishing England as a more powerful kingdom than France and Spain
(D) establishing the principle of constitutional government
(E) stabilizing political and economic relationships among English, French, and Spanish kingdoms

54. Which colonial power in the New World was the LEAST successful in establishing stable relationships with Amerindians?

(A) Spain
(B) Portugal
(C) France
(D) The Netherlands
(E) Britain

55. All of the following were factors that weakened Ming China during the early 1600s EXCEPT:

    (A) climatic change, with the weather turning much colder
    (B) loss of control of Silk Road trade to Tibet
    (C) pirates that attacked ships going in and out of Chinese ports
    (D) inept rulers
    (E) nomadic invasions

56. What was the main purpose of "alternate attendance" required by the Tokugawa Court in Japan?

    (A) to strengthen the power of the military
    (B) to illustrate the wealth and power of the emperor
    (C) to show the shogun's superior political power over the emperor
    (D) to limit the power of the daimyos
    (E) to "close" Japan to trade with the outside world

57. Which type of economic system is the most susceptible to dramatic swings between economic hard times to recovery and growth?

    (A) capitalism
    (B) communism
    (C) socialism
    (D) agricultural economic base with limited trade
    (E) economies characterized by unequal trade

58. The philosophical and political movement that most directly questioned the assumptions of absolute government was

    (A) the Renaissance
    (B) the Reformation
    (C) the Industrial Revolution
    (D) the Scientific Revolution
    (E) the Enlightenment

59. Which of the following best describes the changes that took place in the French government in the years following the Revolution, from about 1789 to 1805?

   (A) The government went from absolutism to radical egalitarianism back to absolutism again.
   (B) The government gradually changed from a constitutional monarchy to a representative democracy.
   (C) The government changed from absolutism to a constitutional monarchy.
   (D) The government changed from a constitutional monarchy to absolutism.
   (E) The government changed from absolutism to constitutional monarchy to radical egalitarianism.

60. Which of the following clearly limited the success of Latin American constitutional experiments during the 19th and 20th centuries?

   (A) Latin American newly independent nations were led by inexperienced peasants.
   (B) Unlike North American political leaders, their generals often became presidents.
   (C) Latin America lacked strong, independent military leaders.
   (D) Latin American colonies were unable to gain independence until after World War II.
   (E) Latin American colonies had little experience with popular politics.

61. The best example of a radical political and economic ideology of 19th century Europe is

   (A) liberalism
   (B) Marxism
   (C) fascism
   (D) nationalism
   (E) conservatism

62. An important consequence of the political organization of Germany by Otto von Bismarck in the late 19th century was

   (A) the decline of nationalism as a political force in Europe
   (B) the dismantling of European empires around the globe
   (C) the decline of the importance of the military in European politics
   (D) a change in the balance of power among European nations
   (E) a decline in the power of Spain in European politics

63. The Young Turks were instrumental in bringing about a decline in the political power of

   (A) the Ottoman Empire
   (B) Russia
   (C) the Mongol Khanates
   (D) Israel
   (E) the Byzantine Empire

64. Perestroika, glasnost, democratization formed the three-pronged revival program of

   (A) Mao Zedong
   (B) Deng Xiaoping
   (C) Boris Yeltsin
   (D) Adolf Hitler
   (E) Mikhail Gorbachev

65. Which of the following is an accurate comparison between the nature of the warfare during World War I and World War II?

   (A) World War I was fought on two fronts; World War II took place in arenas, or "theatres."
   (B) World War I was fought primarily with gunpowder; World War II armies relied much more on nuclear power.
   (C) World War I was fought only in Western Europe; World War II was also fought in the Pacific Ocean.
   (D) World War I had no tanks nor airplanes; World War II warfare depended heavily on tanks and airplanes.
   (E) A larger proportion of deaths during World War I were of ordinary citizens rather than soldiers.

66. The formation of the North Atlantic Treaty Organization (NATO) in 1949 was a direct reflection of

   (A) the growing power of eastern European nations
   (B) the massive genocides that took place during World War II
   (C) Cold War politics
   (D) the declining power of western European nations
   (E) the growing economic influence of countries in East Asia

Sample Examination III

67. Which of the following is the best reason why India gained independence from Britain in 1947?

    (A) The British Government had a major change in leadership.
    (B) The British were more interested in maintaining their ties with other colonial possessions.
    (C) Few British Citizens were interested in moving to India to keep control of the colony.
    (D) As a result of shifting world markets, India became much less attractive possession that it had been before.
    (E) The nationalist movement in India gained intensity during the early 20th century.

68. Which of the following characterized most Latin American government during the 20th century?

    (A) Most had become stable democracies.
    (B) Most teetered back and forth between authoritarian and democratic politics and leaders.
    (C) Most remained firmly in the hands of authoritarian elite political leaders.
    (D) Most governments were weak because they had no strong military leaders to protect them.
    (E) Most governments were taken over by communist leaders.

69. The concept of the "Third World" describes an aspect of world politics during

    (A) the late 1800s
    (B) World War I
    (C) The Great Depression
    (D) World War II
    (E) The Cold War

70. World War I is best understood as a Marker Event in world history because it was the first in a series of events that led to

    (A) declining European power and ascending power for the United States
    (B) the rise of western powers in dominating the globe
    (C) globalization of world trade and communication
    (D) the establishment of a relatively stable balance of power among world nations
    (E) the decline of the influence of religion in world politics

DOCUMENT-BASED QUESTION

(suggested writing time – 40 minutes)

Directions: The following question is based on the accompanying Documents 1-7. This question is designed to test your ability to work with and understand historical documents. Write an essay that:

- Has a relevant thesis and supports that thesis with evidence from the documents.
- Uses all or all but one of the documents.
- Analyzes the documents by grouping them in as many appropriate ways as possible. Does not simply summarize the documents individually.
- Takes into account both the sources of the documents and the authors' points of view.

You may refer to relevant historical information not mentioned in the documents.

Between about 1600 and 1800 C.E. a "scientific revolution" occurred in Europe. How revolutionary was it? Making use of the documents below, analyze how innovative the scientific revolution was in terms of its impact on the course of world history. What kinds of additional documentation would help you better evaluate the importance of the scientific revolution?

Document 1

"Description of the drug (*dawa'*) that you put in the cannon (*midfa'*)- Its composition (*'lyaruhu*) is: potassium nitrate (barud) ten, charcoal (*fahm*) two *dirhams* and sulphur (*kibrit*) one and a half *dirhams*. Grind it finely and fill one third of the cannon (*midfa'*). Do not fill more otherwise it will split. Then let the wood turner make a wooden plug (*midfa'*) of the same size as the mouth of the cannon (*midfa'*). Ram (the gunpowder) tightly and place on it the ball (*bunduga*) or the arrow, and give it fire at the ammunition (*al-dhakhira*). Measure the cannon (*midfa'*) at the hole; if it (i.e. the *midfa'*) is deeper than the hole then it is defective and it will punch the gunner (*al-rami*), do understand this.""Description of *furga'a* (firecracker): fold a sheet of paper four or five folds on a mould. The mould is a rod that is turned to the thickness of a finger. Fold it very tightly, five or six plies. Take it off the mould. Seal its head very tightly, and fill it with *barud* and the charcoal of willow tree mixed together, and close its end very securely. If you want to give it fire pierce the head with a small piercing iron and insert a fuse that has been twisted very well. Glue the fuse to the hole, give it fire and move away. It will crack and move with explosive noise."

14th century Arabic descriptions of gunpowder technology

Document 2

"Not more than seven or eight observatories seem to have been constructed in the world. Mamum Khalifa made one with which the *Mamumi* Tables were written. Batalus [Ptolemy] constructed another. Another was made, in Hindustan, in the time of Raja Vikamaditya Hindu inUjjain and Dhar…The Hindus of Hindustan use the Tables of this Observatory."

Babar, first ruler of the Mughal Empire, 16th century

Document 3

Some years ago, as Your Serene Highness well knows, I discovered in the heavens many things that had not been seen before our own age. The novelty of these things, as well as some consequences which followed from them in contradiction to the physical notions commonly held among academic philosophers, stirred up against me no small number of professors…They know that as to the arrangement of the parts of the universe, I hold the sun to be situated motionless in the center of the revolution of the celestial orbs while the earth rotates on its axis and revolves about the sun. They know also that I support this position not only by refuting the arguments of Ptolemy and Aristotle, but by producing many counter-arguments…They have endeavored to spread the opinion that such propositions in general are contrary to the Bible and are consequently…heretical…I think that in discussions of physical problems we ought to begin not from the authority of scriptural passages but from sense-experiences and necessary demonstrations…"

"Letter to the Grand Duchess Christina"
Galileo Galilei, 1615

Document 4

"I perceive…philosophy is now become very Mechanical…I value [this universe] the more since I know it resembles a Watch, and the whole order of Nature the more plain and easy it is, to me it appears the more admirable."

"Countess" in Fontenelle's
popular dialogue of 1686

Document 5

"Nature and nature's laws lay hidden in night;/ God said, 'Let Newton be' and all was light."

Alexander Pope, 18th century English poet

Document 6

"Comparing lands of the Eastern seas with those of the Western, we note that their spoken languages are mutually unintelligible and that their written forms are different. Nonetheless, once a computation has been completed, [no matter where,] there will not be the most minute discrepancy when it is checked. The result can be for no other reason than the identity of human minds, the identity of patterns of phenomena, and the identity of numbers [everywhere]. It is not possible that the ingenuity of Europeans surpasses that of China. It is only that Europeans have transmitted [their findings] systematically from father to son and from master to disciple for generations. Hence, after a long period [of progress] their knowledge has become increasingly precise. Confucian scholars, on the other hand, usually denigrated those that were good mathematicians as petty technicians...In ancient times, no one could be a Confucian who did not know mathematics...Chinese methods [now] lag behind Europe's because Confucians do not know mathematics."

Qian Daxin, a leading Chinese scholar, 18th century

Document 7

"The gentleman has five pleasures...That he is born after the opening of the visas of science by the Westerners, and can therefore understand principles not known to the sages and wise men of old – this is the fourth pleasure. That he employs the ethics of the East and the scientific technique of the West, neglecting neither the spiritual nor material aspects of life, combining subjective and objective, and thus bringing benefit to the people and serving the nation – this is the fifth pleasure."

"Reflections on My Errors," 1854
Sakuma Shozan, Japanese government adviser

CHANGE-OVER-TIME ESSAY

(suggested planning and writing time – 40 minutes)

Choose ONE of the areas listed below and analyze how the nature of political ideologies changed from 1750 to the present. Be sure to describe influential political ideologies in each area around 1750 as your starting point, and include continuities that existed throughout the entire time span.

East Asia
Russia
Europe
South America

COMPARATIVE ESSAY

(suggested planning and writing time – 40 minutes)

Compare and contrast migrations of people to TWO of the following regions during the time period before 600 C.E. and assess the differing impact that the migrations had on each area.

West Asia
Europe
East Asia
The Indian Subcontinent
Northern Africa

NOTES

NOTES